INFLUENTIAL PAPERS
FROM THE 1920s

INFLUENTIAL PAPERS FROM THE 1920s

PAPERS FROM THE DECADES IN
INTERNATIONAL JOURNAL OF PSYCHOANALYSIS
KEY PAPERS SERIES

Edited by

R. D. Hinshelwood

International Journal of Psychoanalysis Key Papers Series
Series Editors: Paul Williams and Glen O. Gabbard

KARNAC
LONDON   NEW YORK

First published in 2004 by
H. Karnac (Books) Ltd.
6 Pembroke Buildings, London NW10 6RE

British Library Cataloguing in Publication Data

A C.I.P. for this book is available from the British Library

  ISBN 185575 3901

Edited, designed, and produced by The Studio Publishing Services Ltd,
Exeter EX4 8JN

10 9 8 7 6 5 4 3 2 1

www.karnacbooks.com

CONTENTS

The International Journal of Psychoanalysis Key Papers Series

The IJP "Key Papers" series brings together the most important psychoanalytic papers in the Journal's eighty-year history, in a series of accessible monographs. The idea behind the series is to approach the IJP's intellectual resource from a variety of perspectives in order to highlight important domains of psychoanalytic enquiry. It is hoped that these volumes will be of interest to psychoanalysts, students of the discipline and, in particular, to those who work and write from an interdisciplinary standpoint. The ways in which the papers in the monographs are grouped will vary: for example, a number of "themed" monographs will take as their subject important psychoanalytic topics, while others will stress interdisciplinary links (between neuroscience, anthropology, philosophy etc., and psychoanalysis). Still others will contain review essays on, for example, film and psychoanalysis, art and psychoanalysis and the worldwide IJP Internet Discussion Group, which debates important papers before they appear in the printed journal (cf. www.ijpa.org). The aim of all the monographs is to provide the reader with a substantive contribution of the highest quality that reflects the principal concerns of contemporary psychoanalysts and those with whom they are in dialogue. This volume is the second within the "Key Papers" series that identifies, reproduces, and discusses the most influential psychoanalytic papers produced in each decade since IJP began. By "influential" we mean papers that not only made an important individual contribution to psychoanalytic knowledge at the time, but also went on to influence the development of psychoanalytic thinking and concepts. The objective of this and future volumes in the "decades" collection will be to provide an overview of the development of psychoanalysis, as articulated through its principal scholarly journal.

We hope you will find this and all the "Key Papers" monographs rewarding and pleasurable to read.

Paul Williams and Glen O. Gabbard
Joint Editors-in-Chief,
International Journal of Psychoanalysis
London, 2004

ABOUT THE EDITOR

R. D. Hinshelwood is a Member of the British Psychoanalytic Society, and a Fellow of the Royal College of Psychiatrists. He was previously Clinical Director of The Cassel Hospital and currently is Professor, Centre for Psychoanalytic Studies, University of Essex. He is the author of *A Dictionary of Kleinian Thought* (1989), and *Clinical Klein* (1995). He has written widely on therapeutic communities, and the psychoanalysis of organizations (*Thinking About Institutions* (2001)); and published a book on psychoanalysis and ethics, *Therapy or Coercion* (1997).

Introduction to the journal in the 1920s

R. D. Hinshelwood

The 1920s, the first decade of the journal, was a time of hope and dismay. The phenomenal violence of the First World War was slowly absorbed in Europe and a new realization of what human beings could do to each other was faced. The optimism was to resolve that it should never happen again, and Freud believed that psychoanalysis had a contribution to make to that resolve. In his paper (1919a) "Lines of advance in psychoanalysis" he pointed with some enthusiasm towards innovative developments in psychoanalysis itself.

Curiously, one powerful factor that supported optimism over psychoanalysis was the war. The huge "haemorrhage" of man-power due to "war neurosis"—i.e. post-traumatic stress disorder (PTSD)—led, after the war, in all European (and American) armies, to a search to understand the illness psychologically. At the time it was only psychoanalysis that could offer a credible theory of the condition and, therefore, a method of prevention (see, for instance, Ferenczi *et al.*, 1921). From this, psychoanalysis gained a lot of credit in some quarters, and was widely applied in the treatment and rehabilitation of soldiers. Over the years of the 1920s, the journal reviewed many papers and books on the topic. The topic of war

1

neurosis was of great interest again at the time of the Second World War (see, for instance, Miller, 1940). Freud's reaction to the enormity of the social violence gave rise to at least one of his major texts—"Group psychology and the analysis of the ego (Freud, 1921c); and probably "Beyond the pleasure principle" (Freud, 1920g). Both these works serve as inspiration to much of what was published in the 1920s.

The backdrop of social changes and historical events are rarely addressed explicitly in these papers. The post-war poverty in Germany, and the plight of the working class in mid-decade in Britain, appear to go unmarked. Nor do the events of the developing Soviet regime in Russia warrant mention, despite their devastating effect on Russian psychoanalysts. This seeming neglect of social occurrences is, I presume, on the grounds that they are mere epiphenomena and that psychoanalysis is an investigation of the psychological underpinnings of any social phenomena, a view not necessarily shared by social scientists (see the debate between Malinowski, 1923, and Jones, 1925).

One of the enthusiastic new projects after the First World War was to found an English-language journal. Psychoanalysis had originated in Germany; and though a number of Freud's books had been translated and published in Britain and the United States in English, this new journal was a celebration of the spread of psycho-analysis to international dimensions. As Ernest Jones said in his editorial to the first volume:

> It has long been evident that a periodical published mainly in German could not indefinitely subserve the function of an official international organ, and, since interest in Psycho-Analysis has extended from German-speaking countries to English-speaking countries far more than to any other, it was only a question of time when such a Journal as the present one would have to be founded: with the cessation of the war, the resumption of scientific activities, and the reestablishment of contact between different countries, that time may be judged to have now arrived. [Jones, 1920, p. 3]

Jones clearly saw the creation of this journal as having political nuances—the widening of the psychoanalytic horizons; and, moreover, the insistence that the epicentre of English-speaking psychoanalysis would be Britain.

Jones's editorial hand created a very distinctive style to these early volumes, in line with his intentions. Besides the original papers, a most interesting aspect of the early numbers is the variety of other material. There are many translations of German papers, including new ones by Freud; for instance the first volume, in 1920, has "A child is being beaten", published the year before in the *Zeitschrift für Psychanalyse* and translated for publication in the journal (see Freud, 1919e, pp. 177–204). Jones was enormously industrious in commissioning reviews of books on psychoanalysis, of which there was a multitude at this time. He constantly found people to review literature from other languages, including French, Dutch, Italian, and Spanish in the first issue. And he found people to review current papers on various key psychoanalytic topics such as dreams, childhood, clinical reports, as well as applied psychoanalysis. He drew on his wide contacts as a central figure in international psychoanalysis and constantly reaffirmed that position with this commissioning work.

It is clear he saw the journal as providing a wide-ranging information service for the English-speaking world. During this decade, the *Bulletin of the International Psychoanalytical Association* was actually published within the journal as an integral section with pagination following the rest of the journal. This includes a mass of important details concerning the histories of the growing number of psychoanalytical societies worldwide. There was little more that an Anglophone could want to inform himself of the up-to-the-minute state of the psychoanalytic world. It was more, much more, than a vehicle for the latest discoveries of the new science; it represented a whole community that was of interest to itself.

But this is the psychoanalytic world as presented by Jones, the great statesman and "fixer" of psychoanalysis. Jones's enthusiasm and optimism shine out from these pages, his belief in Freud and psychoanalysis, and its future as an untroubled ascent of the mountain of knowledge facing the fledgling science. The great dissensions are little addressed. Jung hardly appears in these volumes. And Ferenczi's active technique (Ferenczi, 1919; Ferenczi & Rank, 1924), also a post-war enthusiasm, is criticized in rather low key throughout the decade—see Alexander's review of Ferenczi and Rank's book (Alexander, 1925; also Glover, 1924, 1928; Jokl, 1927; Laforgue, 1929; Sachs, 1925).

So, Jones's presence towers magisterially over the journal, as it did over British psychoanalysis during this and later decades. His enormous ambition and dedication are palpable in these pages. In the first issue of the journal, Jones summarized the advances in psychoanalysis hitherto as: technique, characterology, narcissism, and metapsychology (Jones, 1920). He clearly expresses his sense of an advancing powerful science; but what are the advances that will be recorded in the journal in the next ten years?

The decade ahead for the journal was, in fact, punctuated by a series of innovating texts by Freud: "Beyond the pleasure principle" (1920g), "Group psychology and the analysis of the ego" (1921c), "The ego and the id" (1923b), "Inhibitions, symptoms and anxiety" (1926d) and "The question of lay analysis" (1926e). The psychoanalytic world had to accommodate and absorb these new or revised ideas of Freud's; and those advances determine to a considerable degree the themes most common in the journal during the 1920s. Especially, the new structural model described in "The ego and the id" gave rise to important debates which were started in this decade and which are represented in the journal.

One prominent theme is analysis of the ego and characterology (Abraham, 1925, 1926*;[†] Alexander, 1923, 1926; Federn 1926; Edward Glover, 1925; James Glover, 1926; Reich, 1928; Searl, 1929), which presages the development of ego-psychology in the 1930s—and Reich's development of his idea of the defensive character armour.

The super-ego was newly formulated in 1923. It is of some interest that this concept, which seems to have such an intuitively correct quality, raised so many critical questions and debate when it was first postulated (Eder 1929; Fenichel, 1928; Issacs 1929; Jones, 1926*, 1929; Sachs, 1929; Searl, 1929). Jones's paper, presented in Vienna, was given, possibly tactlessly, during his visit for the occasion of Freud's seventieth birthday in May 1926. It was characteristically well thought out and, also characteristically, it was introduced as tentative whilst his style was declamatory. Freud, it would appear, did not pay much attention, since Jones had to write to him later to ask for his opinion, to which he got a mollifying but non-committal response.

---

† An asterisk after the date indicates a paper republished in this volume.

As a result of your reminder [Freud wrote to Jones in November 1926], I have reread your paper on the superego and confirmed my first impression. All the obscurities and difficulties you point out really do exist. But one cannot remove them, even with the criteria which you stress. It does require fresh examination of accumulated impressions and experiences. [Paskauskas 1993, p. 607]

And in the same letter Freud had placatingly said, "I myself have the impression that you sometimes overestimate the importance of the disagreements ('dissensions') that occurred also between us" (*ibid.*, p. 607). This was the year before the dissensions between Melanie Klein and Anna Freud broke into the open—in 1927—when Freud and Jones were engaged in a dispute that taxed each of them to remain friends (Steiner, 1985).

However, topics of interest were developing at this stage outside of Freud's inspiration. One such is female sexuality (Deutsch, 1925; Horney, 1924*, 1926; Jones, 1927; Lampl-De Groot, 1928; Muller-Braunschweig, 1926; Riviere, 1929*; Sachs, 1920, 1929); perhaps it was an interest especially in Berlin. In fact, there were many women coming into the psychoanalytic profession after the war. Women's emancipation in society at large was increasing rapidly in the 1920s, and women considered entering the professions—those that would accept them. Psychoanalysis, as a new profession, was naturally more open to recruits. Statistically, the Berlin Society had more women members and associates than any other psychoanalytical society in the IPA—approaching 50% (the British Society was not so far behind with over 30%, while the rest of the IPA was under 20%). It is not surprising that, especially in Berlin, women analysts began to debate Freud's hesitation in theorizing women's sexuality.

It may be that the interest in psychoanalysing children was also a consequence of the increased numbers of women becoming psychoanalysts. This was an interest that developed in both London and Vienna. Hermine von Hug-Hellmuth (Vienna) published her foundational paper on child psychoanalysis in the journal in 1921*. It influenced both Anna Freud in Vienna and Melanie Klein in Berlin (and in London, from 1926) in their methods of conducting a child analysis. Their paths diverged, not least in 1924 after the murder of Hug-Hellmuth by her adopted nephew, upon whom she had practised a psychoanalytic form of child rearing (MacLean &

Rappen, 1991). This shocking occurrence in Vienna led the Viennese to take a very circumspect, cautious view of the analysis of children, whilst Klein was much more intrepid. She had been booked to give a lecture in Vienna in December 1924—four months after the murder—where she described her rigorous interpretive technique. Its reception can only be imagined in this unhappy atmosphere. Klein's uncompromising stance on deep interpretation led her to follow up contacts, through the Bloomsbury group (Strachey & Strachey, 1986), in London. Two papers of Klein's (1924, 1926) were translated for the journal and, in 1927, after she settled in London, a symposium was published on child analysis in the journal, with papers by six British analysts (Klein*, Riviere, Searl, Sharpe, Glover, and Jones). This symposium was a defensive response to Anna Freud's *Einfürung in die Technik der Kinderanalyse* (*Four Lectures on Child Analysis*) published (in German) in 1927, and believed in Britain to be an unfair appraisal of Klein's play technique method of child analysis (Klein. 1926). Anna Freud's gentle riposte to the journal's symposium, published later, 1929*, in the journal, asserted caution and a unique educational dimension appropriate to child analysis. As is well known, the English publication of her *Four Lectures* was delayed until 1948.

In the same year, 1927, there was also a symposium on lay analysis following Freud's published opinion in 1926. The new profession had absorbed huge numbers of new recruits following the First World War and the question of what qualified a person to practise psychoanalysis was a major question. Particularly in America, there was a spectre of quack medicine that psychoanalysis had to disassociate itself from (see Gay, 1988). In addition, the recent history of dissension had led to a suspicion that psychoanalysts, too, were victims of unconscious and even neurotic components in their relations with Freud and their colleagues as well as with patients. Beginning in Berlin, the various Societies began to establish formal Institutes for the training of new psychoanalysts (Berlin in 1920, London in 1924, Vienna in 1925, the French in 1926), starting with the insistence upon a personal "didactic" analysis.

The papers in this symposium were published prior to the IPA Congress at Innsbruck later that year, 1927, and much in response to Freud's remarks on the subject in his short book (Freud, 1926e). Twenty-four analysts (Jones*, Sachs, Obendorf, Rickman, Glover,

Brill, Jeliffe, Alexander, Muller-Brauschweig, Benedek, Reik, Roheim, Hitschman, Schilder, Nunberg, Felix Deutsch, Reich, Horney, Simmel, Sadger, Hárnik, Waelder, Jokl, and Ophuisjen, and two Societies, the Hungarian and the New York) contributed views.

From this "map" of topics and discussions, it is difficult, even invidious, to make a small selection. I have not made an effort to cover the whole breadth of opinion and debate. I have had to restrict myself in various ways. First of all, I excluded all the papers of Freud's, on the assumption they are all well known and well consulted. Second, there are many rather short clinical accounts which are aimed at providing supporting evidence for psychoanalytic theory. I have excluded all these, too. There are also many brief papers reporting clinical curiosities and adventurous applications of psychoanalytic ideas. One could say that in the first years of the decade there is a curious mixture of naïve British psychoanalysis and mature, sophisticated, continental psychoanalysis. So, I have concentrated on papers that speak to substantial issues in the development of psychoanalysis as perceived with hindsight; and I have chosen only those that seem to have either (a) a high merit or (b) have achieved a classic status and reputation. Some papers had appeared in German previously and so the journal is not the date of first publication; nevertheless, all papers represent the first instance of English publication, which was the set purpose of the journal.

I realize, having made the selection, that there is a strong influence from both Berlin and Vienna. It makes me consider that the restoration of European culture and knowledge pushed psychoanalysis in Berlin to the fore, while Vienna, the foremost city for science before the war, had become merely the rump of the Austro-Hungarian Empire, far too big for the small country Austria had become, and thus impoverished economically and culturally. Berlin, despite the defeat of Germany, nevertheless gained in reputation for its modernity, and this seemed to rub off on the psychoanalytic world. Here the first training institute was established (in 1920), the first policlinic (in 1920, by Eitingon), and eventually, the first psychoanalytically orientated inpatient service (in 1927), the Schloss Tegel, by Ernst Simmel (1929). It was perhaps to Berlin that Jones's ambitions turned first for inspiration rather than Vienna—he sent a number of his would-be trainees to Berlin for their analyses—and wherefrom he attracted Melanie Klein, in 1926, as the analyst for his children and his wife.

My selection includes significant papers on: child analysis, sublimation, female sexuality, active technique, character and libidinal development, super-ego, the reality principle, and lay analysis. Thus, breadth of interest rather than depth of debate is what characterized the early years of the journal.

References

Abraham, K. (1925). The influence of oral erotism on character-formation. *International Journal of Psychoanalysis*, 6: 247–258.

Abraham, K. (1926). Character-formation on the genital level of libido-development. *International Journal of Psychoanalysis*, 7: 214–222.

Alexander, F. (1923). The castration complex in the formation of character. *International Journal of Psychoanalysis*, 4: 11–42.

Alexander, F. (1925). Review of *Entwicklungsziele Der Psychoanalyse* by Sandor Ferenczi & Otto Rank (1924). *International Journal of Psychoanalysis*, 6: 484–496.

Alexander, F. (1926). Neurosis and the whole personality. *International Journal of Psychoanalysis*, 7: 340–352.

Deutsch, H. (1925). The psychology of women in relation to the functions of reproduction. *International Journal of Psychoanalysis*, 6: 405–418.

Eder, D. (1929). On the economics and the future of the super-ego. *International Journal of Psychoanalysis*, 10: 249–255.

Federn, P. (1926). Some variations in ego-feeling. *International Journal of Psychoanalysis*, 7: 434–444.

Fenichel, O. (1928). The clinical aspect of the need for punishment. *International Journal of Psychoanalysis*, 9: 47–70.

Ferenczi, S. (1919). Technical difficulties in the analysis of a case of hysteria. *Zeitschrift für Psychanalyse*, 5: 34–40.

Ferenczi, S., & Rank, O. (1924) *Entwicklungsziele der Psychoanalyse (The Development of Psychoanalysis)*. Vienna: Internationaler psychoanalytischer Verlag.

Ferenczi, S., Abraham, K., Simmel, E., & Jones, E. (1921). *Psychoanalysis and the War Neuroses*. London: The International Psycho-Analytical Press, London.

Freud, A. (1927). *Einfürung in die Technik der Kinderanalyse (Four Lectures on Child Analysis)*. Vienna: Internationaler psychoanalytischer Verlag.

Freud, A. (1929). On the theory of analysis of children. *International Journal of Psychoanalysis, 10*: 29–38.

Freud, S. (1919a). Lines of advance in psychoanalysis. *S.E., 17*: 157–168. London: Hogarth Press.

Freud, S. (1919e). A child is being beaten. *S.E., 17*: 177–204.

Freud, S. (1920g). Beyond the pleasure principle. *S.E., 18*: 7–64. London: Hogarth Press.

Freud, S. (1921c). Group psychology and the analysis of the ego. *S.E., 18*: 67–143. London: Hogarth Press.

Freud, S. (1923b). The ego and the id. *S.E., 19*: 3–66. London: Hogarth Press.

Freud, S. (1926d). Inhibitions, symptoms and anxiety. *S.E., 20*: 77–175. London: Hogarth Press.

Freud, S. (1926e). The question of lay analysis. *S.E., 20*: 179–258. London: Hogarth Press.

Gay, P. (1988). *Freud: A Life for our Time*. London: Dent.

Glover, E. (1924). "Active therapy" and psychoanalysis—a critical review. *International Journal of Psychoanalysis, 5*: 269–311.

Glover, E. (1925). Notes on oral character formation. *International Journal of Psychoanalysis, 6*: 131–154.

Glover, E. (1928). Lectures on technique in psycho-analysis. *International Journal of Psychoanalysis, 9*: 7–46; 181–218.

Glover, J. (1926). The conception of the ego. *International Journal of Psychoanalysis, 7*: 414–419.

Horney, K. (1924). On the genesis of the castration complex in women. *International Journal of Psychoanalysis, 5*: 50–65.

Horney, K. (1926). The flight from womanhood: the masculinity-complex in women, as viewed by men and by women. *International Journal of Psychoanalysis, 7*: 324–339.

Hug-Hellmuth, H. von (1921). On the technique of child-analysis. *International Journal of Psychoanalysis, 2*: 287–305.

Issacs, S. (1929). Privation and guilt. *International Journal of Psychoanalysis, 10*: 335–347.

Jokl, R. H. (1927). The mobilizing of the sense of guilt—a contribution to the problem of active therapy. *International Journal of Psychoanalysis, 8*: 479–485.

Jones, E. (1920). Editorial. *International Journal of Psychoanalysis, 1*: 3–5.

Jones, E. (1925). Mother-right and the sexual ignorance of savages. *International Journal of Psychoanalysis, 6*: 109–130.

Jones, E. (1926). The origin and structure of the super-ego. *International Journal of Psychoanalysis, 7*: 303–311.

Jones, E. (1927). The early development of female sexuality. *International Journal of Psychoanalysis, 8*: 459–472.

Jones, E. (1929). Fear, guilt and hate. *International Journal of Psychoanalysis, 10*: 383–397.

Klein, M. (1924). The role of the school in the libidinal development of the child. *International Journal of Psychoanalysis, 5*: 312–331.

Klein, M. (1926). Infant analysis. *International Journal of Psychoanalysis, 7*: 31–63.

Laforgue, R. (1929) "Active" psycho-analytical technique and the will to recovery. *International Journal of Psychoanalysis, 10*: 411–422.

Lampl-de Groot, A. (1928). The evolution of the Oedipus Complex in women. *International Journal of Psychoanalysis, 9*: 332–345.

MacLean, G., & Rappen, U. (1991). *Hermine Hug-Hellmuth: Her Life and Work*. London: Routledge.

Malinowski, B. (1923). Psychoanalysis and anthropology. *Nature, 112*: 650–651.

Miller, E. (1940). *The Neuroses in War*. London: Macmillan.

Muller-Braunschweig, C. (1926). The genesis of the feminine super-ego. *International Journal of Psychoanalysis, 7*: 359–362.

Paskauskas, A. (1993). *The Complete Correspondence of Sigmund Freud and Ernest Jones, 1908–1939*. Cambridge, MA: Harvard University Press.

Reich, W. (1928). Criticism of recent theories of the problem of neurosis. *International Journal of Psychoanalysis, 9*: 227–240.

Riviere, J. (1929). Womanliness as a masquerade. *International Journal of Psychoanalysis, 10*: 303–313.

Sachs, H. (1920). The wish to be a man. *International Journal of Psychoanalysis, 1*: 262–267.

Sachs, H. (1925). Metapsychological points of view in technique and theory. *International Journal of Psychoanalysis, 6*: 5–12.

Sachs, H. (1929). One of the motive factors in the formation on the super-ego in women. *International Journal of Psychoanalysis, 10*: 39–50.

Searl, N. (1929). Difficulties in child development. *International Journal of Psychoanalysis, 10*: 476–480.

Simmel, E. (1929). Psycho-analytic treatment in a sanatorium. *International Journal of Psychoanalysis, 10*: 70–89.

Steiner, R. (1985). Some thoughts about tradition and change arising from an examination of the British Psychoanalytical Society's controversial discussions (1943–1944). *International Review of Psychoanalysis*, 12: 27–71.

Strachey, J., & Strachey, A. (1986). In: P. Meisel & W. Kendrick (Eds.) *Bloomsbury/Freud: The Letters of James and Alix Strachey, 1924–1925*. London: Chatto and Windus.

CHAPTER ONE

Child analysis

Hug-Hellmuth, Hermine von (1921). On the technique of child-analysis. *International Journal of Psychoanalysis*, 2: 287–305.

Klein, Melanie (1927). Contribution to the symposium on child-analysis. *International Journal of Psychoanalysis*, 8: 339–370.

Freud, Anna (1929). On the theory of analysis of children. *International Journal of Psychoanalysis*, 10: 29–38.

The Little Hans case (Freud, 1909b) showed Freud's interest in child observation as a means of confirming psychoanalytic developmental psychology. From before the First World War, Hermine von Hug-Hellmuth was evolving a practice of psychoanalytically applied principles to treat children. The paper, republished here, by the first non-Jew to become a member of the Viennese Psycho-analytical Society, proposed certain principles for child analysis (Hug-Hellmuth, 1921*). She considered that a child does not come for treatment from his or her own motivation, that the child is in the midst of the family setting in which his or her symptoms arise, so he or she is not suffering from past experiences, and the child has no concept of changing him or herself.

She made many recommendations:

- practise analysis only with older children (her examples are mostly adolescents, and not earlier than seven years of age);
- avoid stirring up powerful feelings;
- exercise circumspection about the golden rule of openness and freedom from censorship;
- use some positive and negative transference from the beginning;
- see younger children at home, not in a consulting-room or in an institution;
- gain a rapport at the beginning and avoid resistances even by using a ruse to undermine them;
- engage in play;
- make use of "active therapy" exercises;
- be aware of the greater susceptibility to suggestion in young persons;
- recognize children's astute awareness of the family environment;
- use non-technical language about psychoanalytic concepts;
- understand the centrality of enquiry about sexuality;
- accept that intuitive empathy is at least as important as insight for the child;
- recognize the need to sustain an explanatory relationship with the child's family, to ensure realistic expectations, to deal with the parents' narcissistic jealousy of the analyst, and to amplify details the child is reluctant to divulge.

In subsequent years both Anna Freud and Melanie Klein mined Hug-Hellmuth's writings. Anna Freud tended to observe the more cautious principles, no doubt reinforced after Hug-Hellmuth's death. She adopted these principles without acknowledgement, perhaps out of respect for Hug-Hellmuth's wishes, but gave them a rigorous theoretical foundation (Anna Freud, 1927). Melanie Klein did acknowledge the use of play and rejected a cautious approach as indicated by one of Klein's supporters in Berlin, Alix Strachey, who wrote in 1924: "Hug-Hellmuth's outpourings [are] a mass of sentimentality covering the old intention of dominating at least one human being—one's own child" (Strachey & Strachey. 1986, p. 200). Klein "wanted in the first place to separate 'Fruhanalyse' entirely from education (unlike Hug-Hell)" (Strachey & Strachey, 1986, p. 203).

However, despite their debt, both Anna Freud and Melanie Klein tended to be silent about Hug-Hellmuth's contribution, and it has disappeared from view. As mentioned in the Introduction, Hermine Hug-Hellmuth was murdered in 1924 by her nephew, Rudolph Hug. He was the illegitimate son of Hermine's sister, Antonia, and Hermine adopted him as her son. She brought him up according to psychoanalytic principles, as she understood them to apply to child development. This was an old Austrian aristocratic family, which was shamed by both the illegitimate birth and the murder. However, the Viennese Society was also drastically affected by this murderous outcome of an upbringing based on psychoanalysis. It suggested a much more cautious approach to applying psychoanalysis to children—hence one of the reasons for the caution characteristic of Anna Freud's approach.

Hug-Hellmuth's death and the seismic tremor it created in the psychoanalytic world, together with her stiff, retiring personality, consigned her to an undeserved oblivion. Moreover, her will, made a few days before her death, stated a wish that no account of her life or work should be published, even in the psychoanalytic literature (Bernfeld, 1925, p. 106). Nevertheless, Hug-Hellmuth's paper (and her many other writings—MacLean & Rappen, 1991) is the foundation of child analysis and her experience is as fresh today as then; hence there is good reason to republish her work.

These divergent approaches led to quite bitter exchanges later in the decade. Melanie Klein's contribution to the symposium is republished here (Klein, 1927*). The symposium was held by the British Psychoanalytical Society, in 1927, to address Anna Freud's criticisms (in *Einführung in die Technik der Kinderanalyse*; translated as *Introduction to the Technique of Child Analysis*), is a detailed rebuttal of many points.[1] Klein's method of child analysis had been presented in the journal (and in the *Zeitschrift*) prior to the symposium (Klein, 1926). Here she claims, in contrast to Anna Freud, that a full analytic situation can be established with children even as young as three years of age, and that there is no need to combine psychoanalysis with an educational aim. There is opportunity, indeed need, to explore the unconscious Oedipus complex of the child to the full depths of the unconscious; and transference, both negative and positive, is fully active and analysable without the need to coax positive feelings and dissipate negative ones. Play is equivalent to free association in adults, and shows the child to be much dominated by the unconscious and by anxiety, meaning that an analysis of children needs to penetrate to the deepest layers of the unconscious. She had found that the child's super-ego is highly active and particularly harsh. And finally she disputed that a successful analysis will harm the child's relations with its parents.

Anna Freud made a further statement, in 1929*. This paper, republished here, was short and clinically rich, offering an elegant argument that implicitly dismissed a number of Klein's claims. Whilst she acknowledged Melanie Klein's play technique, Anna Freud challenged Klein's argument that the use of pedagogic inter-ventions diluted the psychoanalytic. In fact, Anna Freud invited child analysts to discover that precisely this educational attitude in the analyst was what made the significant difference from an adult analysis. In justification she described the formation of the super-ego during latency years, and its particular susceptibility to influ-ence by external figures (as opposed to its intractable nature in older patients); and thus its openness to therapeutic influence at this age by the analyst. Implicitly, she contradicted Klein's view of the inherent harshness of the super-ego. So, by advising the analyst of the latency child to take the opportunity to influence the super-ego through an educational approach, she defended the view that Klein attacked. This paper is characteristically gentle, but firm in the defence of her own technique.

The dispute over the correct method of child analysis was never resolved. Instead it evolved as Klein introduced new ideas into psychoanalysis, such as the depressive position, internal objects, and unconscious phantasy from birth. It erupted as a conflict over the progress of psychoanalytic ideas in general during the 1940s, after the Freud family had fled the Nazis and arrived in London (King & Steiner, 1991).

Note

1. In 1947 Klein added a note to her paper indicating her belief by then that Anna Freud had moved closer to Klein's position (see pages

168–169 of *Love, Guilt and Reparation: The Writings of Melanie Klein, Volume 1*).

References

Bernfeld, S. (1925). Vienna Psycho-Analytical Society. *Bulletin of the International Psycho-Analytical Association, 6*: 106–107.

Freud, A. (1927). *Einfürung in die Technik der Kinderanalyse (Four Lectures on Child Analysis)*. Vienna: Internationaler psychoanalytischer Verlag.

Freud, S. (1909b). Analysis of a phobia in a five-year-old boy. *S.E., 10*: 3–149. London: Hogarth Press.

King, P., & Steiner, R. (1991). *The Freud–Klein Controversies, 1941–1945*. London: Routledge.

Klein, M. (1926). Infant analysis. *International Journal of Psychoanalysis, 7*: 31–63.

MacLean, G., & Rappen, U. (1991). *Hermine Hug-Hellmuth: Her Life and Work*. London: Routledge.

Strachey, J., & Strachey, A. (1986). *Bloomsbury/Freud: The Letters of James and Alix Strachey, 1924–1925*. P. Meisel & W. Kendrick (Eds.). London: Chatto and Windus.

On the technique of child-analysis*†

H. Von Hug-Hellmuth

> The answer to technical problems in psycho-analytic practice
> is never obvious.

> Freud: Sammlung kleiner Schriften zur Neurosenlehre, IV. Folge.

The analysis both of the child and of the adult has the same end and object; namely, the restoration of the psyche to health and equilibrium which have been endangered through influences known and unknown.

The task of the physician is fulfilled when a cure has been effected, no matter what ethical and social standards the patient pursues; it suffices that the individual becomes once more adapted to life and his vocation, and that he is no longer liable to succumb to the demands and disappointments of life.

---

* Read before the Sixth International Psycho-Analytical Congress at the Hague, September 1920. Translated by R. Gabler and Barbara Low.

† Article citation:
Hug-Hellmuth, H. von (1921). On the technique of child-analysis. *International Journal of Psychoanalysis*, 2: 287–305.

The *curative* and educative work of analysis does not consist only in freeing the young creature from his sufferings, it must also furnish him with moral and aesthetic values. The object of such curative and educative treatment is not the mature man who when freed is able to take responsibility for his own actions: but the child, the adolescent, that is human beings who are still in the developing stage, who have to be strengthened through the educative guidance of the analyst, in order to become human beings with strong wills and definite aims. He who is both analyst and educator must never forget that the aim of child-analysis is character-analysis—in other words, education.

The peculiarity of the child-psyche, its special relationship to the outside world, necessitates a special technique for its analysis.

There are three considerations of fundamental importance:

1. The child does not come of his own accord to the analyst, as the grown-up does, but owing to the wish of his parents and only then (and herein he resembles the grown-up) when all other means have proved futile.

2. The child is in the midst of the very experiences which are causing his illness. The grown-up suffers from past experiences, the child from present ones; and his ever-changing experiences create a perpetually-changing relationship between himself and his surroundings.

3. The child, unlike the adult man (but very often in accordance with the attitude of women patients), has no desire at all to change himself or to give up his present attitude towards his external surroundings. His "naughtiness" creates in him a sense of great self-importance, indeed a feeling of omnipotence, owing to which he tyrannizes over the people who surround him, and his narcissism which rejoices in the continual attention which he wins from his surroundings will not allow him to give up his wickedness. To the child with strong sadistic tendencies as well as to the child with pronounced masochism, constantly recurring outbursts of fury and punishments are essential to his neurotic personality. We must also include those fortunate natures who adapt themselves even as children to every different phase of life, who remember only the pleasure of "making it up" in the continual quarrels of childhood, and

who take a temporary exile in a boarding-school as a pleasant change—we mean, in short, those who can adapt themselves to every change in their environment.

For instance, a small boy, a habitual pilferer, whom I had for treatment, took all his experiences in school and at home just as "a lark" and squared his conscience in regard to his complete failure at school with the reflection: "My father did not like learning either, and yet we are doing so well." Another twelve-year-old boy, a little truant, whom I analysed in the Vienna children's clinic, enjoyed his stay there so much, on account of the nice food he got, that in spite of his often expressed longing for his parents, he had no desire whatever to depart.

Experience has taught me that girls at the age of puberty are more helpless when confronted by conflicts in the home life, and more sensitive to them, than are boys of the same age. The explanation of this lies partly in the fact that the girl has stronger links with her home life on account of her education aiming more at repression, partly in the fact that she has less power to overcome, by way of sublimation, the incestuous impulses which are ready to burst out at this critical period.

In the case of phobia in a five-year-old boy, Freud has shown us the method (and this has become the basis of psycho-analytic child-therapy) by which we can throw light on these psychic depths in a small child where the libidinous stirrings change into childish anxiety. At this stage of life an analysis similar to the analytic treatment of the adult is not possible. One can only apply educational methods founded on psycho-analytical knowledge. A full understanding of the child's world of thoughts and feelings will call out its unlimited confidence, and thus a way is discovered to safeguard the child from various errors and injuries. As the training of the young child, both physical and mental, rests especially with women, it becomes essential that we should train understanding and kind-hearted women for educational psychoanalytic work.

A proper analysis according to psycho-analytical principles can only be carried out after the seventh or eighth year. But even with children at this early age the analyst must, as I will show later, turn aside from the usual routine, and satisfy himself with partial results, where he thinks that the child might be intimidated by too powerful a stirring-up of his feelings and ideas, or that too high demands upon his powers of assimilation are being made, or that his soul is disturbed instead of freed.

Generally speaking, there are two groups of these child-patients; namely, those who know from the beginning, or soon learn, in what the treatment consists, its aim and object, and those others who owing to their tender age, or to the fact that they do not suffer personally from their symptoms (for example, in the case of marked homosexual tendencies) or owing to individual factors (such as a feeble constitution) cannot be enlightened as to the object of the analytic treatment. Such children can be safely left to the idea that the analyst spends these hours with them in order to communicate some knowledge to them or to wean them from some misbehaviour, or to play with them, or from a special interest in them.

For instance a delicate thirteen-year-old boy did not doubt for a moment that I was, as his mother said, a friend of his father who was in the war, and that I came to wish the youngster Many Happy Returns of the Day. As he had an impediment in his speech he also accepted quite trustingly the further explanation that I would teach him to speak distinctly, and he actually tried himself to speak more clearly.

The mother of an eleven-year-old boy, who lived completely in his phantasies and dreams, chose, without my sanction, a form of introduction which I thought might have proved harmful. She said that a friend of hers was very much interested in children's dreams and would like him to talk to her about his own. However the course of the analysis convinced me that no harm had been done, for the somewhat artificial accounts of dreams given in the beginning were after all only reflections of his conscious and unconscious day-dreams.

No rule can be laid down for the appropriate moment to tell the patient the aim of these talks; experience and personal tact are the only reliable guides.

In close connection with the above matter is the formulating of the obligations which must be carried out by the adult patient at the beginning as a *sine qua non* if a cure is to be effected. Right from the beginning one understands that in the case of the second type of psycho-analytic patients one must abandon the demand for absolute openness, and uncensored expression of everything which comes into the mind, and instead put forward this obligation only at some favourable opportunity. In the case of the first-mentioned group, however, those more mature young people who often have already had instruction concerning psycho-analysis from some other member of the family who has already undergone treatment, it is often suitable in the very first hour to demand that they shall be completely frank and shall not talk over the treatment with their comrades, their brothers and sisters, or other members of the family. Of course, in connection with this enjoining of secrecy, we must not overlook that commands and prohibitions are the very means of tempting the young to transgress.

The period of time devoted to the child's analysis is generally conditioned by the attendance at school, which the parents do not want on any account to be shortened. Apart from the few cases where the young patient has special difficulties in preserving the continuity, I have always found that three or four hours a week, if the analysis is carried on long enough, leads to successful results. An exact keeping to time appears to me of the greatest importance. It involves a self-education which the young person must undergo. Sometimes it needs strong self-control to reject some important communication which the child has kept back till the end of the hour, but to concede to such demands would mean that the patient was allowed to get the upper hand.

While the educative analysis of children of more mature age (say from fourteen to eighteen) resembles more that of the grown-up—for in the very first hours, we can speak of the factors in the treatment, of positive and negative transference, of resistance, and of the significance of the unconscious psychic tendencies in the whole of our experience—the analysis of the younger or backward child proceeds on different lines from the beginning.

I consider it inadvisable to take the young patient to the consultation with the analyst. The child feels himself exposed and humiliated while he waits in another room during the consultation, and often this creates in him excitement, may be anxiety, resentment, defiance, shame, all of which endangers the subsequent treatment, or at least makes the beginning much more difficult. If one has to break down a resistance before getting an opportunity to build a bridge of mutual understanding, one is, so to speak, confronted with a task similar to that of clearing away a heap of débris which lies at the other side of a yawning chasm.

Just as the first meeting between the analyst and the young patient should take place in the latter's home, so should it be with the treatment itself. The analysis must go on independently of the whims of the patient, who can very cleverly contrive to have a slight indisposition which prevents him coming, or arriving in time, or he may play truant in the analysis hour. The child not only lacks interest in the money problem (which for the grown-up is a continual stimulus to make him continue the treatment uninterruptedly), but in addition he knows that he has an opportunity of causing his parents expense and of satisfying his own defiance and desires for revenge. Of course, every child when at the height of a positive transference tries to transfer the analysis to the home of the analyst; but I have always gained the conviction that even when external circumstances demanded this change of place, such a change proved not to be lasting. However much the time and energy of the analyst is burdened by this demand, since he can only see daily half the number of patients as compared with those treated by his medical colleagues, and although an absolutely undisturbed and private talk in the patient's own house is difficult to obtain, nevertheless these evils seem to me trifling compared with the greater one of letting the child decide the external conditions of the analysis. Another consideration is that the parents, in spite of all their devotion, very soon feel that chaperoning of the child to and from the analyst's house becomes impossible and this difficulty is used as a reason for terminating the treatment—a situation well-known to every child-analyst.

However favourable may be a temporary absence from home for difficult children, nevertheless I have my doubts as to the value of psycho-analytic treatment for them in any kind of institution, whether they are boarders or day-pupils, for one reason because the child finds the necessity for secrecy in a situation where he feels himself more important than his comrades very difficult to endure, and for another, because he easily becomes a target for their ridicule when he has to have a special "treatment hour", about the aim and object of which the other children cannot obtain information. What the treatment will be like in future happier times when perhaps some of my ideas for the founding of psycho-analytic homes for young children have been realized I cannot foretell, but I believe that it will need quite special tact, great educational skill and experience, to meet successfully the great difficulties which will arise in psycho-analytic treatment owing to collective life. The jealousy among the patients themselves, the making of comparisons not always favourable to one's own analyst, the exchange of confidences between the children about their analysis which cannot be prevented—all these things are difficulties which must not be underrated. Nevertheless, I believe that the creation of psycho-analytic "homes" will either solve the problem of the guidance of the "difficult" child which so many parents and schools fail in, or at least make the problem easier.

An important difference between the analysis of the child and of the grown-up results from what seems a merely external circumstance; namely, whether the patient should lie down or sit up during treatment. For the very juvenile patient, this question is already answered by the limitations which his age imposes. But also in the case of the older child the notion of "lying down" produces in the child an anxiety-situation. To lie down awakens in the child the memory of some real or imagined scene of being overpowered: one will be afraid of a beating, another of an operation, and both are overcome by their secret feeling of guilt, a fear of castration. Adolescent patients imagine themselves while lying down to be under hypnosis and exposed to rape. Seduction phantasies of both homosexual and heterosexual nature which are projected on to the analyst play a great part with so-called "nervous" boys and girls when they have to lie down.

A fifteen-year-old boy who came for my educative treatment on account of a serious phobia of thunderstorms and earthquakes, confessed to me in the course of analysis that he would certainly have resisted the treatment if he had been obliged to lie down on the sofa which, he had heard, a family acquaintance had had to do in his analysis, for he was in continual dread of being hypnotized. As a matter of fact this boy had worked himself into such a serious condition of excitement during a consultation with a nerve specialist at home, who tried to hypnotize him, that he cried out "Police" and finally dashed out of the house in a panic into the street.

I have never noticed that the success of the analysis is in any way imperilled by the fact that the analyst faces the patient.

The first hour in treatment is of the utmost importance; it is the opportunity for establishing a *rapport* with the young creature, and for "breaking the ice". It causes much strain and stress to the beginner and opens up even to the experienced analyst nearly always new methods of approach and new guiding lines. But no rules and no programme can be laid down; the intellectual development, the age, and the temperament of the patient must decide which course to pursue.

In the case of more mature patients, often the right course is for the analyst to confess himself as such openly, in order to gain their confidence whole heartedly.

The mother of a nervous girl of fourteen introduced me to her daughter as a friend whom she had not seen for many years, but the girl was not to be deceived by this; after a little while she enquired: "But who are you really?" My honest explanation, namely, that I was interested in young people who find life very difficult and are unable to grapple with it, and that I should like to help her, too, to get on better with her mother, had the desired effect. The girl became strongly attached to me and came to me for advice about all matters which disturbed her, as to her "second and real mother".

Sometimes, in the case of those patients who obstinately shut themselves up, a ruse is helpful. For example, a nine-year-old boy with suicidal impulses, during the first hour took not the slightest notice of me, but simply laid his head on the table and made no response to any remark. A fly passing close to my face suggested to me the idea of pretending that I had got something in my eye. At once the boy, who always wished to be in the limelight, jumped up, saying: "Please let me see, I will get it out; but you must not rub your eye." Thus, with his proffered help the ice was broken, because he felt himself of use to me. Every time, after this, when a strong resistance made him retire into silence, I had only to ask for his advice or his help, and the analysis once more progressed favourably.

A ruse, which, in my opinion, never fails, is to tell the young patient about the misdeeds of other children. As one has already been sufficiently informed by the parents about the misdemeanours and peculiarities of one's little patient, one need not be afraid of inciting the child, by such accounts of others, to similar naughtiness which he has not indulged in up to the present. No child has so far been harmed either in a sexual, or any other way, by a properly-conducted analysis. Though a temporary increase in bad behaviour may lead the layman to such an idea, the analyst is able to appreciate it as a sign of progress.

The reaction of the child to this kind of beginning may be of three types. Often the patient reacts with a story of similar misdeeds, which at first are described as having been done by another child, and only later on admitted as his own. Or secondly he may reply with a fierce denial: "I have never done such things!" From the analysis of the grown-up, we are aware that such emphatic denials are tantamount to admissions. Thirdly, the child may accept the information with absolute indifference. Then we can scarcely be wrong in assuming that the parents have misunderstood something in the behaviour of the child, or that behind the known facts something more is hidden.

When dealing with children of seven or eight years of age, the analyst can often pave the way by sharing in the play activities, and thus he can recognise several symptoms, peculiar habits, and character traits; and in the case of these very young patients, very often play will enact an important part throughout the whole treatment.

A seven-year-old boy, who suffered from severe insomnia accompanied with compulsive laughter and tic, which made me suspect he had watched the parental sex-life, manifested during daytime complete apathy: he lay on the carpet for hours without speaking or playing; he ate a great deal but without enjoyment or selection, and apparently had lost quite suddenly his former strongly-marked desire for caresses. In the analysis he would allow me to play with his toys for the whole hour, with scarcely any reaction on his part, and seldom gave me answer, so that it was difficult to decide whether he had taken in at all that I said. In one of the first treatment hours I told him about a little boy who would not go to sleep at night, and made such a noise that his parents could not sleep either. I told also how little Rudi made a noise too in the afternoons when his father wanted to rest; so his father became angry and Rudi was whipped (Little Hans's reaction to this was to run to the sideboard and take down a "Krampus'[1] and to beat me on the arm, saying: "You are naughty!"). I went on to tell how Rudi was then cross with his father, and wished his father were somewhere else. (To this the reaction was: "My father is at the war." Actually his father, an officer of high rank, was on active service throughout the war, and had only returned to his family in Vienna on short leave.) Suddenly Hans took his little gun and said: "Puff, puff."

The next day his death-wishes towards his father showed themselves more clearly. He was playing with his toy motor-car and several times ran over the chauffeur, whom I had made out to be little Rudi's father. I pretended to telephone the news of his father's accident to the little boy. Rudi was supposed to weep bitterly at the news, and then I said that although Rudi had formerly wished his strict father away, now he felt very sad, because in spite of this wish, he really loved his father very much. The reaction of little Hans was very characteristic; he listened to me, lying on the floor, asking me eagerly now and then, "What does little Rudi do next?" Suddenly he jumped up and ran out of the room. On the following day he reacted in the same way when our game was repeated, at his request. In his sudden going out of the room, we can see clearly the working of the unconscious. It also shows us an important difference in the course of psychic functionings in the grown-up and in the child. Whereas in the analysis of the adult, we aim at bringing about full insight into unconscious impulses and feelings, in the case of a child, this kind of avowal expressed, without words, in a symbolic act, is quite sufficient. We learn, indeed, from the analysis of the child that in him the psychic events take place in quite different layers from those of the grown-up, that they may be more closely or more remotely connected with each other and that in the child many impressions leave clearly-marked traces in spite of never having reached the threshold of consciousness. Even analysis does not make conscious these fragmentary memories of "primordial scenes"[2] the blending of new impressions with these former takes place, perhaps, in the preconscious, and it is left to later experiences at a higher stage of development to bring them into consciousness. This would supply a further explanation of the fact that the very earliest impressions which are very much alike for all human beings (such for example, as the methods of upbringing) lay the foundation for neurosis in some whilst others pass through them unharmed.

It is most rare for the young patient to put out his psychic feelers, or to talk freely during the first treatment hour, since he is full of mistrust towards his analyst, who is the father- or mother-*imago*, unless it so happens that an extreme bitterness against his parents or brothers and sisters compels the child to break out into complaints and abuse. In such case, it is necessary to manifest to the young patient the greatest forbearance and a full consideration of his troubles.

The communications or symptomatic actions in the first treatment hour are of the greatest importance, for they demonstrate the nuclear-complex of the infantile neurosis.

A fifteen-year-old boy came to me for analytic treatment on account of severe anxiety conditions, which he himself speedily declared to be "anxiety of anxiety". The first thing he said was: "In our form at school, the two best pupils are Jews, I come next, and again after that, the next best are Jews, and the rest are Gentiles." By this formulation the boy betrayed his ever-gnawing feeling of reproach against the father, who owing to marriage with a Gentile, had become a convert from Judaism to Protestantism.

Little Hans, to whom we are indebted for valuable insight into the mechanism of the child's psychic functioning, was aroused from his complete apathy by the following game: I saw in the looking-glass that he poked his finger into his nose, and I said: "Oh dear, whatever is Hans doing? I don't want to see such a sight!" Whereupon he stood in front of the mirror, smiling roguishly, and said. "Don't look!" poking his finger again into his nose. Of course he expects me to forbid him and untiringly repeats this game, only exchanging his nose-poking for putting out his tongue. This game symbolizes to him the oft-experienced strictness of his father which he tries to evade by keeping secret his little misdeed.

A sixteen-year-old girl suffered in a marked degree from inferiority feelings, owing to squinting. She covered up spontaneously my spectacles which lay on the table—a symptomatic action which revealed that she was unwilling to be reminded of eyes or their abnormalities. She admitted to me later on that this defect of mine had for a long time disturbed her affectionate relations towards me.

A ten-year-old boy, who was rather a failure at his work owing to his very extreme habit of phantasying, in the first treatment hour informed me how greatly he disliked the pose of the hero in a performance of *Lohengrin* which he had witnessed. He ostentatiously turned his back towards me, imitating the singer's position, declaring it unsuitable for a performer on the stage, asking me:

"Surely, Doctor, an actor should not stand in such a position in front of the public?" After a short course of analysis, my original suspicion was confirmed, namely, that the boy was suffering from a strongly repressed exhibitionism.

The first communication of a fourteen-year-old girl, who was harrassed by painful broodings, was a very contemptuous criticism of the geographical teaching which she received at the age of ten or eleven, which consisted of continual repetition about "climate" and even now in the high school it was the same subject all over again: climate, the position of the sun and its shadow—these were pursued with the same persistency. "Whatever is the object of teaching the movements of the sun to an eleven-year-old child who cares nothing about the subject," and so forth—this complaint filled up the whole hour of treatment with the greatest monotony, and in the subsequent hours she continually returned to this subject, until at last was revealed the connection between this question and what was really the girl's main interest—sexual intercourse between human beings. In a roundabout way (first under the guise of her great liking for horses—she was greatly interested in books on horse-breeding—then of her interest in descriptions of travels and the love relations of foreign peoples) the main preoccupation finally emerged: "For how long a period do the men and women of foreign races have intimate relations with one another" (having in mind her own father and mother).

The demand for "active therapy" which is made for the analysis of the adult is also of importance in child-analysis. It is certainly advisable for quite a number of patients that during the course of analysis they should be given small tasks to perform. Especially in the case of the patient who suffers from strong inferiority feelings, if a due measure of work be demanded of him, his self-confidence will be strengthened.

The shy, dependent weak boy (of whom I spoke above) who had difficulty with his speech and suffered a great deal from the ridicule of street-boys, surprised his grandfather after a six months treatment by his manly self-reliant behaviour with his seniors. The boy, who formerly would scarcely go outside the house, improved so much by analysis that he joined in walks, and went along, first for me, then for his mother, to execute little commissions for us—which he carried out very successfully.

More important than making positive requests is the avoidance, as far as possible, of any direct prohibitions, and, again, more valuable than both prohibitions and commissions, is talking over things together. This mutual weighing up of the pros and cons of a given situation will influence the self-confidence of the patient repressed by his inferiority feelings.

No more for the child than for the adult can a programme for the course of analysis be laid down. Kind and sympathetic attention, encouraging occasionally, joking words at the right moment, a loving interest in all the trifles which are by no means trifles to the child, indicate the way to gain the full confidence of the young creature. In addition, to forget nothing and to confuse nothing said in previous sittings—this completes the demands made by the child upon the analyst. How far, and when, free association should be made use of, can only be decided as the circumstances arise. So far as my own experience goes, Abraham's remark that older people need more guidance in analysis than the younger ones holds good for both the young child and the adolescent. Perhaps we would add that in the case of these latter, greater care has to be used than with the grown-up. True, it is difficult to disentangle deep-rooted and rigid ideas and feelings, but the greater plasticity of the youthful mind lends itself easily to the danger of unintended suggestion instead of yielding to the patient the clearest possible insight. Over and over again I have been able to prove to myself that children know far more about the things that go on in their surroundings than we grown-ups, owing to our anxious solicitude, wish to admit. Does it not sound almost tragi-comic to receive unexpectedly the confession of an eleven-year-old girl (whose repeated questions about the sexual act I have carefully tried to answer step by step) that when she was five her mother enticed her to look through the keyhole and thus spy on her father when having intercourse with a prostitute!

Of course, dreams play their part in child-analysis also, but we need not fear, any more than in the case of adults, that resistance will produce a more intense or imaginary dream-experience. The so-called night-dream signifies only a day-dream to which perhaps the child would never otherwise give expression. And here I wish to emphasize the difficulty there is in getting some children to speak out freely all their ideas because they cannot free themselves from the habit fixed by the daily teaching, namely: "not to talk nonsense" and so forth.

Although naturally in child-analysis technical expressions, such as the Oedipus and castration-complex, exhibitionism, etc. cannot be made use of, nevertheless the real facts must be made clear. Even in the case of a very young patient it is necessary to explain certain phenomena in the course of treatment. He will quite easily understand the meaning of "resistance" if first it is explained to him in connection with "the negative transference", that is, his refusal to speak out of a spirit of defiance; and later in connection with the "positive transference", that is, his feeling of shame at making a confession to the analyst which is humiliating to himself or his family; and in the end he will understand the readily acquired phrase: "Now I have no more to say".

Out of the resistance which expresses itself in the form of unwillingness to humiliate his family we can find a way of explanation concerning the negative transference, which is generally much more readily accepted than the idea of the positive transference. Discussion about this latter, even when it is quite clearly recognised, demands special caution in formulating it, because at bottom the child is unwilling to exchange his own parents for any stranger, even when there is every good reason for so doing. In spite of this, however, the child's first attitude at the beginning of the treatment is generally a strong positive transference, owing to the fact that the analyst, by sympathetic and dispassionate listening, realizes the child's secret father—or mother—ideal. Of course he makes use of this attitude at once against his own family. This results in those intensely irritating remarks made by the child to his people, such as: "Doctor said I need not do this or that", or, "I must ask Doctor first about this". The child takes for granted that the analyst by listening to his complaints in the treatment hour, is in agreement with him, and from this he builds up his phantasies and attributes to them the value of reality. Also the juvenile patient is continually ready to plot against his parents, and in this he relies upon the support of his analyst. The child, just like the grown-up, when at the height of his positive transference, is unwilling to end the treatment.

The negative transference usually appears first in the form of a fear of being deceived. For everything they say, they demand oaths of secrecy, for their mistrust towards the analyst is the product both of unwillingness to lay themselves bare, and of the countless disappointments which even the most favourable home conditions provide for the child from his earliest years. This is also the reason why he anxiously and jealously watches the interviews between the analyst and his parents and tries to overhear them and shorten them.

We know what an important part is played in the child's psychic life by sexuality, and its observation, and by the diverting of this childish interest by the family circle. The child is accustomed to get very unsatisfactory answers from his parents and other grown-up members of the family to the riddle of sex, and therefore he reacts in two ways to the straight-forward talk in the analysis about sexual matters. He feels more important, like a grown-up man, and tries hard to reward the analyst's frankness by greater friendship: on the other hand, as soon as stronger resistance sets in, he is at once ready (owing to his earlier repressions) to belittle the analyst because he has talked on tabooed matters. So strong with the child is the parental authority and the first educational influence, that he expects the same claims to be made upon himself, and the same outlook in life, from every grown-up who is interested in him. To him the analyst embodies, but in much stronger form than to the adult, the father- or mother-*imago*. On that account it takes a long time before he can feel convinced that the analyst does not take the parent's part, and that he can expect from the analyst full freedom and complete understanding for all his utterances. The child's overestimation of authority, in both positive and negative sense, makes the analysis difficult, for the patient watches with a keen eye for any defect in the analyst which will give him an excuse for gainsaying his belief in authority. And the young person, especially the child, thinks he finds this wished-for defect in the analyst's frank talk about sexual problems, and therefore in this phase of the treatment the ambivalency of the patient towards his guide and adviser is most apparent. The notable difference between his parents as they are in reality and their image in his phantasy re-awakens once more in its original intensity the very earliest child-wish, namely, that his little heart should once more be able to confide in his father and mother and with this all the old feelings of early disappointment are revived. Owing to this unavoidable conflict which has its foundation in the childish memories of the young soul, and in its attitude to the analyst, arise the fundamental demands made upon the latter by the patient. The chief thing in the analysis of children and young people is the analyst's power of intuition in regard to the sufferer. It does not matter so much whether many complexes are made conscious to the young patient, or how much "insight" he gains, the reaction is sufficient at the beginning. Often, much later, some chance word from the child shows that he has preserved and appreciated at its true value the explanation which he had at an earlier stage. But this acceptance does not take place by means of conscious work: a great part of the psycho-analytic process in the child takes place in his unconscious, and contrary to the case of the grown-up, it remains permanently there, and only a change in his behaviour proves to the analyst that his trouble has not been in vain. In my experience, it is those children whose seeming compliance might tempt one to satisfaction, who are the most difficult type for treatment: they are the well-drilled kind, who say "yes" to everything, but in their hearts say "no" and act accordingly.

Intuition and patience, these are the foundations which must be laid from the first meeting with the young patient, in order that confidence may rest on solid ground.

An important factor in child-analysis is the relationship between the analyst and the young patient's family. One might think that in this respect the analyst-educator would have an advantage over his medical colleagues, since the child comes for treatment owing to the parents' wish, whereas the adult comes of his own accord, very often quite against the wish of his family. Unfortunately this idea is quite incorrect. In the case of the child as well, psycho-analysis is looked upon as the last resource, and the parents, who have found all other educational measures fail, have a good deal of mistrust even of psycho-analysis. In spite of this, they expect a "miraculous cure" which shall remedy in the course of days the mistakes of years. And the relatives cling to this expectation, in spite of the analyst's quite explicit information that the duration of the treatment cannot be fixed in advance because it is dependent upon the individual character of the child, but that it will certainly stretch over several months. I have proved over and over again that the relatives from the very beginning of the treatment have privately settled in their own minds a time-limit, and this they maintain, incapable of sufficient insight to understand that to break off treatment half-way through means waste of time, trouble, and money. Of course, the psycho-analytic treatment itself is held responsible for the consequence of the premature breaking-off, namely, that there is a considerable intensification of the original trouble—and this is produced by the child (in part consciously, in part unconsciously) owing to his revolt against the loss of treatment which though at first compulsory has become indispensable to him. The parents' criticism of the treatment is made more poignant owing to their painful consciousness, mingled with shame, anxiety and bitterness, of having failed in regard to their children's successful training. In addition the knowledge that the analysis reveals all the mistakes made in the upbringing of the child in spite of the best intentions, and that the analyst obtains an insight (very undesirable from the parents' point of view), into intimate family affairs creates in most parents distrustful and anxious feelings. This reluctance to lay bare family affairs proves a greater hindrance in the case of child-analysis than in the case of the adult, for the latter is willing to sacrifice, for the sake of his own recovery, the consideration he holds for his family. Another difficulty arises from the over-anxiety of the parents to further and hasten the analysis by their co-operation. The mothers, at all events, nearly always show a desire to make use of "active therapy". It is terribly difficult to convince them that their work lies in quite another direction and that they are really acting as helpers if they show the child during the treatment the greatest possible measure of patience and forbearance. They must develop the understanding that the young mind during the analysis has to go through a process of re-crystallization, during which first the old values are destroyed; and this destructive process cannot take place without disturbances, and these shocks have an outlet in an increase of the very difficulties and peculiarities which have to be eliminated. Quite usually after a striking temporary improvement in the symptoms (arousing in the parents premature expectation of cure in a few weeks or even hours in spite of the analyst's emphatic warning as to the duration of the analysis) a marked change for the worse takes place. Some children rebel more violently than ever against the parents' rules and regulations: others who have failed in their work owing to their extreme phantasy-life, will take advantage of the unwonted freedom to express now without check their secret thoughts and feelings. They lose themselves in their day-dreams, and for the time being, they turn away from their work more completely than before. This apparent deterioration in the outward behaviour of the child, which reveals his psychic condition, is regarded quite differently by the parents and by the analyst: the latter sees in it a good sign for the further progress of the analysis.

It is not easy to convince the parents that the renunciation of the desire for the children's success in work during the process of analysis holds out the promise of that very success when the treatment is over. They are very unwilling to allow as much importance to a psychic trouble as to a physical one. Just as no father would think of sending his child to school when suffering from pneumonia, so no demands must be made for study from the child suffering psychically.

The narcissism of the parents explains their extreme jealousy, experienced especially by the mother, when they see their child so ardently attaching himself to the analyst. In this connection an important task devolves upon the analyst who has to explain to the mother that the positive transference is a passing phenomen but one necessary to the success of the analysis, and in no way deprives her permanently of her child's love.

In spite of the difficulties which prevent the relations between the parents and analyst being so friendly as might be desirable in the interests of the child, this relationship is inevitable. It is a legitimate demand on the part of the parents and furthers the treatment. For the child passes over, instinctively and, unlike the adult, without conscious criticism, everything which has no "feeling-tone" for him and which is settled and done with. Consequently, very often we learn nothing in the analysis of difficulties at home or at school, because the child does not feel the need to revise these scenes, and his interest in them disappears as soon as they have played their part according to his expectations. In addition we must not forget that the child consciously also keeps secrets. In order to ascertain some special date, or the accuracy of some memory, it is sometimes useful to question the parents; and further it is valuable for obtaining an insight into the earliest stage of the patient's life. It is here that the parents can satisfy their desire for active co-operation in the analysis, by means of written replies to the analyst's series of questions, concerning the physical and psychic development of the child in early infancy, and these communications throw a valuable light upon the surroundings, the outlook on life and the educational system in which the child has grown up. It is of special importance in the process of analysis to refrain from touching on certain matters, such as infantile masturbation and how it ceased, and to overlook a decided denial in respect to certain matters which we all know (just like the interest in the digestive process, etc.) must be answered in the affirmative by every child. This emphatic denial of all kinds of "nastiness" affords the analyst guiding-lines for the treatment of the sexual problem.

I consider it impossible for anyone to analyse properly his own child. This is so not only because the child hardly ever reveals its deepest desires and thoughts, conscious or unconscious, to father and mother, but because in this case the analyst is often driven to re-construct too freely, and also because the narcissism of the parents would make it almost unbearable to hear from their own child the psycho-analytic revelations.

The relations between the analyst and the patient's brothers and sisters has also a bearing on the course of the treatment. Usually the younger ones are eager to share the patient's confidence, whereas the elder ones, owing to a secret feeling of envy and animosity, and a half-expectation of betrayal of themselves, keep aloof. Both of these attitudes are judged with equal hostility by the patient, who watches with jealous mistrust the relations of his special confidant with his brothers and sisters and is unwilling to give up his phantasy of the analyst's hostile attitude towards the latter.

We may sum up our knowledge obtained from child-analysis in a few sentences. Almost always we find mistakes in education, through which a bad disposition or a harmful experience, instead of decreasing in destructive effects, is fostered. Too much strictness on the one hand, and too much leniency on the other, with nearly always a lack of consistency in the upbringing, bring about these evils, from which both parents and children alike suffer. If the parents themselves were analysed, in all probability fewer children would be in need of analysis.

Notes

1. The dressed-up figure of a little man, holding a birch-rod.
2. Cf. Freud: A child is being beaten, *International Journal of Psychoanalysis*, Vol. I, p. 380.

Symposium on child-analysis*

Melanie Klein

I will begin my remarks with a short retrospect of the development of child-analysis in general. Its beginnings date from the year 1909, when Freud published the "Analysis of a phobia in a five-year-old boy". This publication was of the greatest theoretical importance, confirming as it did in the person of the child who was its subject the truth of what Freud, proceeding from the analysis of adults, had discovered to exist in children. The paper had, however, yet another significance, the greatness of which could not at that time at all be gauged. This analysis was destined to be the foundation-stone of subsequent child-analysis. For not only did it show the presence and the evolution of the Oedipus complex in children and demonstrate the forms in which it operates in them; it showed also that these unconscious tendencies could safely and most profitably be brought into consciousness. Freud himself describes this discovery as follows:[1]

> But I must now inquire what harm was done to Hans by dragging to light in him complexes such as are not only repressed by children

---

* Held before the British Psycho-Analytical Society, May 4 and 18, 1927.

but dreaded by their parents. Did the little boy proceed to take some serious action as regards what he wanted from his mother? or did his evil intentions against his father give place to evil deeds? *Such misgivings will no doubt have occurred to many doctors, who misunderstand the nature of psycho-analysis and think that wicked instincts are strengthened by being made conscious.*[2]

And again, on p. 285:

On the contrary, the only results of the analysis were that Hans recovered, that he ceased to be afraid of horses and that he got on to rather familiar terms with his father, as the latter reported with some amusement. But whatever his father may have lost in the boy's respect he won back in his confidence: "I thought", said Hans, "you knew everything as you knew that about the horse". For analysis does not undo the *effects* of repression. The instincts which were formerly suppressed remain suppressed; but the same effect is produced in a different way. Analysis replaces the process of repression, which is an automatic and excessive one, by a temperate and purposeful control on the part of the highest mental faculties. In a word, *analysis replaces repression by condemnation.* This seems to bring us the long-looked-for evidence that consciousness has a biological function, and that with its entrance upon the scene an important advantage is secured.

H. Hug-Hellmuth, who had the honourable distinction of having been the first to undertake the systematic analysis of children, approached her task with certain preconceptions in her mind, which she also retained to the last. In her paper entitled "On the technique of child-analysis", written after four years' work in this field, which gives us the clearest idea of her principles and her technique,[3] she makes it very clear that she deprecated the idea of analysing very young children, that she considered it necessary to content oneself with "partial success" and not to penetrate too deep in analysis with children, for fear of stirring up too powerfully the repressed tendencies and impulses or of making demands which their powers of assimilation are unable to meet.

From this paper, as well as from her other writings, we know that she shrank from penetrating at all deeply into the Oedipus complex. Another assumption to which she held in her work was that in the case of children not only analytic treatment but also a definite educative influence is required of the analyst.

As early as 1921, when I published my first paper "The development of a child",[4] I had arrived at very different conclusions. In my analysis of a boy of five and a quarter I found (what all my later analyses confirmed) that it was perfectly possible and also salutary to probe the Oedipus complex to its depths and that by so doing one could obtain results at least equal to those of adult analysis. But, side by side with this, I found out that in an analysis so conducted not only was it unnecessary for the analyst to endeavour to exert an educative influence but that the two things were incompatible. I took these discoveries as the guiding principles in my work and advocated them in all my writings, and this is how I have come to attempt the analysis of quite little children, that is, from three to six years old, and to find it both successful and full of promise.

Let us now first of all select from Anna Freud's book what seem to be her four principal points. Here we meet again with the fundamental idea which we have already mentioned as being also H. Hug-Hellmuth's, namely, the conviction that the analysis of children should not be pressed too far. By this, as is clear also from the more immediate conclusions drawn, is meant that the child's relation to the parents should not be too much handled, that is, that the Oedipus complex must not be searchingly examined. The examples which Anna Freud gives do in fact show no analysis of the Oedipus complex.

The second leading idea is, here again, that the analysis of children should be combined with exerting an educational influence upon them.

It is remarkable and should give food for thought that, though child-analysis was first attempted some eighteen years ago and has been practised ever since, we have to face the fact that its most fundamental principles have not yet been clearly enunciated. If we compare with this fact the development of adult psychoanalysis we shall find that, within a similar period of time, all the basic principles for the latter work were not only laid down but were empirically tested and proved beyond refutation, and that a technique was evolved the details of which had certainly to be perfected but whose fundamental principles have remained unshaken.

What is the explanation of the fact that just the analysis of children should have been so much less fortunate in its development? The argument often heard in analytical circles that children are not suitable objects for analysis does not seem to be valid. H. Hug-Hellmuth was indeed very sceptical about the results to be obtained with children. She said she "had to content herself with partial success and also to reckon with relapses". Moreover she restricted the treatment to a limited number of cases. Anna Freud also sets very definite limits to its applicability, but on the other hand she takes a more optimistic view than did H. Hug-Hellmuth of the potentialities of child-analysis. At the end of her book she says: "In child-analysis, in spite of all the difficulties I have enumerated, we do bring about changes, improvements and cures such as we dare not even dream of in analysing adults" (p. 86).

In order to answer the question I have suggested, I want now to make certain statements which it will be my business to prove as I go on. I think that child-analysis, as compared with that of adults, has developed so much less favourably in the past because it was not approached in a spirit of free and unprejudiced enquiry, as adult analysis was, but was hampered and burdened from the outset by certain preconceptions. If we look back at that first child-analysis, the foundation of all others (that of little Hans), we discover that it did not suffer from this limitation. Certainly there was as yet no special technique: the child's father who carried out this partial analysis under Freud's directions was quite unversed in the practice of analysis. In spite of this he had the courage to go quite a long way in the analysis and his results were good. In the summary to which I referred earlier in this article Freud says that he himself would have liked to go further. What he says shows, too, that he did not see any danger in a thorough analysis of the Oedipus complex, so evidently he did not think that this complex should on grounds of principle be left unanalysed in children. But H. Hug-Hellmuth, who for so many years was almost alone and certainly pre-eminent in this field of work, approached it from the outset with principles which were bound to limit it and therefore make it less fruitful, not only in respect of its practical results, the number of cases in which analysis was to be used, etc., but also in respect of theoretical findings. For, during all these years, child-analysis, which might have reasonably been expected to contribute directly to the development of psycho-analytical theory, has done nothing in this direction worth speaking of. Anna Freud, as well as H. Hug-Hellmuth, has the idea that in analysing children we can discover not only no more, but actually less about the early period of life than when we analyse adults.

Here I come upon another pretext which is put forward as a reason for the slow progress made in the field of child-analysis. It is said that a child's behaviour in analysis is obviously different from that of an adult, and that therefore a different technique must be used. I think this argument is incorrect. If I may adapt the saying, "It is the spirit which builds the body", I should like to maintain that it is the attitude, the inner conviction which finds the necessary technique. I must reiterate what I have said: if one approaches child-analysis with an open mind one will discover ways and means of probing to the deepest depths. And then, from the results of the procedure one will realize what is the child's *true nature* and will perceive that there is no need to impose any restriction on the analysis, either as to the depth to which it may penetrate or the method by which it may work.

In what I have now said I have already touched on the principal point in my criticism of Anna Freud's book.

A number of technical devices employed by Anna Freud may, I think, be explained from two points of view: (1) she assumes that the analytic situation cannot be established with children; and (2) in the case of children she regards pure analysis without any pedagogic admixture as unsuitable or questionable.

The first thesis follows directly from the assumption of the second.

If we compare this with the technique of adult analysis, we perceive that we assume unconditionally that a true *analytic* situation can be brought about only by *analytic* means. We should regard it as a grave error to ensure for ourselves a positive transference from the patient by employing measures such as Anna Freud describes in Chapter One of her book, or to utilize his anxiety in order to make him submissive, or otherwise to intimidate or win him over by means of authority. We should think that even if such an introduction as this secured for us partial access to the patient's Ucs, we yet could never expect to establish a true analytic situation and to carry through a complete analysis which should penetrate the deeper layers of the mind. We know that we constantly have to analyse the fact that patients wish to see us as an authority—whether a hated or a loved one—and that only by analysing this attitude do we gain access to these deeper layers.

All the means which we should regard as incorrect in the analysis of adults are specially stressed by Anna Freud as valuable in analysing children, the object being that introduction to the treatment which she believes to be necessary and which she calls the "breaking-in" to analysis. It would appear obvious that after this "breaking-in" she will never wholly succeed in establishing a true analytic situation. Now I think it surprising and illogical that Anna Freud, who does not use the necessary measures to establish the analytic situation but substitutes others at variance with these, yet continually refers to her assumption, and tries to prove it theoretically, that it is *not possible* to establish an analytic situation with children nor, therefore, to carry through with them a pure analysis in the sense of adult analysis.

Anna Freud gives a number of reasons to justify the elaborate and troublesome means which she considers it necessary to employ with children in order to bring about a situation which shall make analytic work possible. These reasons do not seem to me sound. She departs in so many respects from the proved analytic rules, because she thinks that children are such *different* beings from adults. Yet the sole purpose of all these elaborate measures is to make the child like the adult in his attitude to analysis. This seems contradictory and I think is to be explained by the fact that in her comparisons Anna Freud puts the Cs and the ego of the child and the adult in the foreground, while we (though we give all necessary consideration to the ego) surely have to work first and foremost with the Ucs. But in the Ucs (and here I am basing my statement on deep analytical work with both children and adults) the former are by no means so fundamentally different from the latter. It is only that in children the ego has not yet attained to its full development, and therefore they are very much more under the sway of their Ucs. It is this which we must approach and this that we must regard as the central point of our work if we want to learn to know children as they really are and to analyse them.

I do not attach any special value to the goal which Anna Freud so ardently strives after—that of bringing about in children an attitude towards analysis analogous to the attitude of adults. I think, too, that if Anna Freud does attain this goal by the means which she describes (and this can be only in a certain limited number of cases) the result is not that towards which her work is directed but something very different. The "acknowledgment of illness or of naughtiness" which she has succeeded in awaking in the child emanates from the anxiety which she has mobilised in him for her own purposes: castration-anxiety and the sense of guilt. (I will not here go into the question how far in adults too the reasonable and conscious desire to get well is simply a façade screening this anxiety.) With children we cannot expect to find any lasting basis for our analytic work in a conscious purpose which, as we know, even in adults, would not long hold firm as the sole support for the analysis.

Anna Freud too, it is true, thinks that this purpose is necessary in the first instance as a preparation for the work, but she further believes that, when once the purpose is there, she can rely upon it as the analysis progresses. I think this idea is mistaken and that whenever she appeals to this insight she is really having recourse to the child's anxiety and sense of guilt. In itself there would be nothing objectionable about this, for feelings of anxiety and guilt are undoubtedly most important factors in the possibility of our work. Only I think it necessary for us to be clear *what* are the supports upon which we are relying and *how* we are using them. Analysis is not in itself a gentle method: it cannot spare the patient *any suffering*, and this applies equally to children. In fact, it must force the suffering into consciousness and bring about abreaction if the patients are to be spared permanent and more fatal suffering later. So my criticism is not that Anna Freud *activates* anxiety and the sense of guilt, but on the contrary that she does not *resolve* them *sufficiently*. It seems to me an unnecessary harshness towards a child when, as for instance she describes on p. 9, she brings into his consciousness the anxiety lest he should go mad, without immediately attacking this anxiety at its unconscious roots and thus as far as possible allaying it again.

But if it is really to feelings of anxiety and guilt that we have to appeal in our work, why should we not regard these two as factors to be reckoned with and work with them systematically from the outset?

I myself always do this, and I have found that I can place complete reliance in a technique which goes on the principle of taking into account and working analytically with the quantities of anxiety and of feelings of guilt which are so strong in all children and are much clearer and more easily laid hold of than in adults.

Anna Freud states (p. 56) that a hostile or anxious attitude towards me in a child does not justify me in concluding immediately that there is a negative transference at work, for "the more tenderly a little child is attached to his own mother, the fewer friendly impulses are left in him for strangers". I do not think we can draw a comparison, as she does, with tiny infants who reject what is strange to them. We do not know a great deal about tiny infants, but it is possible to learn a great deal from an early analysis about the mind of a child of, say, three years old, and there we see that it is only very ambivalent neurotic children who manifest fear or hostility towards strangers. My experience has confirmed my belief that if I construe this dislike at once as anxiety and negative transference feeling, and interpret it as such in connection with material which the child at the same time produces and then trace it back to its original object, the mother, I can at once observe that the anxiety diminishes. This manifests itself in the beginning of a more positive transference and, with it, of more vigorous play. In older children the situation is analogous though it differs in detail. Of course, my method presupposes that I have from the beginning been willing to attract to myself the negative as well as the positive transference and, further, to investigate it to its source in the Oedipus situation. Both these measures are in full agreement with analytical principles, but Anna Freud rejects them for reasons which I think are unfounded.

I believe then that a radical difference between our attitudes to anxiety and a sense of guilt in children is this: that Anna Freud makes use of these feelings to attach the child to herself, while I from the outset enlist them in the service of the analytic work. There cannot in any case be any very large number of children in whom one can stir up anxiety without its proving an element which will most painfully disturb or even make impossible the progress of the work, unless one immediately proceeds to resolve it analytically.

Anna Freud, moreover, as far as I can understand from her book, employs this means only in particular cases. In other she tries by every means to bring about a positive transference, in order to fulfil the condition, which she regards as necessary for her work, of attaching the child to her own personality.

This method, again, seems to me unsound, for surely we could work more certainly and more effectually by purely analytic means. It is not every child who responds to us from the beginning with fear and dislike. My experience bears me out when I say that if a child's attitude to us is friendly and playful we are justified in assuming that there is a positive transference and in at once making use of this in our work. And we have another excellent and well-tried weapon which we use in an analogous fashion to that in which we employ it in the analyses of adults, though there, it is true, we do not have so speedy and so plain an opportunity to intervene. I mean that we *interpret* this positive transference, that is, in both children's as in adults' analyses we trace it back to the original object. In general, we shall probably notice both the positive and the negative transference and we shall be given every opportunity for analytic work if we handle both from the outset analytically. By resolving some part of the negative transference we shall then obtain, just as with adults, an increase in the positive transference and this, in accordance with the ambivalence of childhood, will soon in its turn be succeeded by a re-emerging of the negative. Now this is true analytic work and an analytic situation has been established. Moreover, we have then found the basis upon which to build in the child itself, and we can often be to a great extent independent of a knowledge of its surroundings. In short, we have achieved the conditions necessary for analysis and not only are we spared the laborious, difficult and unreliable measures described by Anna Freud, but (and this seems even more important) we can ensure for our work the full value and success of an analyses in every sense equivalent to adult analysis.

At this point, however, I encounter an objection raised by Anna Freud in the second chapter of her book, entitled "The means employed in child-analysis". To work in the way I have described we must get material from the child's associations. Anna Freud and I and probably everyone who analyses children agree that they neither can nor will give associations in the same way as grown-ups and so sufficient material cannot be collected by means of speech alone. Amongst the means which Anna Freud suggests as useful for making up for the lack of verbal associations are some which I too have found valuable in my experience. If we examine these means rather more closely—take, for instance, drawing, or telling day-dreams, etc.—we shall see that their object is to collect material in some other way than that of association according to rule, and that it is above all important with children to set their phantasy free and to induce them to phantasy. In one of Anna Freud's statements we have a clue, which must be carefully considered, as to how this is to be done. She states that "there is nothing easier than to make children understand dream-interpretation". And again (p. 31) "even children of poor intelligence, who seemed in every other respect as unfit as possible for analysis, succeeded in dream-interpretation". I think that these children would perhaps not have been so unsuitable for analysis at all if Anna Freud had made more use, in other ways as well as in dream-interpretation, of the understanding of symbolism which they so plainly manifested. For it is my experience that, if this is done, no child, not even the least intelligent, is unfit for analysis.

For this is just the lever which we must make use of in child-analysis. A child will bring us an abundance of phantasies if we follow him along this path with the conviction that what he recounts is symbolic. In Chapter Three Anna Freud puts forward a number of theoretical arguments against the play-technique which I have devised, at least when it is applied for the purpose of analysis and not merely of observation. She thinks it doubtful whether one is justified in interpreting the content of the drama enacted in children's play as symbolic and thinks that they might very likely be occasioned simply by actual observations or experiences of daily life. Here I must say that from Anna Freud's illustrations of my technique, I can see that she misunderstands it. "If a child upsets a lamp-post or one of the figures in the game, she [Melanie Klein] interprets the action probably as due to aggressive tendencies towards the father, while, if the child makes two carts collide, it is construed as implying observation of parental coitus". I should never attempt any such "wild" symbolic interpretations of children's play. On the contrary I emphasized this very specially in my last paper.[5] Supposing that a child gives expression to the same psychic material in various repetitions—often actually through various media, i.e. toys, water, by cutting-out, drawing, etc.—and supposing that, besides, I can observe that these particular activities are mostly accompanied at the time by a sense of guilt, manifesting itself either as anxiety or in representations which imply over-compensation, which are the expression of reaction-formations—supposing, then, that I have arrived at an insight into certain connections: then I interpret these phenomena and link them up with the Ucs and the analytic situation. The practical and theoretical conditions for the interpretation are precisely the same as in the analysis of adults.

The little toys I use are only one means I provide; paper, pencils, scissors, string, balls, bricks and, above all, water are others. They are at the child's disposal to use if he likes and the purpose of them all is simply to gain access to and to liberate his phantasy. There are some children who for a long time will not touch a toy or perhaps for weeks on end will only cut things out. In the case of children altogether inhibited in play the toys may possibly simply be a means of studying more closely the reasons for their inhibition. Some children, often the very little ones, as soon as the playthings have given them the opportunity of dramatizing some of the phantasies or experiences by which they are dominated, often put the toys aside altogether and pass on to every imaginable kind of game in which they themselves, various objects in my room and I have to take part.

I have gone into this detail of my technique at some length because I want to make clear the principle which, in my experience, makes it possible to handle children's associations in the greatest abundance and to penetrate into the deepest Ucs strata.

We can establish a quicker and surer contact with the Ucs of children if, acting on the conviction that they are much more deeply under the sway of the Ucs and their instinctual impulses than are adults, we shorten the route which adult analysis takes by way of contact with the ego and *make direct connection with the child's Ucs*. It is obvious that, if this preponderance of the Ucs is a fact, we should also expect that the mode of representation by symbols which prevails in the Ucs would be much more natural to children than to adults, in fact, that the former will be dominated by it. Let us follow them along this path, that is to say, let us come into contact with their Ucs, making use of its language through our interpretation. If we do this we shall have won access to the children themselves. Of course this is not all so easily and quickly to be accomplished as it appears; if it were, the analysis of little children would take only a short time, and this is not by any means the case. In child-analysis, we shall again and again detect resistance no less markedly than in that of adults, in children very often in the form still the more natural to them, namely, in anxiety.

This, then, is the second factor which seems to me so essential if we wish to penetrate into the child's Ucs. If we watch the alterations in his manner of representing what is going on within him (whether it is that he changes his game or gives it up or that there is a direct onset of anxiety) and try to see what there is in the nexus of the material to cause these alterations, we shall be convinced that we are always coming up against the sense of guilt and have to interpret this in its turn.

These two factors, which I have found to be the most reliable aids in the technique of child-analysis, are mutually dependent and complementary. Only by *interpreting* and so *allaying* the child's anxiety whenever we can reach it shall we gain access to his Ucs and get him *to phantasy*. Then, if we follow out the symbolism that his phantasies contain, we shall soon see anxiety reappear, and thus we shall ensure the progress of the work.

The account given of my technique and the importance attributed by me to the symbolism contained in children's actions might be misconstrued as implying that in child-analysis one has to do without the help of free association in the true sense.

In an earlier passage of my paper I pointed out that Anna Freud and I and all of us who work at child-analysis are agreed that children cannot and will not associate in the same way as adults. I should like here to add that probably it is chiefly that children *cannot*, not because they lack the capacity to put their thoughts into words (to some degree this would apply only to quite small children), but because *anxiety* resists verbal associations. It does not lie within the scope of this paper to discuss this interesting special question in greater detail: I will just briefly mention some facts of experience.

Representation by means of toys—indeed, symbolic representation in general, as being to some extent removed from the subject's own person—is less invested with anxiety than is confession by word of mouth. If, then, we succeed in allaying anxiety and in getting in the first instance more indirect representations, we shall be able to convince ourselves that we can elicit for analysis the fullest verbal expression of which the child is capable. And then we find repeatedly that at times when anxiety becomes more marked the indirect representations once more occupy the foreground. Let me give a brief illustration. When I had advanced quite a long way in the analysis of a five-year-old boy, he produced a dream the interpretation of which went very deep and was fruitful in results. This interpretation occupied the whole analytic hour, all the associations being *exclusively verbal*. On the two following days he again brought dreams which turned out to be continuations of the first. But verbal associations to the second dream could be elicited only with great difficulty and one at a time. The resistance was plain and the anxiety markedly greater than on the day before. But the child turned to the box of toys and by means of dolls and other play-things depicted for me his associations, helping himself out with words again whenever he overcame some resistance. On the third day the anxiety was even greater, on account of the material which had come to light on the two previous days. The associations were given almost exclusively by means of play with toys and water.

If we are logical in our application of the two principles that I have emphasized, namely, that we should follow up the child's symbolic mode of representation and that we should take into account the facility with which anxiety is roused in children, we shall be able also to count on their associations as a very important means in analysis, but, as I have said, only at times and as one means amongst several.

I think therefore that Anna Freud's statement is incomplete when she says: "Every now and again, too, unintentional and invol-untary associations come to our aid" (p. 41). Whether associations appear or not depends quite regularly on certain definite attitudes in the analysand and in no way on chance. In my opinion we can make use of this means to a far greater extent than seems likely. Over and over again it bridges the gulf to reality, and this is one reason why it is more closely associated with anxiety than is the unreal, indirect mode of representation. On this account I would not regard any child-analysis, not even that of a quite little child, as terminated unless I could finally succeed in its being expressed in speech, to the degree to which the child is capable of this, and so of linking it up with reality.

We have then a perfect analogy with the technique of adult analysis. The only difference is that with children we find that the Ucs prevails to a far greater extent and that therefore its mode of expression is far more predominant than in adults, and further that we have to take into account the child's greater tendency to anxiety.

But this is also very decidedly true of analysis during the latency and prepubertal periods and even to some extent during puberty. In a number of analyses in which the subjects were at one or other of these phases of development I was forced to adopt a modified form of the same technique as I use with children.

I think that what I have now said robs of their force Anna Freud's two main objections to my play-technique. She questioned (1) whether we were justified in assuming that the symbolic content of children's play is its main motive, and (2) whether we could regard children's play as equivalent to verbal association in adults. For, she argues, such play lacks the idea of purpose which the adult brings to his analysis and which "enables him when associating to exclude all conscious directing and influencing of his trains of thought".

To this latter objection I should like to reply further that these intentions in adult patients (which in my experience are not so effective as Anna Freud supposes even with them) are quite super-fluous for children, and by this I do not mean very little children.

It is clear from what I have said that children are so much domi-nated by their Ucs that it is really unnecessary for them deliberately to exclude conscious ideas.[6] Anna Freud herself too has weighed this possibility in her mind (p. 49).

I have devoted so much space to the question of the technique to be employed with children because this seems to me fundamen-tal in the whole problem of child-analysis. When Anna Freud rejects the play-technique her argument applies not only to the analysis of little children but also in my opinion to the basic principle of the analysis of older children, as I understand it. The play-technique provides us with a rich abundance of material and gives us access to the deepest strata of the mind. If we make use of it we arrive unconditionally at the analysis of the Oedipus complex, and once arrived, we cannot mark out limits for analysis in any direction. If then we really wish to avoid analysing the Oedipus complex we must not make use of the play-technique, even in its modified application to older children.

It follows that the question is not whether the analysis of children *can* go so deep as that of adults, but whether it *ought* to go so deep. To answer this question we must examine the reasons which Anna Freud gives, in Chapter Four of her book, *against* penetrating so far.

Before we do this, however, I should like to discuss Anna Freud's conclusions, given in Chapter Three of her book, about the part played by the transference in child-analysis.

Anna Freud describes certain essential differences between the transference situation in adults and in children. She comes to the conclusion that in the latter there may be a satisfactory transference, but that no transference-neurosis is produced. In support of this statement she adduces the following theoretical argument. Children, she says, are not ready like adults to enter upon a new edition of their love-relations, because the original love-objects, the parents, still exist as objects in reality.

In order to refute this statement, which I believe to be incorrect, I should have to enter into a detailed discussion of the structure of the super-ego in children. But as this is contained in a later passage I will content myself here with a few statements which are supported by my subsequent exposition.

The analysis of very young children has shewn me that even a three-year-old child has left behind him the most important part of the development of his Oedipus complex. Consequently he is already far removed, through repression and feelings of guilt, from the objects whom he originally desired. His relations to them have undergone distortion and transformation so that the present love-objects are now *imagos* of the original objects.

Hence in reference to the analyst children can very well enter upon a new edition of their love-relations in all the fundamental and therefore decisive points. But here we encounter a second theoretical objection. Anna Freud considers that in analysing children the analyst is not, as he is when the patient is an adult, "impersonal, shadowy, a blank page upon which the patient can inscribe his phantasies", one who avoids imposing prohibitions and permitting gratifications. But according to my experience it is exactly thus that a children's analyst can and ought to behave, when once he has established the analytic situation. His activity is only apparent, for even when he throws himself wholly into all the play-phantasies of the child, conforming to the modes of representation peculiar to children, he is doing just the same as the analyst of adults, who, we know, also willingly follows the phantasies of his patients. But beyond this I do not permit child-patients any personal gratifications, either in the form of presents or caresses or personal encounters outside analysis and so forth. In short, I keep on the whole to the approved rules of adult analysis. What I give to the child-patient is analytic help and relief, which he feels comparatively quickly even if he has not had any sense of illness before. Besides this, in response to his trust in me he can absolutely rely on perfect sincerity and honesty on my part towards him.

I must, however, contest Anna Freud's conclusion no less than her premises. In my experience a full transference-neurosis does occur in children, in a manner analogous to that in which it arises with adults. When analysing children I observe that their symptoms change, are accentuated or lessened in accordance with the analytic situation. I observe in them the abreaction of affects in close connection with the progress of the work and in relation to myself. I observe that anxiety arises and that the children's reactions work themselves out on this analytic ground. Parents who watch their children carefully have often told me that they have been surprised to see habits, etc., which had long disappeared come back again. I have not found that children work off their reactions when they are at home as well as when with me: for the most part they are reserved for abreaction in the analytic hour. Of course it does happen that at times, when very powerful affects are violently emerging, something of the disturbance becomes noticeable to those with whom the children are associated, but this is only temporary and it cannot be avoided in the analysis of adults either.

On this point, therefore, my experience is in complete contradiction to Anna Freud's observations. The reason for this difference in our findings is easy to see: it depends on the different way in which she and I handle the transference. Let me sum up what I have already said. Anna Freud thinks that a *positive* transference is a necessary condition for all analytic work with children. She regards a negative transference as undesirable.

In the case of children [she writes], it is especially inconvenient to have negative tendencies directed against the analyst, in spite of the light they may throw on many points. We shall endeavour to demolish or modify them as soon as possible. The really fruitful work will always be done when the attachment to the analyst is positive. [p. 51]

We know that one of the principal factors in analytic work is the handling of the transference, strictly and objectively, in accordance with the facts, in the manner which our analytic knowledge has taught us to be the right one. A thorough resolution of the transference is regarded as one of the signs that an analysis has been satisfactorily concluded. On this basis psycho-analysis has laid down a number of important rules which prove necessary in every case. Anna Freud sets aside these rules for the most part in child-analysis. With her the transference, the clear recognition of which we know to be an important condition of our work, becomes an uncertain and doubtful concept. She says that the analyst "*probably* has to share with the parents the child's love or hate" (p. 56). And I do not understand what is intended by "demolishing or modifying" the inconvenient negative tendencies.

Here premises and conclusions move in a circle. If the analytic situation is not produced by analytic means, if the positive and the negative transference are not handled logically, then neither shall we bring about a transference-neurosis nor can we expect the child's reactions to work themselves out in relation to analysis and the analyst. Later in this paper I will deal with this point more thoroughly, but at present I will just briefly sum up what I have already said by stating that Anna Freud's method of attracting the positive transference by all possible means to herself and of lessening the negative transference when it is directed against herself seems to me not only technically incorrect but, in effect, to militate far more against the parents than my method. For it is only natural that the negative transference will then remain directed against those with whom the child is associated in daily life.

In her fourth chapter Anna Freud comes to a number of conclusions which seem to me again to display this vicious circle, this time specially clearly. The term "vicious circle" I have explained elsewhere as meaning that from certain premises conclusions are drawn which are then used to confirm those same premises. As one of the conclusions which seem to me erroneous I would instance Anna Freud's statement that in child-analysis it is impossible to surmount the barrier of the child's imperfect mastery of speech. It is true she makes a reservation: "As far as my experience goes up till now, with the technique I have described". But the very next sentence contains an explanation of a general theoretical nature. She says that what we discover about early childhood when we are analysing adults "is revealed by these very methods of free association and interpretation of the transference-reactions, i.e. by those means which fail us in child-analysis". In various passages in her book Anna Freud stresses the idea that child-analysis, adapting itself to the child's mind, must alter its methods. Yet she bases her doubts of the technique which I have evolved on a number of theoretical considerations, without having submitted it to a practical test. But I have proved by practical application that this technique helps us to get the child's associations in even greater abundance than we get in adult analysis and thus to penetrate far deeper than we can in the latter.

From what my own experience has taught me, then, I really can only emphatically combat Anna Freud's statement that both the methods used in adult analysis (namely, free association and the interpretation of the transference-reactions), in order to investigate the patient's early childhood, fail us in analysing children. I am even convinced that it is the special province of child-analysis, particularly that of quite young children, to make valuable contributions to our theory, just because with children analysis can go far deeper and therefore can bring to light details which do not appear so clearly in the case of adults.

Anna Freud compares the situation of an analyst of children with that of an ethnologist "who should try by contact with a primitive people to acquire information about prehistoric times more easily than by studying the civilized races" (p. 66). This again strikes me as a theoretical statement which contradicts practical experience. The analysis of little children, as well as that of older children if it is carried far enough, gives a very clear picture of the enormous complexity of development which we find even in very little ones and shews that children of the age of, say, three years, just because they are already so much the products of civilization, have gone and are going through severe conflicts. To keep to Anna Freud's illustration, I should say that precisely from the standpoint of research a children's analyst finds himself in a fortunate situation which is never vouchsafed to an ethnologist, namely that of finding the civilized people in closest association with the primitive and, in consequence of this rare association, of receiving the most valuable information about both the earliest and later times.

I will now deal in greater detail with Anna Freud's conceptions of the child's super-ego. In Chapter Four of her book are certain statements which have special significance, both because of the importance of the theoretical question to which they relate and also because of the wide conclusions which Anna Freud draws from them.

The deep analysis of children, and particularly of little children, has led me to form quite a different picture of the super-ego in early childhood from that painted by Anna Freud principally as a result of theoretical considerations. It is certain that the ego of children is not comparable to that of adults. The super-ego, on the other hand, approximates closely to that of the adult and is not radically influenced by later development as is the ego. The dependence of children on external objects is naturally greater than that of adults and this fact produces results which are indisputable, but which I think Anna Freud very much over-estimates, and therefore does not rightly interpret. For these external objects are certainly not identical with the already developed super-ego of the child, even though they have at one time contributed to its development. It is only thus that we can explain the astonishing fact that in children of three, four or five years old we encounter a super-ego of a severity which is often in the sharpest contradiction to the real love-objects, the parents. I should like to instance the case of a four-year-old boy whose parents have not only never punished or threatened him but who are really unusually kind and loving. The conflict between the ego and the super-ego in this case (and I am taking it only as one example of many) shews that the super-ego is of a phantastic severity. On account of the well-known formula which prevails in the Ucs this child anticipates, by reason of his own cannibalistic and sadistic impulses, such punishments as castration, being cut to pieces, eaten up, etc., and lives in perpetual dread of them. The contrast between his tender and loving mother and the punishment threatened by the child's super-ego is actually grotesque and is an illustration of the fact that we must on no account identify the real objects with those which children introject.

We know that the formation of the super-ego takes place on the basis of various identifications. My results shew that this process, which terminates with the passing of the Oedipus complex, i.e. with the beginning of the latency period, commences at a very early age. In my last paper I have indicated, basing my remarks on my findings in the analysis of very young children, that the Oedipus complex ensues upon the deprivation experienced at weaning, that is, at the end of the first or the beginning of the second year of life. But, hand in hand with this, we see the beginnings of the formation of the super-ego. The analyses both of older and of quite young children give a clear picture of the various elements out of which the super-ego develops and the different strata in which the development takes place. We see how many stages there are in this evolution before it terminates with the beginning of the latency period. It is really a case of *terminating*, for, in contrast to Anna Freud, I am led to believe from the analysis of children that their super-ego is a highly resistant product, at heart unalterable, and is not essentially different from that of adults. The difference is only that the *maturer ego* of adults is better able to come to terms with their super-ego. This, however, is often only *apparently* the case. Further, adults can defend themselves better against those authorities which represent the super-ego in the outside world; children are inevitably more dependent on these. But this does not imply, as Anna Freud concludes, that the child's super-ego is still "too immature, too dependent on its object, spontaneously to control the demands of the instincts, when analysis has got rid of the neurosis". Even in children these objects—the parents—are not identical with the super-ego. Their influence on the child's super-ego is entirely analogous to that which we can prove to be at work on adults when life places them in somewhat similar situations, e.g. in a position of peculiar dependence. The influence of dreaded authorities in examinations, of officers in military service, and so forth, is quite comparable to the effect which Anna Freud perceives in the "constant correlations in children between the super-ego and the love-objects, which may be likened to those of two vessels with a communicating duct". Under the pressure of those situations in life such as I have mentioned, or others similar to them, adults, like children, react with an increase in their difficulties. This is because the old conflicts are reactivated or reinforced through the harshness of reality, and here a predominant part is played precisely by the intensified operation of the super-ego. Now this is exactly the same process as that to which Anna Freud refers, namely, the influencing of the (child's) super-ego by objects still actually present. It is true that good and bad influences on character and all the other dependent relations of childhood exert a stronger pressure on children than is undergone by adults. Yet in adults too such things are undoubtedly important.[7]

Anna Freud quotes an example (pp. 70–71) which she thinks illustrates particularly well the weakness and dependence of the claims of the ego-ideal in children. A boy in the period of life immediately preceding puberty, when he had an uncontrollable impulse to steal, found that the highest agency which influenced him was his fear of his father. She regards this as a proof that here the father who actually existed could still be substituted for the super-ego.

Now I think that quite often we can find in adults similar developments of the super-ego. There are many people who (often all through their lives) ultimately control their asocial instincts only through fear of a "father" in a somewhat different guise: the police, the law, loss of caste, etc. The same is true too of the "double morality" which Anna Freud observes in children. It is not only children who keep one moral code for the world of adults and another for themselves and their boon companions. Many grown-ups behave in just the same way and adopt one attitude when they are alone or with their equals, and another towards superiors and strangers.

I think that one reason for the difference of opinion between Anna Freud and myself on this very important point is the following. By the super-ego I understand (and here I am in complete agreement with what Freud has taught us of its development) the faculty which has resulted from the Oedipus development through the introjection of the Oedipus objects, and, with the passing of the Oedipus complex, has assumed a lasting and unalterable form. As I have already explained, this faculty, both during its evolution and still more when it is completely formed, differs fundamentally from those objects which really initiated its development. Of course children (but also adults) will set up all kinds of ego-ideals, installing various "super-egos", but this surely takes place in the more super-ficial strata and is at bottom determined by that one super-ego which is firmly rooted in the child and whose nature is immutable. The super-ego which Anna Freud thinks is still operative in the persons of the parents is not identical with this inner super-ego in the true sense, though I do not dispute its influence in itself. If we wish to reach the real super-ego, to reduce its power of operation and to influence it, our only means of doing so is analysis. But by this I mean an analysis which investigates the whole development of the Oedipus complex and the structure of the super-ego.

To return to Anna Freud's illustration which I mentioned before. In the boy whose highest weapon against the onslaught of his instincts was his fear of his father we encounter a super-ego which was certainly immature. I would rather not call such a super-ego typically "childish". To take another example: The four-year-old boy of whom I reported that he suffered from the pressure of a castrating and cannibalistic super-ego, in complete contrast to his kind and loving parents, has certainly not only this one super-ego. I discovered in him identifications which corresponded more closely to his real parents, though not by any means identical with them. These figures, who appeared good and helpful and ready to forgive, he called his "fairy papa and mamma", and, when his atti-tude towards me was positive, he allowed me in the analysis to play the part of the "fairy mamma" to whom everything could be confessed. At other times—always when the negative transference was reappearing—I played the part of the wicked mamma from whom everything evil that he phantasied was anticipated. When I was the fairy mamma he was able to make the most extraordinary demands and gratify wishes which could have no possible fulfil-ment in reality. I was to help him by bringing him as a present, in the night, an object which represented his father's penis, and this was then to be cut up and eaten. That he and she should kill his father together was one of the wishes which the "fairy mamma" was to gratify. When I was the "fairy papa", we were to do the same sort of things to his mother, and, when he took over the role himself and I enacted that of the son, he not only gave me leave to have coitus with his mother but gave me information about it, encour-aged me and also shewed me how the phantasied coitus could be performed with the mother by father and son simultaneously.

A whole series of most varied identifications, which were in opposition to one another, originated in widely different strata and periods and differed fundamentally from the real objects, had in this child resulted as a whole in a super-ego which actually gave the impression of being normal and well developed. An additional reason for selecting this case from many analogous ones is that it was that of a child who would be called *perfectly normal* and who was having analytic treatment only for prophylactic reasons. It was only after we had done analysis for some time and the development of his Oedipus complex had been probed to the depths that I was able to recognize the complete structure and the different parts of this child's super-ego. He shewed the reactions of a sense of guilt on a really high level ethically. He condemned anything that he regarded as wrong or ugly in a manner which, while appropriate to the ego of a child, was analogous to the functioning of the super-ego of an adult on a high ethical level.

The development of the child's super-ego, but not less that of the adult, depends on various factors which need not here be discussed in greater detail. If for any reason this development has not been fully accomplished and the identifications are not wholly successful, then anxiety, in which the whole formation of the super-ego originated, will preponderate in its functioning.

The case which Anna Freud quotes does not seem to me to prove anything but that such developments of the super-ego exist. I do not think it shews that this is an instance of a specifically childish development, for we meet with the same phenomenon in those adults in whom the super-ego is undeveloped. And so I think that the conclusions which she draws from this case are erroneous.

What Anna Freud says in this connection gives me the impression that she believes the development of the super-ego, with reaction-formations and screen-memories, to take place to a large extent during the period of latency. My analytic knowledge of little children forces me to differ from her quite definitely on this point. My observations have taught me that all these mechanisms are set going when the Oedipus complex arises and are activated by that complex. With its passing they have accomplished their fundamental work; the subsequent developments and reactions are rather the super-structure on a substratum which has assumed a fixed form and persists unchanged. At certain times and in certain circumstances the reaction-formations are accentuated, and, again, when the pressure from without is more powerful, the super-ego will operate more powerfully.

These, however, are phenomena which are not peculiar to child-hood.

That which Anna Freud regards as a further extension of the super-ego and reaction-formations in the periods of latency and immediately before puberty is simply an apparent outward adaptation to the pressure and requirements of the outside world, and has nothing to do with the true development of the super-ego. As they grow older, children (like adults) learn how to handle the "double moral code" more skilfully than little children who are as yet less conventional and more honest about things.

Let us now pass on to the deductions which the author makes from her statements about the dependent nature of the super-ego of children and their double moral code in relation to the emotions of shame and disgust.

On pp. 73–75 of her book Anna Freud argues that children differ from adults in this respect: that when the child's instinctual tendencies have been brought into consciousness the super-ego by itself should not be expected to assume complete responsibility for their direction. For she believes that children, left to themselves on this point, can only discover "a single short and convenient path, namely, that which leads to direct gratification". Anna Freud is reluctant—and gives good reasons for her reluctance—that the decision as to the way in which the instinctual forces liberated from repression are to be employed should be left to the persons responsible for the child's training. She therefore considers that the only thing to be done is that "the analyst should guide the child in this most important point". She gives an example to illustrate the necessity for educational intervention on the part of the analyst. Let us see what she says. If my objections to her theoretical propositions are valid they must stand the test of a practical example.

The case in question is one which she discusses in several passages of her book: that of a six-year-old girl who suffered from an obsessional neurosis. This child, who before treatment displayed inhibitions and obsessional symptoms, became for the time being naughty and lacking in restraint. Anna Freud drew the inference that at this point she ought to have intervened in the role of educator. She thought she recognized that the fact that the child gratified its anal impulses outside analysis, when once they were free from repression, indicated that she herself had made a mistake and had relied too much on the strength of the childish ego-ideal. She felt that this as yet insufficiently established super-ego had needed temporary educative influence on the part of the analyst and therefore was not at that point capable of controlling the child's impulses unaided.

I think it will be a good thing if I too select an illustration in support of my view, which is contrary to Anna Freud's. The case which I shall cite was a very severe one, that of a six-year-old girl who, at the beginning of the analysis, was suffering from an obsessional neurosis.[8]

Erna, whose behaviour at home was unbearable and who displayed marked asocial tendencies in all her relations, suffered from great sleeplessness, excessive obsessional onanism, complete inhibition in learning, moods of deep depression, obsessive brooding, and a number of other serious symptoms. She was treated analytically for two years, and that the result was a cure is evident from the fact that for more than a year now she has been at a school which on principle takes only "normal children" and that she is standing the test of the life there. As goes without saying, in such a severe case of obsessional neurosis the child suffered from excessive inhibitions and deep remorse. She displayed the characteristic cleavage of personality into "devil and angel", "good and wicked princess", etc. In her, too, analysis naturally liberated enormous quantities of affect as well as anal-sadistic impulses. During the analytic hours extraordinary abreactions took place: rages which were vented on objects in my room, such as cushions, etc.; dirtying and destroying of playthings, smearing paper with water, plasticine, pencils, and so forth. In all this the child gave the impression of a very considerable freedom from inhibition and seemed to take a remarkable pleasure in this often quite wild behaviour. But I discovered that it was not simply a case of "uninhibited" gratification of her anal fixations, but that other factors were playing a decisive part. She was not by any means so "happy" as might have been thought at first sight and as those with whom the child was associated assumed to be the case in the instance quoted by Anna Freud. To a great extent what lay behind Erna's "lack of restraint" was anxiety and also the need for punishment which compelled her to repeat her behaviour. In it, too, there was clear evidence of all the hate and defiance which dated from the period when she was being trained in cleanliness. The situation changed completely when we had analysed these early fixations, their connection with the development of the Oedipus complex, and the sense of guilt associated with it.

In these periods when anal-sadistic impulses were being liberated in such force Erna shewed a passing inclination to abreact and gratify these outside analysis. I came to the same conclusion as Anna Freud: that the analyst must have made a mistake. Only—and here is probably one of the most salient and fundamental differences in our views—I concluded that I had failed somehow on the *analytic* side, and not on the educational. I mean that I realized that I had failed to resolve the resistances completely in the analytic hour and to release in its fullness the negative transference. I have found in this and in every other case that if we want to make it possible for children to control their impulses better without fretting themselves in a laborious struggle with them, the Oedipus development must be laid bare analytically as completely as possible, and the feelings of hate and guilt which result from it must be investigated down to their earliest beginnings.[9]

Now if we look to see at what point Anna Freud found it necessary to substitute educational for analytic measures we find that the little patient herself gives us quite exact information about it. After Anna Freud had clearly demonstrated to her (p. 41) that people could only behave so badly to some one they hated, the child asked "*why* she should have any such feeling of hate towards her mother, whom she supposed she loved very much". This question was well justified and shews that good understanding of the essence of analysis that we often find in even quite little patients of a certain obsessional type. The question points the way which the analysis ought to have taken; it should have penetrated deeper. Anna Freud, however, did not take this way, for we read: "Here I refused to tell her any more, for I too had come to the end of what I knew". The little patient then tried herself to help to find the way which should lead them further. She repeated a dream which she had already mentioned the meaning of which was a reproach against her mother for always going away just when the child needed her most.

Some days later she produced another dream which clearly indicated jealousy of her younger brothers and sisters.

Anna Freud, then, stopped and ceased to press the analysis any further just at the point where she would have had to analyse the child's hatred against her mother, that is, where it really meant first clearing up the whole Oedipus situation. We see that it is true that she had liberated and brought to abreaction some of the anal-sadistic impulses, but she did not follow up the connection of these impulses with the Oedipus development; on the contrary she confined her investigations to superficial conscious or preconscious strata, for, as far as one can judge from what she writes, she seems also to have omitted to follow up the child's jealousy of her brothers and sisters to her unconscious death-wishes against them. Had Anna Freud done so this would again have led on to the death-wishes against the mother. Moreover, up till then she must also have avoided analysing the attitude of rivalry with the mother, for otherwise both patient and analyst must by this time have known something of the causes of the child's hatred of her mother.

In the fourth chapter of her book, where Anna Freud quotes this analysis as an illustration of the necessity for the analyst to intervene for a time in the educational role, she is apparently considering that turning-point in the analysis which I have just discussed. But I picture the situation as follows: the child became partially conscious of her anal-sadistic tendencies but was not given the opportunity through a further analysis of her Oedipus situation to become largely and fundamentally free of them. In my view it was not a question of directing her to a painful mastery and control of the impulses liberated from repression. What was needed was rather to subject to a further and fuller analysis the motive-force behind these impulses.

But I have the same criticism to make of certain other illustrations given by Anna Freud. She refers several times to confessions of onanism which she received from patients. The nine-year-old girl who made such admissions in two dreams which she related (pp. 31–32) was, I think, telling much more than that and something very important. Her dread of fire and the dream of the explosion in the geyser, which took place on account of wrongdoing on her part and was visited with punishment, seem to me clearly to indicate observations of parental coitus. This is evident in the second dream as well. In it there were "two bricks of different colours and a house which they set on fire". These, as my experience of child-analysis enables me to say quite generally, regularly represent the primal scene. That this was true in the case of this little girl, with her dreams of fire, is to my mind plain from her drawings of the monsters (described by Anna Freud, pp. 37, 38) which she called "biters" and of the witch pulling out a giant's hair. Anna Freud is certainly right in interpreting these drawings as indicating the child's castration-anxiety, as well as her masturbation. But I have no doubt that the witch, who castrates the giant, and the "biter" represent parental coitus, construed by the child as a sadistic acid of castration, and further that, when she received this impression, she herself conceived sadistic desires against her parents (the explosion of the geyser caused by her in the dream), that her masturbation was associated with these and that therefore, from its connection with the Oedipus complex, it involved a deep sense of guilt and, on that account, involved the compulsion to repetition and part of the fixation.

What then was left out in Anna Freud's interpretation? Everything which would have led deeper into the Oedipus situation. But this means that she omitted to explain the deeper causes of the sense of guilt and of the fixation, and made it impossible to reduce the latter. I am compelled to draw the same conclusion as in the case of the little obsessional neurotic: If Anna Freud had submitted the instinctual impulses to a more thorough analysis, there would have been no necessity to teach the child how to control them. And at the same time the cure would have been more complete. For we know that the Oedipus complex is the nuclear complex in neurosis; hence analysis, if it shrinks from analysing that complex, cannot resolve the neurosis either.

Now what are Anna Freud's reasons for refraining from thorough analysis, which should without reservation investigate the child's relation to his parents and to the Oedipus complex? There are a number of important arguments which we come upon in different passages of the book. Let us summarize them and consider what they amount to.

Anna Freud has the feeling that she ought not to intervene between child and parents and that the home training would be endangered and conflicts aroused in the child if his opposition to his parents were brought into consciousness.

Now I think that this is the point which chiefly determines the difference between Anna Freud's and my views and our opposite methods of work. She herself says (p. 14) that she has a bad conscience in relation to the child's parents as her employers if she, as she calls it, "turns against them". In the case of a nurse who was hostile to her (pp. 20–21) she did everything she could to prejudice the child against the woman and to detach the positive feeling from her and attach it to herself. She hesitates to do this where the parents are in question, and I think she is entirely right. The difference in our point of view is this: that I never attempt in any way to prejudice a child against those with whom he is associated. But if his parents have entrusted him to me to analyse, either in order to cure a neurosis or for other reasons, I think I am justified in taking the line which seems to me in the child's interest the most advantageous and the only possible one. I mean that of analysing without reservation his relation to those about him, and therefore in particular to his parents and brothers and sisters.

There are several dangers which Anna Freud apprehends from analysis of the relation to the parents and which she thinks would arise from that weakness assumed by her to characterize the child's super-ego. Let me mention some of them.—When the transference is successfully resolved, the child could no longer find his way back to the proper love-objects, and he might be forced either "to fall back into neurosis or, if this way were closed to him on account of the success of the analytic treatment, to take the opposite direction: that of open rebellion" (pp. 61, 62). Or again: if the parents use their influence in opposition to the analyst, the result would be, "since the child is emotionally attached to both parties, a situation similar to that which arises in an unhappy marriage where the child has become a bone of contention" (p. 77). And again: "Where the child's analysis cannot become an organic part of his whole life but intrudes itself like a foreign body into his other relations and disturbs them we shall probably only involve him in more conflicts than our treatment solves" (p. 84).

In so far as it is the idea that the child's super-ego is as yet not strong enough which makes the author fear that, when he is freed from neurosis, he will no longer adapt himself satisfactorily to the necessary demands of education and of the persons with whom he is associated, I would reply as follows:

My experience has taught me that, if we analyse a child *without any preconceptions* whatever in our minds, we shall form a different picture of him, just because we are able to penetrate further into that critical period before the age of two years. There is then revealed in a far greater degree the severity of the child's super-ego, a feature Anna Freud herself has on occasion discovered. We find that what is needed is not to reinforce this super-ego but to tone it down. Let us not forget that educational influences and cultural demands are not suspended during analysis, even if the analyst, who acts as a quite unbiassed third person, does not assume responsibility for them. If the super-ego has been strong enough to lead to conflict and to neurosis, it will surely retain sufficient influence, even if in the analysis we modify it by little and little.

I have never finished an analysis with the feeling that this faculty had become too much weakened; on the other hand there have been a good many at the conclusion of which I have wished that its exaggerated power could be still further reduced.

Anna Freud justly emphasizes the fact that, if we secure a positive transference, children will contribute much in the way of co-operation and in other kinds of sacrifice. But I think this surely proves that, besides the strictness of the super-ego, this craving for love is an adequate security that the child will have a strong enough motive to comply with reasonable cultural requirements, if only his capacity for love be liberated by analysis.

We must not forget that the demands made by reality on the adult ego are far heavier than the much less exacting demands with which the much weaker ego of the child is confronted.

Of course it is possible that, if the child has to associate with people lacking in insight, neurotic, or otherwise harmful to him, the result may be that we cannot completely clear up his own neurosis or that it may be evoked again by his surroundings. According to my experience, however, we can even in these cases do much to mitigate matters and to induce a better development. Moreover, the neurosis on its reappearance will be milder and easier to cure in the future. Anna Freud's fears that a child who has been analysed and remains in surroundings wholly adverse to analysis will, on account of his detachment from his love-objects, become more opposed to them, and hence more of a prey to conflicts, seem to me theoretical considerations which are refuted by experience. Even in such cases I have found that the children were enabled by analysis to adapt themselves better and therefore better to stand the test of an unfavourable *milieu* and to suffer less than before being analysed.

And I have proved repeatedly that when a child becomes less neurotic it becomes less tiresome to those around it who are themselves neurotic or lacking in insight, and in this way too analysis will exercise only a favourable influence on their relationships.

In the last eight years I have analysed a large number of children; and my findings in regard to this point, which is crucial in the question of child-analysis, have been constantly confirmed. I would summarize them by saying that the danger apprehended by Anna Freud, that the analysis of a child's negative feelings to its parents will spoil their relationship, is always and in all circumstances non-existent. Rather, the exact opposite is the case. Exactly the same thing takes place as with adults: the analysis of the Oedipus situation not only releases the negative feelings of the child towards its parents and brothers and sisters but it also in part resolves them, and thus makes it possible for the positive impulses to be greatly strengthened. It is just the analysis of the earliest period which brings to light the hate-tendencies and feelings of guilt originating in the early oral deprivation, the training in cleanliness and the deprivation connected with the Oedipus situation. And it is this bringing of them to light which largely frees the child from them. The final result is a deeper and better relation to those around him, and by no means a detachment in the sense of an estrangement. The same applies to the age of puberty, only that at this period the capacity for detachment and transference necessary in that particular phase of development is powerfully reinforced by analysis. So far I have never had complaints from the family, after the analysis terminated or even while it was going on, that the child's relation to those around him had become worse. Now this means a good deal when we remember the ambivalence of the relations. On the other hand I have frequently received assurances that children have become much more social and amenable to training. So in the end I do the parents as well as the child a great service in this very matter of *improving* the relation between them.

Undoubtedly it is desirable and helpful that the parents should support us in our work both during and after the analysis. I must, however, say that such gratifying instances are decidedly in the minority: they represent the *ideal case*, and upon this we cannot base, our method. Anna Freud says (p. 83): "It is not only definite illness which will decide us to analyse a child. The place of child-analysis is above all in the analytic *milieu*; for the present we must confine it to children whose parents are analysts, have themselves been analysed or have a certain confidence in and respect for analysis". In reply I would say that we must discriminate very clearly between the Cs and the Ucs attitudes of the parents themselves, and I have repeatedly found that the Ucs attitude is by no means guaranteed by the conditions desiderated by Anna Freud. Parents may be theoretically entirely convinced of the necessity of analysis and may ostensibly wish to help us with all their might and yet for complexive reasons they may hinder us in our work all the way along. On the other hand I have constantly found that people who knew nothing about analysis—sometimes just a homely nurse who met me with personal confidence—have been most helpful owing to a favourable Ucs attitude. However, in my experience, anyone who analyses children has to reckon with a certain hostility and jealousy in nurses, governesses, and even mothers and has to try to accomplish the analysis in spite of and against these feelings. At first sight this seems impossible and it certainly is a special and very considerable difficulty in child-analysis. Nevertheless in most cases I have not found it insuperable. Of course I presuppose that we have not "to share with the parents in the child's love and hate", but that we handle both positive and negative transference in such a way as to enable us to establish the analytic situation and to rely upon it. It is amazing how children, even little children, then support us by their insight and their need for help and how we are able to include in our work the resistances caused by those with whom the little patients are associated.

My experience, therefore, has gradually led me to emancipate myself in my work as far as possible from these persons. Valuable as their communications at times may be, when they tell us about important changes which are taking place in the children and afford us insight into the real situation, we must of necessity be able to manage without this aid. I do not of course imply that an analysis may never come to grief through the fault of those associated with the child, but I can only say that so long as the parents send their children to be analysed at all I see no particular reason why it should be impossible to carry the analysis through simply because their attitude shews a lack of insight or is otherwise unfavourable.

From all that I have said it will be clear that my position with regard to the advisability of analysis in various cases is entirely different from Anna Freud's in other respects as well. I consider analysis helpful not only in every case of obvious mental disturbance and faulty development, but also as a means of diminishing the difficulties of normal children. The way may be indirect, but I am sure that it is not too hard, too costly, or too tedious.

In this second part of my paper my intention was to prove that it is impossible to combine in the person of the analyst analytical and educational work, and I hoped to shew why this is so. Anna Freud herself describes these functions (p. 82) as "two difficult and contradictory tasks". And again she says: "To analyse and to educate, i.e. at one and the same time to allow and to forbid, to loose and to bind again". I may sum up my arguments by saying that the one activity in effect cancels the other. If the analyst, even only temporarily, becomes the representative of the educative agencies, if he assumes the role of the super-ego, at that point he blocks the way of the instinctual impulses to Cs: he becomes the representative of the repressing faculties. I will go a step further and say that, in my experience, what we have to do with children as well as with adults is not simply to establish and maintain the analytic situation by every analytic means and to refrain from all *direct* educative influence, but, more than that, a children's analyst must have the same Ucs attitude as we require in the analyst of adults, if he is to be successful. It must enable him to be really willing *only to analyse* and not to wish to mould and direct the minds of his patients. If anxiety does not prevent him, he will be able calmly to wait for the development of the correct issue, and in this way that issue will be achieved.

If he does this, however, he will prove the validity of the second principle which I represent in opposition to Anna Freud: namely, that we must analyse completely and without reservation the child's relation to his parents and his Oedipus complex.

Notes

1. *Collected Papers*, Vol. III, p. 284.
2. The italics are mine.
3. *International Journal of Psychoanalysis*, Vol. II, 1921.
4. Translated in *International Journal of Psychoanalysis*, Vol. IV, 1923.
5. *International Journal of Psychoanalysis*, Vol. VIII, 1927.
6. I must go yet a step further. I do not think that the problem is to induce a child in the analytic hour "to exclude all conscious directing and influencing of his trains of thought", but rather that we must aim at inducing him to recognize all that lies outside his Ucs, not only in the analytic hour, but also in life in general. The special relation of children to reality rests (as I shewed in greater detail in my last paper already quoted: "The psychological principles of infant analysis") on the fact that they endeavour to exclude and repudiate everything which is not in accordance with their Ucs impulses, and in this is included reality in the broader sense.
7. In *Psycho-analytische Studien zur Charakterbildung* (Internationaler Psychoanalytischer Verlag, Leipsic, Vienna, Munich) Abraham says (ss. 57–58): "But the dependence of character-traits on the general fate of the libido is not confined to one particular period of life but is universally valid for the whole of life. The proverb *'Jugend kennt keine Tugend'* [Youth knows no virtue] voices the fact that at a tender age character is immature and lacking in firmness. We should, however, not over-estimate the stability of character even in later years."
8. I discussed this case-history in greater detail at the Würzburger Tagung Deutscher Analytiker (autumn 1924) and in one of my lectures in London in the summer of 1925. I propose later to publish the history. As the analysis went on I discovered that the severe obsessional neurosis masked a paranoia.
9. Anna Freud's little patient recognized this too quite correctly when, after recounting how she had come off victorious in a fight with her devil, she defined the object of her analysis thus (p. 22): "You must help me not to be so unhappy if I have to be stronger than he is." I think, however, that this object can be fully attained only when we have been able to clear up the earliest oral and anal-sadistic fixations and the feelings of guilt connected with them.

On the theory of analysis of children*†

Anna Freud

Ladies and gentlemen,

Three papers on the subject of analysing children are being read before you at this Congress—instead of only one, which has hitherto been the order of the day—and this alone illustrates the importance that the subject has acquired in the eyes of the International Association during the last few years. I think that the reason for this accession of interest in child-analysis lies in the three-fold contribution it can make to our psycho-analytical knowledge. It gives us welcome confirmations of those conceptions of the mental life of children which, in the course of years, have been deduced by psycho-analytical theory from the analyses of adults. Secondly, as Mrs Klein's paper has just demonstrated, the direct observation thus employed leads us to fresh conclusions and

* Read before the Tenth International Psycho-Analytical Congress, Innsbruck, September 3, 1927.

† Article citation:
Freud, A. (1929). On the theory of analysis of children. *International Journal of Psychoanalysis*, 10: 29–38.

supplementary conceptions, and, finally, it serves as a point of transition to a field of applied analysis which, as many hold, will in the future be one of the most important. I refer to pedagogy.

Thus, strong in the sense of its threefold usefulness, child-analysis ventures to claim liberty and independence in various directions. It demands a new technique. This is willingly conceded: even the most conservative person realizes without difficulty that a difference in the object with which one is dealing demands different methods of approach. Thus Melanie Klein has evolved the play-technique for the analysis of little children, and, later, I myself put forward suggestions for the analysis of children in the latency period. But certain advocates of child-analysis (myself amongst them) go further still. They begin to ponder the question whether the processes in child-analysis are always wholly identical, from the theoretical standpoint, with those in the analysis of adults, and whether the aims and objects of the two forms of treatment are exactly the same. The people who follow this line of thought hold that those who analyse children should possess not only the correct analytical training and mental attitude but something further: something which is called for by the idiosyncrasies of childhood, namely, the training and the mental attitude of the pedagogue. I think we ought not to be dismayed by this word or to conclude offhand that to combine the two attitudes is somehow derogatory to analysis. It is worth while to take some concrete examples and see whether the demand for such a combination can at all be justified or whether the right thing is to reject it as illegitimate.

The first example I shall select for this purpose is a fragment from the analysis of an eleven-year-old boy. When he first came for treatment his disposition was of the feminine-masochistic type, his original object-relation with his mother being wholly overlaid by his identification of himself with her. His original masculine aggressive tendencies only occasionally found a vent in hostile behaviour to his brothers and sisters and isolated asocial acts; these were succeeded by violent outbreaks of remorse and by depression of spirits. I am now quoting from a period in his analysis in which his mind was occupied with countless thoughts, phantasies and dreams about death, or, more precisely, about killing.

Just at this time a very intimate friend of his mother's was seriously ill, and his mother was informed by telegram of her friend's danger. The patient seized upon this opportunity to weave phantasies in this connection. He phantasied that another telegram came saying: "She is dead". His mother was much grieved. Then yet another telegram arrived saying that it was a mistake, the friend was alive again. His mother rejoiced. Then, in his phantasy, he caused telegrams to arrive in rapid succession—one saying that the friend was dead and the next that she had come to life again. The whole phantasy ended with the news that it was all a joke which had been played on his mother. It is not difficult to interpret the phantasy. We see clearly the boy's ambivalence, his desire to kill the person whom his mother loved and his inability actually to carry his purpose through.

Soon after this he told me of the following obsessive act. When he was sitting in the w.c. he felt impelled to touch a knob on the wall on one side three times with his hand and immediately afterwards to do the same to a knob on the other side. At first this action seemed incomprehensible, but a few days later we found the explanation in a phantasy which he recounted in another connection. He imagined God as an old man sitting on a great throne in the courts of Heaven. To the right and left of Him were knobs or switches on the wall. If he pressed a knob on one side, some human being died: if he pressed one on the other side a child was born into the world. I think, if we compare the boy's obsessive action with this daydream, it will be superfluous to interpret it further. The number three is probably explained by the number of the other children in the family.

Soon after this, a friend of the family, the father of one of his play-fellows and a man whom his mother knew very intimately, fell ill. On the way to his analysis the patient heard the telephone-bell ring, and, while with me, he made up the following phantasy: His mother had been sent for to the sick man's house. She went in, entered the sick-room, went up to the bed and tried to speak to her friend, the patient. But he did not answer, and then she saw that he was dead. It was a great shock to her. At that moment the dead man's little son came in. She called him and said: "Come and look, your father is dead". The boy went up to the bed and spoke to his father, whereupon the father came to life and answered him. The child then turned to my patient's mother and said: "What do you mean? He is *alive*". The mother then spoke to the man again; once more he did not reply, for he was dead. But when the little boy came in again and spoke to him, the father came to life.

I have recounted this phantasy in such detail because it is so instructive and transparent, and contains in itself the interpretation of the two previously quoted. We see that the father is dead as far as his relation to the mother is concerned: as soon as it is a question of himself and his son, he is alive. In the earlier phantasies the ambivalent feelings to the same person—the desire to kill and the opposite desire to keep alive or to bring back to life—were simply separated into two different actions, cancelling one another. This last phantasy however, contains in addition a specification of the person threatened (on the one hand as husband and on the other a father), and here we have the historic explanation of the boy's twofold attitude. Obviously the two tendencies originate in different phases of his development. The death-wish against the father as the rival for the mother's love springs from the normal Oedipus phase with the positive object-love (since repressed) to the mother. Here his masculine aggressive impulses are directed against the father, who is to be killed to leave the way clear for the boy himself. But the other tendency—the desire to keep the father for himself—originates on the one hand in the early period, when the son's attitude to the father was one of pure admiration and love, undisturbed by the rivalry connected with the Oedipus complex, and on the other (and this is the more important here) belongs to the phase of identification with the mother which has succeeded to the normal Oedipus attitude. Out of dread of the castration with which he is menaced by the father the boy has renounced his love for his mother and let himself be forced into the feminine position. Here he is forced to try to keep his father as the object of his homosexual love.

It is tempting to go on and describe the transition by which this boy passed from the desire to kill to a dread of death which awoke in him at night, and hence to gain access to the complicated structure of this neurosis of the latency period. But you know that that is not part of my purpose here. I have cited this fragment simply in order that you may confirm my impression that this part of the analysis of a child differs in no way from that of an adult. What we have to do is to free some of his masculine aggression and his object-love for his mother from repression and from being buried beneath his now feminine-masochistic character and his identification of himself with his mother. The conflict which we come upon here is an inner one. Even if originally dread of his real father in the outside world impelled him to make the repression, its success now depends on forces within himself. The father has been internalized, and the super-ego has become the representative of his power; the boy's dread of him is experienced as dread of castration. Outbreaks of this castration-anxiety hinder every step which the analysis endeavours to make towards bringing the repressed Oedipus tendencies into consciousness. Only the slow analytical dissection of the super-ego, in historical sequence, makes it possible for my work of liberation to advance. Thus you see that, as far as this part of the task is concerned, the work and the attitude of the analyst are purely analytical. There is no place here for the introduction of educational methods.

Now let me give you an example where the opposite is the case. It is taken from the analysis of a little girl of six, part of which I have already published elsewhere for a different purpose. Here again (as always) it is a question of the impulses arising out of the Oedipus complex and once more the attitude towards killing comes in. The analysis shewed that the little girl had passed through an early phase of passionate love for her father and, in the usual way, had been disappointed by him through the birth of younger brothers and sisters. Her reaction to this disappointment was extraordinarily strong. Having barely attained to the genital phase, she abandoned it and regressed completely to the level of anal sadism. She turned her hostile impulses against the newly arrived younger children. She attempted to retain her father, from whom her love had almost entirely withdrawn itself, by incorporation if in no other way. But her efforts to feel herself a male came to grief in competition with an elder brother, for she realized that he was physically better equipped in this direction than she herself. The result was intense hostility to her mother: hate, first, because she had taken the father away from herself; secondly, because she had not made her herself a boy; and, finally, because the mother had borne the brothers and sisters whom she herself would have liked to bring into the world. But at this point—when my patient was about four years old—something of importance happened. She realized dimly that because of her hate-reaction she was on the way to losing the happy relation with her mother, whom she had loved dearly, in spite of all, from her earliest infancy. And in order not to lose this love for her mother and, still more, her mother's love for her, without which she could not live, she made a tremendous effort to become "good". Suddenly and, as it were, at a single blow she dissociated herself from all this hatred and with it from her whole sexual life, consisting of anal and sadistic behaviour and phantasies. She opposed it to her own personality as something alien, no longer part of herself, something which came from "the devil". There was not much left: a tiny, cramped personality, whose emotional life was not wholly her own to control and whose very considerable intelligence and energy were devoted to keeping "the devil" in his state of forcible repression. In her relations with the outside world she was merely apathetic, while the lukewarm feelings of tenderness and affection for her mother were not strong enough to bear the slightest strain. And more than this: the dissociation which she had striven to accomplish could not be permanently maintained in spite of her great expenditure of effort. At times "the devil" would get the better of her for a short while and she fell into states in which without any adequate external cause she would throw herself on the ground and scream in a way which in the old days would certainly have been described as "possession". Or she would suddenly surrender herself to the other side of her nature and luxuriate with the utmost enjoyment in sadistic phantasies, as, for example, that she roamed through her parents' house from attic to cellar, breaking up all the furniture and every object she came across and throwing them out of the window, and without more ado cutting off the heads of all the people she met. Such occasions of being overmastered by the devil were invariably followed by anxiety and remorse. But there was another, still more dangerous way in which the dissociated evil tendencies used to break out. "The devil" loved fæces and dirt: she herself began gradually to develop a peculiar anxiety in regard to habits of cleanliness. "The devil" particularly enjoyed cutting off people's heads, so at certain times she was compelled to creep to the beds of her brothers and sisters early in the morning and see that they were still all alive. "The devil" took a delight in energetically transgressing every human commandment, and so the child began to suffer from a dread of earthquakes, at night before she went to sleep, because someone had told her that an earthquake was the most terrific punishment which God was wont to inflict on human beings. Thus her daily life was in all sorts of ways made up of actions which either were substitutes for those of the dissociated evil nature or represented her remorse and endeavours to atone. So we may say that her magnificently conceived attempt to retain her mother's love and to conform to social requirements and become "good" had failed miserably. The only result was an obsessional neurosis.

Now I did not enlist your interest in this infantile neurosis because of its fine structure and the fact that the symptoms were defined with a clearness unusual in so young a patient. My reason for describing it to you was a peculiar circumstance which struck me while I was treating the child.

In the case of the eleven-year-old boy which I described before you will remember that the motive factor in the repression was the dread of castration by the father. Naturally, the resistance which I observed in the analysis was this same castration-anxiety. But in the case of the little girl it was different. The repression, or rather the cleavage, in the childish personality was brought about under the stress of a dread of loss of love. According to our notions, the anxiety must have been very intense to be able so to disturb the child's whole life. But in the analysis this very anxiety could hardly be detected as a serious resistance. Finding that my interest remained uniformly friendly, the little patient began to display to me her bad side quite calmly and frankly. You will reply that that is not very surprising. I know that we often meet with adult patients who anxiously and with an uneasy conscience keep their symptoms a secret from the whole world and begin to expose them only in the secure atmosphere of analysis with its freedom from criticism. Often, indeed, it is only then that they come to know what they really are. But this applies only to their describing of their symptoms: the analyst's friendly interest and the absence of the criticism the patients anticipate never actually bring about a trans-formation in the symptoms. But that was exactly what happened in the case of this little girl. When she found that not only was I interested and refrained from condemning her, but that also less strict demands were made upon her at home, her anxiety was transformed under my very eyes in analysis into the wish which it concealed, while the reaction-formation turned into the instinct which it was designed to keep at bay and the precautionary measure into the threat to kill which lay behind it. But of the dread of loss of love, which surely should have broken out violently in opposition to such a reversal, there was scarcely a sign. The resistance was weaker on this side than on any other. It was as though the little girl said to herself: "If you don't think it so very bad, then I don't either". And, as her demands upon herself became less exacting, gradually, as the analysis went on, she incorporated once more within herself all the tendencies which she had rejected at the cost of so much energy—her incestuous love for her father, her desire to be a boy, her death-wishes against her brothers and sisters and the recognition of her infantile sexuality. The only check was a temporary one due to the sole serious resistance when she came to what seemed the worst of all: the recognition of the direct death-wish against her mother.

Now this is not the behaviour which we are accustomed to see in the normal super-ego. Surely, adult neurotics teach us how impervious to reason that super-ego is, how obstinately it opposes every attempt at influence from without and how it refuses to modify its demands until it has been dissected in the analysis in historical sequence and every individual command and prohibition has been traced to someone who was important and beloved by the patient in childhood.

Ladies and gentlemen, I think that here we have lighted on the most important, fundamental difference between the analysis of adults and that of children. In the analysis of the adult we are at a point where the super-ego has already established its independence—an independence which is unshakable by any influence from the outside world. Here the only thing for us to do is to bring into consciousness, and thus raise to the same level, all the tendencies belonging to the id, the ego and the super-ego respectively which have played a part in the neurotic conflict. On this new level of consciousness the battle may be fought out in a new way and be brought to a different issue. But child-analysis must include all those cases in which the super-ego has as yet not reached any true independence. Only too clearly it strives to please its task-masters, the child's parents and others responsible for his training, and in its demands it reflects every oscillation in the relation to these beloved persons and all the changes in their own views. Here, as in the analysis of adults, we work on purely analytical lines in so far as our object is to free from the unconscious those parts of the id and the ego which have already been repressed. But our work in relation to the childish super-ego is twofold: on the one hand, as analysts, in so far as the super-ego has already attained to independence, we have to assist in the dissection of the material from within, following the historical sequence, but, in addition to this, we have to use our influence from without in an educational manner by changing the child's relation to those who are bringing him up, by providing him with new ideas and by revising the demands which the outside world is making upon him.

Let us go back once more to my little girl patient. If she had not come for treatment at the age of six probably her infantile neurosis would, like so many others, have spontaneously cleared up. In that case it is certain that it would have bequeathed to her a strict super-ego which would have made implacable demands on the ego and have opposed any subsequent analysis in the form of a resistance hard to overcome. But my view is that this strict super-ego appears at the end and not at the beginning of children's neuroses.

In order to illustrate this point I would refer you to a case recently described by Dr M. W. Wulff.[1] He gives an account of anxiety-attacks of the nature of phobias in a baby girl of eighteen months. It is plain that the parents of this child had exacted habits of cleanliness from her too early. The baby was unable to obey them and began to be mentally disturbed and afraid that they might send her away. Her anxiety reached the pitch of actual attacks when it was dark or when she heard strange noises, e.g. if someone knocked at the door. She asked over and over again if she were good and begged them not to send her away. The parents, much concerned, consulted Dr Wulff.

I think that the interesting thing about this early symptom is that the baby's anxiety, which Dr Wulff immediately diagnosed as dread of the loss of love, could in no way be differentiated from the anxiety of conscience in an adult neurotic. Now, in this case, are we to believe that conscience (i.e. the super-ego) had developed so early? Dr Wulff explained to the parents that the little girl obviously was for some reason or other unequal to the demand for cleanliness, and he advised them to defer her training in this respect for a time. The parents had sufficient understanding to agree. They explained to the child that they loved her even when she wetted herself, and, whenever this happened, they repeatedly tried to calm her with assurances of their love. The success of this experiment was, as Dr Wulff tells us, striking. After a few days the child was calm and free from anxiety.

Naturally treatment of this sort is applicable but rarely, and only with very little children. I do not want you to receive the impression that I am recommending it as the only possible course. But here Dr Wulff was making the patient's cure the test of his treatment, and this is the only test which can reveal to us what is the play of forces which is giving rise to anxiety. If the child had really fallen ill because of the excessive demands of her own super-ego, her parents' reassurances could not have had any influence at all on her symptoms. But if the cause of her anxiety was a real fear of the displeasure of her parents as they actually existed in the outside world (and not of her imagos of them), we can easily understand her illness being cured. For Dr Wulff had removed the cause.

Quite a number of other childish reactions can be similarly explained only by the super-ego's accessibility to influence in the early years of life. By the kindness of Dr Ferenczi I have had an opportunity of seeing the notes of a mistress at one of the modern American schools, the Walden School. This mistress, who has had a psycho-analytical training, describes how neurotic children whose home-standards are strict, and who come to her school while still at the kindgarten age, after a longer or shorter period of holding back in amazement, grow accustomed to the extraordinarily free atmosphere and gradually lose their neurotic symptoms, most of which are reactions to breaking the habit of onanism. We know that with an adult neurotic it would be impossible to produce a similar effect. The freer the environment into which he finds himself transplanted the greater is his dread of the instinct in question and, therewith, the more marked the accentuation of his neurotic defence-reactions, i.e. his symptoms. The demands made on him by his super-ego are no longer susceptible to influence from his environment. A child, on the contrary, once he begins to modify his standards, is inclined rather to go a long way in this direction and allow himself more latitude than even the freest surroundings could permit him. In this respect, as in others, he cannot do without influence from others.

And now, in conclusion, let me give a very innocent example. A little time ago I had an opportunity of listening to the talk of a five-year-old boy and his mother. The child had conceived a wish for a live horse, and the mother, for good reasons, refused to give it to him. "It doesn't matter", he said, nothing daunted, "I will ask for it on my next birthday". His mother assured him that he would not have it even then. "Then I'll ask for it at Christmas", he said, "you can have anything then". "No, not even at Christmas", said his mother, trying to disillusion him. He thought for a moment. "Well, it *doesn't* matter", he said triumphantly, "I'll buy it for myself. *I* will let myself have it". You see, ladies and gentlemen, that already between his inner permission and the prohibition imposed from without there arises the conflict which may terminate in all sorts of ways: in rebellion and asocial behaviour, in neurosis and, fortunately, often in health.

Now let me say just one word about the attitude of the children's analyst as an educationist. We have recognized that the forces arrayed against us in our fight to cure neurosis in children are not merely internal but also in part external. This gives us the right to require that the analyst shall understand aright the part played by the outward situation in which the child is placed, just as we require that he shall grasp the child's inner situation. But in order to fulfil this part of his task a children's analyst must have a knowledge of the theory and practice of pedagogy. This will enable him to ascertain the influences being brought to bear on the child by those who are training him, to criticize them and (if it proves necessary) to take the work of his up-bringing out of their hands for the period of the analysis and to undertake it himself.

Note

1. *International Journal of Psychoanalysis*, Vol. IX., Part 3, 1928.

CHAPTER TWO

Phantasy and sublimation

Freud, Anna (1923). The relation of beating-phantasies to a day-dream. *International Journal of Psychoanalysis*, 4: 89–102.[1]

Freud's paper "A child is being beaten" (Freud, 1919e—translated for the journal in 1920) is at a conceptual cross-roads. His intention was a discussion and elucidation of masochism,[2] but the paper actually discussed the vicissitudes of fantasy and sublimation.

It is almost certain that one of Freud's four cases was his daughter, Anna (Young-Bruehl, 1988, see also Blass, 1993) whom he analysed from 1918 to 1922. The clinical case in the paper of Anna Freud's, republished here, which was her membership paper for the Viennese Psychoanalytical Society, is probably an expansion of her own analysis. She used the case to make a contribution to the understanding of fantasy. Freud had understood masochistic fantasies to be an inherent part of the libido, a component instinct, and therefore inherited. It is akin to, and a part of, the Oedipus complex; and his 1919 paper showed the various ways that sadomasochism can be inverted and expressed. Anna Freud's paper adds a further vicissitude. The primary fantasy can be desexualized, which advances it from being merely gratification to a potential for the capacity to represent, and thus to enable, a creative sublimation. As Blum (1995) commented about the "taming" of the masochism, it became "what would later be called progressive ego and super-ego modification and the development of sublimation" (p. 44). Ultimately, the distinction Anna Freud discerns points to the divergence of aesthetic literature away from pornography (as masturbatory gratification). Anna Freud is elaborating Freud's unfinished thoughts expressed in 1908 ("Creative writers and day-dreaming"), about the difference between the creative process and wishful thinking, although she does not mention that work. It was a concern of Freud's which he returned to in his papers on Leonardo (1910c) and Michelangelo's Moses (1914b).

Anna Freud's contribution to sublimation and creativity later became an important point of contention with other views on the nature and occurrence of primary fantasies (or phantasies). Given the unusual circumstances for the clinical evidence, some doubt can always be thrown on whether this is a valid contribution to the nature of fantasy *per se*. Eiferman (1997) postulates it is, instead, an evasion of the sadomasochism between a father and daughter when one is analyst and the other his analysand. Nevertheless, it is still an example of "sublimation of sensual love into tender friendship" (Eiferman, 1997, p. 100) for her father/analyst.

Thus, there are two ways to read this paper: one is in the terms in which it is given, as deductions from the evidence of clinical material; or, second, as a sublimatory process within a psychoanalytic transference. Either way we are introduced to the sublimation underlying creative fantasy life.

Notes

1. Subsequently known as "Beating fantasies and daydreams" see *The Writings of Anna Freud, Volume 1*. New York: International Universities Press, where a revised version was published.
2. Freud's study is, in effect, a study of female masochism, without acknowledgement of any gender specificity (Deutsch, 1930).

References

Blass, R. (1993). Insights into the struggle of creativity—a reading of Anna Freud's "Beating fantasies and daydreams". *Psychoanalytic Study of the Child, 48*: 161–187.

Blum, H. (1995). The clinical value of daydreams and a note on their role in character analysis. In: E. S. Person, P. Fonagy, & S. A. Figueira (Eds.), *On Freud's "Creative writing and day-dreaming"* (pp. 39–52). New Haven: Yale University Press.

Deutsch, H. (1930). The significance of masochism in the mental life of women. *International Journal of Psychoanalysis, 11*: 48–60.

Eiferman, R. (1997). The exceptional position of "A child is being beaten" in the learning and teaching of Freud. In: E. S. Person (Ed.), *On Freud's "A child is being beaten"* (pp. 157–178). New Haven: Yale University Press.

Freud, S. (1908e). Creative writers and day-dreaming. *S.E., 9*: 143–153. London: Hogarth Press.

Freud, S. (1910c). Leonardo da Vinci and a memory of his childhood. *S.E., 11*: 59–137. London: Hogarth Press.

Freud, S. (1914b). The Moses of Michaelangelo. *S.E., 13*: 211–238. London: Hogarth Press.

Freud, S. (1919e). A child is being beaten. *S.E., 17*: 177–204. London: Hogarth Press.

Young-Bruehl, E. (1988). *Anna Freud.* London: Macmillan.

The relation of beating-phantasies to a day-dream*†

Anna Freud

In his paper "A child is being beaten"[1] Freud deals with a phantasy which, according to him, is met with in a surprising number of the people who come in search of analytic treatment on account of an hysteria or of an obsessional neurosis. He thinks it very probable that it occurs even more often in other people who have not been obliged by a manifest illness to come to this decision. This "beating-phantasy" is invariably charged with a high degree of pleasure and has its issue in an act of pleasurable auto-erotic gratification. I shall take for granted that the content of Freud's paper—the description of the phantasy, the reconstruction of the phases which preceded it, and its derivation from the Oedipus complex—is known to the reader. In the course of my paper I shall return to and dwell on it at some length.

In one paragraph of his paper Freud says:

---

* The following paper was written on the basis of several discussions which I had with Frau Lou Andreas-Salomé.—A. F.

† Article citation:
Freud, A. (1923). The relation of beating-phantasies to a day-dream. *International Journal of Psychoanalysis*, 4: 89–102.

In two of my four female cases an artistic superstructure of day-dreams, which was of great significance for the life of the person concerned, had grown up over the masochistic phantasy of beating. The function of this superstructure was to make possible the feeling of gratified excitement, even though the onanistic act was abstained from.

Now I have been able from a variety of day-dreams to select one which seemed especially well calculated to illustrate this short remark. This day-dream was formed by a girl of fifteen, whose phantasy-life, in spite of its abundance, had never come into conflict with reality; the origin, evolution and termination of the day-dream could be established with certainty; and its derivation from and dependence on a beating-phantasy of long standing was proved in analysis.

I

I shall now trace the course of development of the phantasy-life of this day-dreamer. When in her fifth or sixth year—before school, certainly—she began to entertain a beating-phantasy of the type described by Freud. In the beginning its content remained monotonous: "A boy is being beaten by a grown-up person". Later on it was changed to: "Many boys are being beaten by many grown-up persons". The boys, however, as well as the grown-ups remained indeterminate and so did the misdeed for which the castigation was administered. It is to be supposed that when enacted before the imagination of the girl the various scenes were very vivid; the record, however, given of them during analysis was anything but circumstantial or illuminating. Whenever the phantasy was called up it was accompanied by strong sexual excitement and terminated in an onanistic act.

The sense of guilt which attaches itself to the phantasy in his cases, as with this child also, is explained by Freud in the following way. He says that the form of beating-phantasy just described is not the initial one, but is the substitute in consciousness for an earlier unconscious phase. In this unconscious phase the persons who afterwards became unrecognizable and indifferent were very well-known and important—the boy who was being punished was the child who produced the phantasy, the adult who dealt out the punishment was the dreamer's own father. Further, according to Freud's paper even this phase is not the primary one, but is only a transformation of a preceding first phase, which belongs to the period of the greatest activity of the parental complex. This first phase had in common with the second that the person beating was the dreamer's father; the child that was being beaten, however, was not the one who produced the phantasy but some other one, a brother or sister, i.e., a rival in the struggle for the father's affection. The content and meaning of the phantasy of beating was, in its first phase, therefore: that the child claimed the whole of its father's love for itself and left the others to his anger and wrath. Later on a process of repression took place, a sense of guilt appeared and, to reverse the former triumph, the punishment was turned back upon the child itself. At the same time, however, in consequence of a regression from the genital to the pregenital anal-sadistic organization, the phantasy of being beaten still stood to the child for a phantasy of being loved. Thus the second phase was formed; but it remained unconscious because of its all-too-significant content, and was substituted in consciousness by a third phase, better calculated to meet the demands of the censorship. To this third phase, however, was attached the libidinal excitement and the sense of guilt, since the secret meaning hidden under its strange form still ran: "My father loves only me."

With the child mentioned this sense of guilt attached itself less to the content of the phantasy itself—though the latter too was disapproved of from the beginning—than to the auto-erotic gratification which regularly occurred at its climax. The little girl therefore for a number of years made ever-renewed but ever-failing attempts to separate the one from the other, i.e., to retain the phantasy as a source of pleasure and, at the same time, to break herself of the auto-erotic habit, which was felt to be irreconcilable with the moral standard demanded by her ego. The content of the phantasy at that period went through the most complicated alterations and elaborations. In the attempt to enjoy the legitimate pleasure as long as possible, and to put off its tabooed climax indefinitely, she added on descriptions of a wealth of details indifferent in themselves. She constructed whole institutions, schools and reformatories in which the scenes of beating were imagined to take place, and established definite rules which determined the construction of the various scenes. The persons beating were at that time invariably teachers; only later and in exceptional cases the fathers of the boys were added—as spectators mostly. But even in this elaborate embroidering of the phantasy the day-dreamer left the figures indeterminate and denied them all characteristic traits, as for instance, individual faces and names, or personal histories.

I certainly do not want to imply that postponing the pleasurable situation in this way by prolonging and amplifying the whole phantasy is in all cases the manifestation of a sense of guilt, i.e., the consequence of an attempt to separate the phantasy from an onanistic act. The same technical device may be met with in phantasies which have never given rise to a sense of guilt. With these it simply serves to reinforce the excitation and thus to heighten the final pleasure gained by the dreamer.

In the case of this girl the phantasies of beating after a time entered upon a new phase of development. As years went on the ego-tendencies in which the moral demands set up by her environment were incorporated slowly gained strength. Consequently she resisted more and more the temptation to indulge in the phantasy in which her libidinal tendencies had become concentrated. She gave up as a failure all her attempts to separate the phantasy of beating from the onanistic act, and consequently the content of the phantasy fell under the same taboo as the sexual gratification. Every re-activation of the phantasy meant a serious struggle with strong opposing forces and was followed by self-reproaches, pangs of conscience and a short period of depression. The pleasure derived from the phantasy was more and more confined to the climax itself, which was preceded as well as followed by "pain". Since in the course of time the phantasies of beating came to serve less and less as a source of pleasure, they were largely restricted in their activity.

II

At about the same time—apparently between her eighth and tenth year—the girl began to entertain a new kind of phantasies, which she herself distinguished by the name of "nice stories", to separate them from the unpleasant phantasies of beating. These "nice stories" seemed, at first sight at least, to contain a wealth of pleasurable, agreeable situations describing instances of kind, considerate and affectionate behaviour. The figures in these nice stories were distinguished by individual names, their looks and personal appearance were described in detail and their life-histories given, the latter sometimes reaching far back into their imaginary past. The circumstances of the various persons, their acquaintance and relationship with one another, were laid down and the details of their daily life moulded after the pattern of reality. Alterations in the surroundings of the day-dreamer were followed by alterations in the imaginary scenes, and the effects of reading could also be easily traced in the latter. The climax of each situation was invariably accompanied by a strong feeling of pleasure; no sense of guilt appeared and no auto-erotic gratification took place in connection with it. The girl consequently felt no resistance against indulging largely in this kind of day-dreaming. This was, therefore, the artistic superstructure of day-dreams referred to in Freud's paper. How far one is justified in assuming that it had grown up over the masochistic phantasies of beating I hope to show in the further course of this analysis.

The day-dreamer herself knew nothing about any connection which her pleasant stories might have with the phantasies of beating. If a possibility of this kind had been pointed out to her at that time she would certainly have rejected the idea energetically. The phantasies of beating were to her the personification of everything she considered ugly, prohibited and depraved, whereas the "nice stories" stood to her for beauty and pleasure. She was firmly convinced of the mutual independence of the two kinds of phantasies, the more so since no figure out of a "nice story" ever penetrated into the sphere of the beating-phantasies. The two were kept apart very carefully—even in regard to time: for every re-activation of the phantasies of beating had to be followed by a temporary renunciation of the "nice stories".

Even during analysis, as was mentioned before, the girl never gave any detailed account of any individual scene of beating. Owing to her shame and resistance all she could ever be induced to give were short and covert allusions which left to the analyst the task of completing and reconstructing a picture of the original situation. She behaved quite differently in regard to the "nice stories". As soon as her first resistance to free talking had been overcome, she volunteered vivid and circumstantial descriptions of her various day-dreams. Her eagerness in doing so was such that she even gave the impression of experiencing while she was talking a similar or even greater pleasure than while actually day-dreaming. In these circumstances it was comparatively easy to get a general survey of the wealth of figures and situations produced by her fantasy. It turned out that the girl had formed not one but a whole series of so-called "continued stories", each having a different plot and describing a different set of figures. One of these "continued stories" may be considered the cardinal and most important one; it contained the largest number of figures, existed for years, and underwent various transformations; moreover, other stories branched off from it, which—just as in legends or mythology—acquired in the course of time complete independence. Alongside this main story the girl maintained various smaller and less important ones which she employed in turn. All these day-dreams invariably belonged to the type termed "continued stories". To gain insight into their organization we will now turn our attention to one particular "nice story" which, because of its brevity and clearness, is best suited to serve the purposes of this paper.

In her fourteenth or fifteenth year, after having formed a number of continued stories which she maintained side by side, the girl accidentally came upon a boy's story-book; it contained among others a short story of which the action was laid in the Middle Ages. She went through it once or twice with great interest; when she had finished, she returned the book to its owner and did not see it again. Her imagination, however, had already taken possession of the various figures and a number of the details described in the book. She immediately took up the thread of the story, continued to spin out the action and, retaining it henceforward as one of her "nice stories", she behaved exactly as if she were dealing with a spontaneous product of her own imagination.

In spite of various attempts made during analysis it remained impossible to establish with certainty what had been included in the original story. Its content had been dismembered and devoured by her active imagination, and new phantasies had overlaid it until every attempt at distinction between spontaneous and borrowed details was bound to fail. There remained nothing, therefore, but to leave aside the question of origin and to deal with the content of the imaginary scenes without regard to the sources it had sprung from.

The subject of the story was as follows: A mediaeval Knight has for years been at feud with a number of nobles who have leagued together against him. In the course of a battle a noble youth of fifteen (the age of the day-dreamer) is captured by the Knight's henchmen. He is taken to the Knight's castle and there kept prisoner some time, until at last he gains his freedom again.

Instead of spinning out and continuing the tale (as in a novel published by instalments), the girl made use of the plot as a sort of outer frame for her day-dream. Into this frame she inserted a wealth of scenes, every single one of which was organized like an independent story, containing an introduction, development of the plot and climax. Thus there was no logical sequence in the working out of the whole tale. She was free at any moment to choose between the different parts of the tale according to her mood; and she could always interpose a new situation between two others which had been finished and previously joined up with each other.

In this comparatively simple day-dream there are only two really important figures; all the others may be disregarded, as of episodical importance merely. One of these main figures is the young prisoner, who is endowed in the day-dream with various noble and pleasing character-traits; the other is the Knight who is described as harsh and brutal. Several incidents relating to their past and their family-histories were worked out and added to the plot to deepen the hostility between them. This furnished a basis of an apparently irreconcilable antagonism between one character who is strong and mighty and another who is weak and in the power of the former.

Their first meeting was described in a great introductory scene during which the Knight threatens to put the prisoner on the rack, so as to force him to betray important secrets. The youth thus becomes aware of his utter helplessness and begins to dread his enemy. On these two factors—fear and helplessness—all the subsequent situations were based; e.g., in pursuance of his plan, the Knight nearly goes as far as to torture the prisoner, but at the last moment he desists. He nearly kills him through imprisonment in the dungeon of his castle, but has him nursed back to life again before it is too late for recovery. As soon as the prisoner has recovered the Knight returns to his original plan, but a second time he gives way before the prisoner's fortitude. And while he is apparently bent upon doing harm to the youth, he actually grants him one favour after the other. Similar situations form the later part of the tale, e.g., the prisoner accidentally goes beyond the boundaries of the castle; the Knight meets him there, but does not punish him by renewed imprisonment, as he would have expected. Another time the Knight discovers a similar transgression on the part of the prisoner, but he himself saves him from the humiliating consequences of the deed. Several times the prisoner is subjected to great hardships. These experiences then serve to heighten his enjoyment of some luxuries granted to him by the Knight. All these dramatic scenes were enacted very vividly before the imagination of the girl. In every single one she shared the prisoner's feelings of fear and fortitude in a state of great excitement. At the climax of each situation, i.e., when the anger and rage of the torturer were transformed into kindness and pity, this excitement resolved itself into a feeling of pleasure.

Going through the scenes mentioned and forming some new similar situations usually took the girl from a few days up to one or two weeks. At the beginning of each of these periods of daydreaming the elaboration and development of every single scene was methodically carried out. When forming one particular scene in her imagination, she was able to disregard the existence of all the other adventures which had happened before or after it; consequently at the moment she honestly believed in the prisoner's dangerous position and in the actual possibility of a final catastrophe; so that the prisoner's dread and anxiety, i.e., the anticipation of the climax, were dwelt on at great length. After several days of day-dreaming, however, a disturbing remembrance of the happy issue of scenes already imagined seemed to penetrate into the daydream; dread and anxiety were described with less conviction, the tone of gentleness and clemency which at the beginning had marked the climax spread farther and farther over it and finally absorbed all the interest formerly taken up by the introduction and development of the plot. The final result of this transformation was that the whole story was rendered unfit for further use, and had to be replaced—at least for a period of some weeks—by another story, which after a certain length of time met the same fate. It was only the main day-dream which lasted so immeasurably longer than the other less important continued stories; the reason probably lay in the great wealth of figures contained in it, as well as in its manifold ramifications. On the other hand, it is not unlikely that this broader elaboration was carried through for the very purpose of ensuring it a longer life every time it was re-activated.

A general survey of the various single scenes of the Knight and Prisoner day-dream revealed a surprising monotony in their construction. The day-dreamer herself—though on the whole intelligent and critical of what she read—had never noticed this fact, not even when relating the story during analysis. But on examination of each scene it was only necessary to detach from the plot itself the manifold minor details which at a first glance gave it its appearance of individuality; in every instance the structure then laid bare was as follows: antagonism between a strong and a weak person; a misdeed—mostly unintentional—on the part of the weak one which puts him at the other's mercy; the latter's menacing attitude giving rise to the gravest apprehensions; a slow and sometimes very elaborate intensification almost to the limit of endurance of the dread and anxiety; and finally, as a pleasurable climax, the solution of the conflict, i.e., pardon for the sinner, reconciliation and, for a moment, complete harmony between the former antagonists. With a few variations the same structure held good also for every single scene out of the other "nice stories" invented by the girl.

It is this underlying structure which constitutes the important analogy between the nice stories and the phantasies of beating—an analogy quite unsuspected by the dreamer herself. In the beating-phantasies too, the figures were divided into strong and weak persons, i.e., adults and children respectively; there also it was a matter of a misdeed, though it remained as indefinite as the persons themselves; in the same manner they too contained a period of dread and anxiety. The only decisive disparity between the two kinds of phantasies lies in the difference between their respective solutions, which in the one case consisted of the beating-scene, in the other of the reconciliation-scene.

In the course of analysis the girl became acquainted with these striking points of resemblance in the construction of the two apparently distinct products of her imagination. The suspicion of a connection between them slowly dawned on her; once the possibility of their relationship had been accepted she quickly began to perceive a whole series of connections between them.

Even so the content at least of the beating-phantasies appeared to have nothing in common with that of the nice stories; but this too was disproved by further analysis. Closer observation showed that the theme of the beating-phantasies had in more than one place succeeded in penetrating into the nice stories. As an example we may take the Knight and Prisoner day-dream which has already been discussed. There the Knight threatened to apply torture to the prisoner. This menace always remained unfulfilled; but nevertheless a great number of scenes was built up on it, to which it supplied an unmistakable colouring of anxiety. In the light of previous considerations this menace may easily be recognized as the echo of the earlier scenes of beating: but no description of them was permissible in the nice story. There were other ways in which the theme of beating encroached into the day-dream, not in the Knight and Prisoner day-dream itself, but in the other continued stories produced by the girl.

The following observations are taken from the main story, as far as it was revealed during analysis: In the main story the passive, weak character (corresponding to the youth in the Knight and Prisoner day-dream) was occasionally represented by two figures. After committing identical misdeeds, one of these two had to undergo punishment, while the other was pardoned. Here the scene of punishment was in itself neither pleasurably nor "painfully" accentuated; it simply served to bring the reconciliation into relief and to heighten by contrast the pleasure derived from the latter. In other places the passive person in the day-dream had to live through in memory a past scene of beating while he was actually being treated affectionately. Here again the contrast served to heighten the pleasure. Or, as a third possibility, the active, strong person, dominated by the gentle mood necessary for the climax, remembered a past scene of beating in which, after committing the same misdeed, he had been the punished one.

Besides penetrating into the day-dream in this manner the beating-theme sometimes formed the actual content of a nice story, on the condition that one characteristic indispensable in the beating-phantasy was left out. This characteristic was the humiliation connected with being beaten. In a few impressive scenes in the main day-dream, for example, the climax consisted of a blow or punishment; when it was a blow, however, it was described as unintentional, when a punishment, it took the form of a self-punishment.

These instances of an irruption of the beating-theme into the nice stories all constituted as many arguments proving the relationship already suggested between the two phantasies. In the further course of analysis the girl furnished another convincing proof of this intimate connection. She one day admitted that on a few rare occasions a sudden reversal from nice stories into beating-phantasies had taken place. In hard times, when things were difficult, for instance, a nice story had sometimes failed to fulfil its function and had been replaced at the climax by a beating-scene; so that the sexual gratification connected with the latter had obtained full discharge for the dammed-up excitation. She had afterwards, however, energetically excluded these occurrences from her memory.

Investigation into the relationship between beating-phantasies and nice stories has so far yielded the following results: (1) a striking analogy in the construction of the single scenes; (2) a certain parallelism in the content; (3) the possibility of a sudden change over from the one to the other. The essential difference between the two lies in the fact that in the nice stories affectionate treatment takes the place of the chastisement contained in the phantasies of beating.

Now these considerations lead back to Freud's paper, in which the previous history of the beating-phantasies is reconstructed. As already mentioned, Freud says that the form of beating-phantasy here described is not the initial one, but is a substitute for an incestuous love-scene. The combined influence of repression and of regression to the anal-sadistic phase of libido-organization has transformed the latter into a beating-scene. From this point of view the apparent advance from the beating-phantasies to the nice stories might be explained as a return to a former phase. The nice stories seem to relinquish the original theme of the phantasies of beating; but they simultaneously bring out their original meaning, i.e., the phantasy of love that was hidden in them.

This attempt at explanation is, however, so far deficient in one important point. We have seen that the climax of the beating-phantasies was invariably connected with a compulsive onanistic act, as well as with a subsequent sense of guilt. The climax of the nice stories on the other hand is free from both. At a first glance this seems inexplicable; for the onanistic act as well as the sense of guilt are both derived from the repressed love phantasy, and the latter, though it is disguised in the phantasies of beating, is represented in the nice stories.

A solution of the problem is furnished by the fact that the nice stories do not take up the whole of the incestuous wish-phantasy belonging to early childhood. At that time all the sexual instincts were being concentrated on a first object, the father. Afterwards repression of the Oedipus complex forced the child to renounce most of these infantile sexual ties. The "sensual" object-ties were banned to the unconscious, so that their re-emergence in the phantasies of beating signifies a partial failure of this attempt at repression.

While the phantasies of beating thus represent a return of the repressed, i.e., of the incestuous wish-phantasy, the nice stories on the other hand represent a sublimation of it. The beating-phantasies constitute a gratification for the directly sexual tendencies, the nice stories for those which Freud describes as "inhibited in their aim". Just as in the development of a child's love for its parents, the originally complete sexual current is divided into sensual tendencies which undergo repression (here represented by the beating-phantasies) and into a sublimated and purely tender emotional tie (represented by the nice stories).

The tasks which the two phantasies were each required to fulfil may now be sketched as follows: the beating-phantasies always represent the same sensual love-scene which, expressed in terms of the anal-sadistic phase of libido-organization, comes to be disguised as a beating-scene. The nice stories, on the other hand, contain a variety of tender emotional object-ties. Their theme, however, is also monotonous; it invariably consists of a friendship formed between two characters opposed in strength, in age, or in social position.

The sublimation of sensual love into tender friendship was naturally favoured by the fact that already in the early stages of the beating-phantasy the girl had abandoned the difference of sex and was invariably represented as a boy.

III

It was the object of this paper to examine a special case in which beating-phantasies and day-dreams co-existed side by side. The relationship between them and their dependence on each other has been ascertained. Apart from this, analysis of this particular day-dreamer also provided an opportunity for observing the further development of a continued story.

Some years after the first emergence of the Knight and Prisoner day-dream the girl suddenly made an attempt to write down its content. As a result she produced a sort of short story describing the youth's life during his imprisonment. It began with a description of the torture he underwent and ended with the prisoner's refusal to try to escape from the castle. His readiness to remain in the Knight's power suggested the beginning of their friendship. In contrast to the day-dream all the events were laid in the past and appeared in the form of a conversation between the prisoner's father and the Knight.

Thus, while retaining the theme of the day-dream, the written story completely changed the elaboration of the content. In the day-dream the friendship between the strong and the weak character developed anew in every single scene; in the written story, on the other hand, the friendship developed slowly and its formation took up the whole length of the action. In the new elaboration the single scenes of the day-dream were abandoned; part of the material contained in them was used for the story, their various single climaxes, however, were not replaced by a main climax terminating the latter. The end, i.e., a harmony between the former antagonists, was anticipated but not described in the story. Consequently here the interest, which in the day-dream concentrated on particular points, was more equally diffused over the whole course of the action.

These modifications in the structure corresponded also to modifications in the gratification obtained. In the day-dream every new formation or repetition of a single scene provided another opportunity for pleasurable instinctual gratification. This direct way of obtaining pleasure was abandoned in the written story. The girl indeed did the actual writing in a state of pleasurable excitement, similar to her mental state when day-dreaming; the finished story, however, did not call forth this excitement. Reading the story had no more effect on the girl than reading a story with a similar content produced by a stranger.

This brings the surmise very near that the two essential changes from the day-dream to the written story, i.e., abandoning the single scenes and renouncing the pleasure derived from the various single climaxes, were intimately connected. It seems obvious that the written story had other motives and served another purpose than the day-dream. If this were not so then the development of the Knight's Story out of the day-dream would signify a transformation of something useful into something utterly useless.

When asked the reasons which had induced her to write the story the girl could give only a single conscious one. She said the story had originated at a period when the day-dream had been unusually vivid. Writing it was a defence against over-indulgence in it. The characters were so real to her and took up so much of her time and interest that she formed the purpose of creating a sort of independent existence for them. As a matter of fact, after it was written down the Knight and Prisoner day-dream actually faded away. This explanation, however, does not altogether clear the matter up. If it were the vividness of the scenes which induced her to write the story it remains inexplicable why, in writing it, she abandoned those particular scenes and dwelt on others which were not included in the day-dream (e.g. the torture-scene). The same reasoning holds good for the characters; for in the story some of the characters that were fully developed in the day-dream are lacking and are replaced by others unknown in the former (as, for instance, the prisoner's father).

Another motivation for the written story is shown by following out a remark of Dr Bernfeld's, relating to literary attempts by adolescents. Bernfeld says that in these cases the motive for writing out a day-dream may be extrinsic, not intrinsic. According to him it is most often prompted by certain ambitious ego-tendencies, as, for example, the wish to be regarded as a poet and to win in that capacity the love and esteem of others. In applying this theory to the case under discussion the development from the day-dream to the written story may be represented as follows:

The private phantasy was transformed under the pressure of the ambitious tendencies mentioned above into a communication for others. During the transformation all regard for the dreamer's personal needs were replaced by consideration of the future readers of the story. It was no longer necessary for the girl to gain pleasure directly from the content, since the written story as such gratified her ambition, and was thus indirectly pleasurable. After having renounced the direct way of attaining pleasure, there was then no reason left for retaining the various single climaxes which had been the source of pleasure before. Similarly she was now free to disregard the restrictions which had forbidden her to describe situations derived from the phantasies of beating. The torture, for example, could be introduced. When writing the story she regarded the whole content of the day-dream from the point of view of its suitability for representation and made her choice between the different parts accordingly. The better she succeeded in rounding off the action, the greater would be the impression she created and, simultaneously, the pleasure she indirectly derived from the story. By renouncing her private pleasure in favour of the impression she could create in others she turned from an autistic to a social activity, and thus found her way back from the life of imagination to life in reality.

CHAPTER THREE

Female sexuality

Horney, Karen (1924). On the genesis of the castration complex in women. *International Journal of Psychoanalysis*, 5: 50–65.

Riviere, Joan (1929). Womanliness as a masquerade. *International Journal of Psychoanalysis*, 10: 303–313.

Following the First World War, there was a major move for the advancement of women, and for them to become professionally qualified. At the time, the newness of psychoanalysis made it more open to women than the older professions were. As well as an interest in child analysis, women analysts began to be provoked by Freud's obfuscation of women's sexuality and development:

> Freud has more than once commented on the fact that our knowledge of the early stages in female development is much more obscure and imperfect than that of male development, and Karen Horney has forcibly, though justly, pointed out that this must be connected with the greater tendency to bias that exists on the former subject. [Jones, 1927, p. 459]

Women psychoanalysts began to take questions about female sexuality as their field of enquiry. Helene Deutsch (1925), Josine Muller (1932), Joan Riviere (1929), and others (e.g. Payne, 1936) joined Horney (1924*, 1926, 1933) in this debate, which has continued into the modern period of psychoanalysis (for instance, Arden, 1987; Chasseguet-Smirgel, 1981; Chodorow, 1996; Raphael-Leff & Perelberg, 1997). Freud's case load was predominantly women (e.g., all five cases in "Studies in hysteria", Breuer & Freud, 1895) yet his theory was formulated in terms of male sexuality, based rather explicitly on his own Oedipus complex.

Freud assumed women's development was an analogy of the male, until his paper on "Some psychical consequences of the anatomical distinction between the sexes" (Freud, 1925j). Karen Horney had challenged the standard opinion, at the time, that a woman's castration and Oedipus complexes derive from her penis envy (see Abraham, 1921) and argues, with clinical vignettes, that this is a neurotic camouflage in which an identification with father and the impossible envious wish for a penis overlays an envy of mother and her capacity to bear children. This follows what might possibly be thought of as a characteristic Berlin approach, stemming from Abraham, in which development consists of varying, alternating, and unstable identifications with mother and with father, as much as it depends on the libidinal stages.

I have chosen the paper republished here (Horney, 1924*) because of its clinical emphasis, rather than the later paper published in 1926. In his 1925 paper on anatomical differences, Freud acknowledged Horney's divergent direction from his; and in 1926 Horney responded. She referred in the later paper (Horney, 1926) to the sociologist, Georg Simmel (1911), claiming that it is not merely the bodily difference between the sexes, as Freud claimed, but that the difference itself is viewed from a masculine set of values, which are prevalent socially. She extended her thesis by saying that the male fear of castration is complemented in the female by fear of vaginal damage. The woman therefore flees from the female position towards a male identification and wish for an undamaged penis. Society itself flees in parallel from a female perspective, a thesis elaborated further in a later paper (Horney, 1933).

The link that is suggested in Horney's paper between a vagina and the psychological conception of an inner space where fantasy

resides, has enriched the notion of f/phantasy. Together with Klein
(1928), Horney derived the very concrete idea of inner space as
complicated identifications from Abraham (1924). And Klein influenced many in the British Society with these emphases that originated in Berlin. One of those she influenced was Joan Riviere.
Riviere's paper, republished here, followed a similar direction,
analysing the complex layering of identifications with mother and
father. In certain types of women, the identification as a woman can
have a rather thin, mask-like quality. Riviere followed Klein's recent
views on the Oedipus complex in the separate genders (Klein,
1928), and this rested on similar sources, such as Abraham's work,
which influenced both Horney and Klein. Riviere's clinical descriptions are an early example of the "as-if personality" later formulated by Helene Deutsch (1942) and, together with her later paper
(Riviere, 1932), it places Riviere at the origins of the development of
modern psychoanalysis of femininity and of feminism. Freud
(1933a), somewhat in response to these contributions, supported
these notions, but still stressed the progression and regression
though the libidinal phases, rather then the complex alternating
identifications.

Female sexuality has become a major intellectual and political
issue in recent decades and, when a psychoanalytic perspective is
employed in these debates, these two papers, by Horney and
Riviere, are the important and challenging starting point.

References

Abraham, K. (1921). Manifestations of the female castration complex.
    International Journal of Psychoanalysis, 3: 1–29.
Abraham, K. (1924) [1973]. A short study of the development of the
    libido, viewed in the light of mental disorders. In: K. Abraham (Ed.),
    Selected Papers on Psychoanalysis (pp. 418–501). London: Hogarth.
Arden, M. (1987). "A concept of femininity": Sylvia Payne's 1935 paper
    reassessed. *International Journal of Psychoanalysis*, 14: 237–244.
Breuer, J., & Freud, S. (1895d). Studies in hysteria. *S.E.*, 2: 1–335.
    London: Hogarth Press.
Chasseguet-Smirgel, J. (1981). *Sexuality and Mind*. London: Virago.

Chodorow, N. (1996). Theoretical gender and clinical gender: epistemological reflections on the psychology of women. *Journal of the American Patial Association*, 44S: 215–238.

Deutsch, H. (1925). The psychology of women in relation to the functions of reproduction. *International Journal of Psychoanalysis*, 6: 405–418.

Deutsch, H. (1942). Some forms of emotional disturbance and their relationship to schizophrenia. *Psychoanalytic Quarterly*, 11: 301–321.

Freud, S. (1925j). Some psychical consequences of the anatomical distinction between the sexes. *S.E.*, 19: 243–247. London: Hogarth Press.

Freud, S. (1933a). New introductory lecture: Feminity. *S.E.*, 22: 112–135. London: Hogarth Press.

Horney, K. (1926). The flight from womanhood: the masculinity-complex in women, as viewed by men and by women. *International Journal of Psychoanalysis*, 7: 324–339.

Horney, K. (1933). The denial of the vagina—a contribution to the problem of the genital anxieties specific to women. *International Journal of Psychoanalysis*, 14: 57–70.

Jones, E. (1927). The early development of female sexuality. *International Journal of Psychoanalysis*, 8: 459–472.

Klein, M. (1928). Early stages of the Oedipus conflict. *International Journal of Psychoanalysis*, 9: 167–180.

Müller, J. (1932). A contribution to the problem of libidinal development of the genital phase in girls. *International Journal of Psychoanalysis*, 13: 361–368.

Payne, S. (1936). A conception of feminity. *British Journal of Medical Psychology*, 15: 18–33.

Raphael-Leff, J., & Perelberg, R. (1997). *Female Experience*. London: Routledge.

Riviere, J. (1932). Jealousy as a mechanism of defence. *International Journal of Psychoanalysis*, 13: 414–424.

Simmel, G. (1911) *Philosophische Kultur*. Leipzig: Duncker and Humblot.

On the genesis of the castration complex in women*†

Karen Horney

Whilst our knowledge of the forms which the castration complex may assume in women has become more and more comprehensive,[1] our insight into the nature of the complex as a whole has made no corresponding advance. The very abundance of the material collected which is now familiar to us brings to our minds more strongly than ever the remarkable character of the whole phenomenon, so that the phenomenon in itself becomes a problem. A survey of the forms assumed by the castration complex in women that have hitherto been observed and of the inferences tacitly drawn from them shows that, so far, the prevailing conception is based on a certain fundamental notion which may be briefly formulated as follows (I quote in part *verbatim* from Abraham's work on the subject): Many females, both children and adults, suffer either temporarily or permanently from the fact of their sex.

---

* Paper delivered at the Seventh International Psycho-Analytical Congress, Berlin, September 1922.

† Article citation:
Horney, K. (1924). On the genesis of the castration complex in women. *International Journal of Psychoanalysis*, 5: 50–65.

The manifestations in the mental life of women which spring from the objection to being a woman are traceable to their coveting a penis when they were little girls. The unwelcome idea of being fundamentally lacking in this respect gives rise to passive castration phantasies, while active phantasies spring from a revengeful attitude against the favoured male.

In this formulation we have it assumed as an axiomatic fact that females feel at a disadvantage in this respect of their genital organs, without this being regarded as constituting a problem in itself—possibly because to masculine narcissism this has seemed too self-evident to need explanation. Nevertheless, the conclusion so far drawn from the investigations—amounting as it does to an assertion that one-half of the human race is discontented with the sex assigned to it and can overcome this discontent only in favourable circumstances—is decidedly unsatisfying, not only to feminine narcissism but also to biological science. The question arises, therefore: Is it really the case that the forms of the castration complex met with in women, pregnant with consequences as they are, not only for the development of neurosis but also for the character-formation and destiny of women who for all practical purposes are normal, are based solely on a dissatisfaction with the fact of womanhood—a dissatisfaction due to her coveting a penis? Or is this possibly but a pretext (at any rate, for the most part) put forward by other forces, the dynamic power of which we know already from our study of the formation of neurosis?

I think that this problem can be attacked from several sides. Here I merely wish to put forward from the purely ontogenetic standpoint, in the hope that they may contribute to a solution, certain considerations which have gradually forced themselves upon me in the course of a practice extending over many years, amongst patients the great majority of whom were women and in whom on the whole the castration complex was very marked.

According to the prevailing conception the castration complex in females is entirely centred in the "penis-envy" complex; in fact the term "masculinity-complex" is used as practically synonymous. The first question which then presents itself is: How is it that we can observe this penis-envy occurring as an almost invariable typical phenomenon, even when the subject has not a masculine way of life, where there is no favoured brother to make envy of this sort comprehensible and where no "accidental disasters"[2] in the woman's experience have caused the masculine role to seem the more desirable?

The important point here seems to be the fact of raising the question; once it has been put answers suggest themselves almost spontaneously from the material with which we are sufficiently familiar. For supposing we take as our starting-point the form in which "penis-envy" probably most frequently directly manifests itself, namely, in the desire to urinate like a man, a critical sifting of the material soon shows that this desire is made up of three component parts, of which sometimes one and sometimes another is the more important.

The part about which I can speak most briefly is that of *urethral erotism* itself, for sufficient stress has already been laid on this factor, being as it is the most obvious one. If we want to appraise in all its intensity the envy springing from this source we must above all make ourselves realize the narcissistic overestimation[3] in which the excretory processes are held by children. Phantasies of omnipotence, especially such as are of a sadistic character, are as a matter of fact more easily associated with the jet of urine passed by the male. As an instance of this idea—and it is only one instance amongst many—I can quote something I was told of a class in a boys' school: when two boys, they said, urinate to make a cross the person of whom they think at the moment will die.

Now even though it is certain that a strong feeling of being at a disadvantage must arise in little girls in connection with urethral erotism, yet it is exaggerating the part played by this factor if, as has hitherto been done in many quarters, we straightway attribute to it every symptom and every phantasy of which the content is the desire to urinate like a man. On the contrary, the motive force which originates and maintains this wish is often to be found in quite other instinct-components—above all in active and passive scoptophilia. This connection is due to the circumstance that it is just in the act of urinating that a boy can display his genital and look at himself and is even permitted to do so, and that he can thus in a certain sense satisfy his sexual curiosity, at least as far as his own body is concerned, every time he passes urine.

This factor, which is rooted in the scoptophilic instinct, was particularly evident in a patient of mine in whom the desire to urinate like a male dominated the whole clinical picture for a time. During this period she seldom came to the analysis without declaring that she had seen a man urinating in the street, and once she exclaimed quite spontaneously: "If I might ask a gift of Providence it would be to be able just for once to urinate like a man." Her associations completed this thought beyond all possibility of doubt: "For then I should know how I really am made." The fact that men can see themselves when urinating, while women cannot, was in this patient, whose development was to a great extent arrested at a pregenital stage, actually one of the principal roots of her very marked "penis-envy".

Just as woman, because her genital organs are hidden, is ever the great riddle for man, so man is an object of lively jealousy for woman precisely on account of the ready visibility of his organ.

The close connection between urethral erotism and the scoptophilic instinct was obvious in yet another patient, a woman whom I will call Y. She practised masturbation in a very peculiar way which stood for urinating like her father. In the obsessional neurosis from which this patient suffered, the chief agent was the scoptophilic instinct; she had the most acute feelings of anxiety consequent on the idea of being seen by others whilst thus practising masturbation. She was therefore giving expression to the far-back wish of the little girl: I wish I had a genital too, which I could show, like father, every time I pass urine.

I think, moreover, that this factor plays a leading part in every case of exaggerated embarrassment and prudery in girls, and I further conjecture that the difference in the dress of men and women, at least in our civilized races, may be traced to this very circumstance that the girl cannot exhibit her genital organs and that therefore in respect of her exhibitionistic tendencies she regresses to a stage at which this desire to display herself still applied to her whole body. This puts us on the track of the reason of why a woman wears a low neck, while a man wears a dress-coat. I think too that this connection explains to some extent the criterion which is always mentioned first when the points of difference between men and women are under discussion—namely, the greater subjectivity of women as compared with the greater objectivity of men. The explanation would be that the man's impulse to investigate finds satisfaction in the examination of his own body and may, or must, subsequently be directed to external objects; while the woman, on the other hand, can arrive at no clear knowledge about her own person, and therefore finds it far harder to become free of herself.

Finally, the wish which I have assumed to be the prototype of "penis-envy" has in it a third element, namely, suppressed onanistic wishes, as a rule deeply hidden but none the less important on that account. This element may be traced to a connection of ideas (mostly unconscious) by which the fact that boys are permitted to take hold of their genital when urinating is construed as a permission to masturbate.

Thus a patient who had witnessed a father reproving his little daughter for touching that part of her body with her tiny hands said to me quite indignantly: "He forbids her to do that and yet does it himself five or six times a day." You will easily recognize the same connection of ideas in the case of the patient Y., in whom the male way of urinating became the decisive factor in the form of masturbation that she practised. Moreover, in this case it became clear that she could not become completely free from the compulsion to masturbate so long as she unconsciously maintained the claim that she should be a man. The conclusion I drew from my observation of this case is, I think, quite a typical one: girls have a very special difficulty in overcoming masturbation because they feel that they are unjustly forbidden something which boys are allowed to do on account of their different bodily formation. Or, in terms of the problem before us, we may put it in another way and say that the difference in bodily formation may easily give rise to a bitter feeling of injury, so that the argument which is used later to account for the repudiation of womanhood, namely, that men have greater freedom in their sexual life, is really based upon actual experiences to that effect in early childhood. Van Ophuijsen at the conclusion of his work on the masculinity-complex in women lays stress on the strong impression he received in analysis of the existence of an intimate connection between the masculinity-complex, infantile masturbation of the clitoris and urethral erotism. The connecting link would probably be found in the considerations I have just put before you.

These considerations, which constitute the answer to our initial question about the reason why "penis-envy" is of typical occurrence, may be summarized shortly as follows: The little girl's sense of inferiority is (as Abraham has also pointed out in one passage) by no means primary. But it seems to her that, in comparison with boys, she is subject to restrictions as regards the possibility of gratifying certain instinct-components which are of the greatest importance in the pregenital period. Indeed, I think I should put the matter even more accurately if I said that *as an actual fact*, from the point of view of a child at this stage of development, little girls *are* at a disadvantage compared with boys in respect of certain possibilities of gratification. For unless we are quite clear about the *reality* of this disadvantage we shall not understand that "penis-envy" is an almost inevitable phenomenon in the life of female children, and one which cannot but complicate female development. The fact that later when she reaches maturity a great part in sexual life (as regards creative power perhaps even a greater part than that of men) devolves upon a woman—I mean when she becomes a mother—cannot be any compensation to the little girl at this early stage, for it still lies outside her potentialities of direct gratification.

I shall here break off this line of thought, for I now come to the second, more comprehensive, problem: Does the complex we are discussing really rest on "penis-envy" and is the latter to be regarded as the ultimate force behind it?

Taking this question as our starting-point, we have to consider what factors determine whether the penis-complex is more or less successfully overcome or whether it becomes regressively reinforced so that fixation occurs. A consideration of these possibilities compels us to examine more closely *the form of object-libido* in such cases. We then find that the girls and women whose desire to be men is often so glaringly evident have at the very outset of life passed through a phase of extremely strong father-fixation. In other words: They tried first of all to master the Oedipus complex in the normal way by retaining their original identification with the mother and, like the mother, taking the father as love-object.

We know that at this stage there are two possible ways in which a girl may overcome the "penis-envy" complex without detriment to herself. She may pass from the auto-erotic narcissistic desire for the penis to the woman's desire for the man (= the father), precisely in virtue of her identification of herself with her mother; or to the material desire for a child (by the father). With regard to the subsequent love-life of healthy as well as abnormal women it is illuminating to reflect that (even in the most favourable instances) the origin, or at any rate one origin, of either attitude was narcissistic in character and of the nature of a desire for possession.

Now in the cases under consideration it is evident that this womanly and maternal development has taken place to a very marked degree. Thus in the patient Y., whose neurosis, like all those which I shall cite here, bore throughout the stamp of the castration complex, many phantasies of rape occurred which were indicative of this phase. The men whom she thought of as committing rape upon her were one and all unmistakably father-imagines; hence these phantasies had necessarily to be construed as the compulsive repetition of a primal phantasy in which the patient, who till late in life felt herself one with her mother, had experienced with her the father's act of complete sexual appropriation. It is noteworthy that this patient, who in other respects was perfectly clear in her mind, was at the beginning of the analysis strongly inclined to regard these phantasies of rape as actual fact.

Other cases also manifest—in another form—a similar clinging to the fiction that this primal feminine phantasy is real. From another patient, whom I will call X., I heard innumerable remarks constituting direct proof of how very real this love-relation with the father had seemed to her. Once, for instance, she recollected how her father had sung a love-song to her, and with the recollection there broke from her a cry of disillusion and despair: "And yet it was all a lie!" The same thought was expressed in one of her symptoms which I should like to cite here as typical of a whole similar group: at times she was under a compulsion to eat quantities of salt. Her mother had been obliged to eat salt on account of hæmorrhages of the lungs, which had occurred in the patient's early childhood; she had unconsciously construed them as the result of her parents' intercourse. This symptom therefore stood for her unconscious claim to have suffered the same experience from her father as her mother had undergone. It was the same claim that made her regard herself as a prostitute (actually she was a virgin) and that made her feel a compelling need to make a confession of some kind to any new love-object.

The numerous unmistakable observations of this kind show us how important it is to realize that at this early stage—as an ontogenetic repetition of a phylogenetic experience—the child constructs, on the basis of a (hostile or loving) identification with its mother, a phantasy that it has suffered full sexual appropriation by the father; and further, that in phantasy this experience presents itself as having actually taken place—as much a fact as it must have been at that distant time when all women were primarily the property of the father.

We know that the natural fate of this love-phantasy is a denial of it by reality. In cases which are subsequently dominated by the castration complex this frustration often changes into a profound *disappointment*, deep traces of which remain in the neurosis. Thus there arises a more or less extensive disturbance in the development of the sense of reality. One often receives the impression that the emotional intensity of this attachment to the father is too strong to admit of a recognition of the essential unreality of the relation; in other cases again it seems as though from the outset there had been an excessive power of phantasy, making it difficult to grasp actuality correctly; finally the real relations with the parents are often so unhappy as to account for a clinging to phantasy.

These patients feel as if their fathers had actually once been their lovers and had afterwards been false to them or deserted them. Sometimes this again is the starting-point of doubt: Did I only imagine the whole thing, or was it true? In a patient whom I will call Z., of whom I shall have to speak in a moment, this doubting attitude betrayed itself in a repetition-compulsion which took the form of anxiety whenever a man appeared attracted to her, lest she might only be imagining this liking on his part. Even when she was actually engaged to be married she had to be constantly reassuring herself that she had not simply imagined the whole thing. In a day-dream she pictured herself as assailed by a man whom she knocked down with a blow on the nose, treading upon his penis with her foot. Continuing the phantasy, she wished to give him in charge but refrained because she was afraid he might declare she had imagined the scene. When speaking of the patient Y., I mentioned the doubt she felt as to the actuality of her phantasies of rape, and that this doubt had reference to the original experience with the father. In her it was possible to trace out the way in which the doubt from this source extended to every occurrence in her life and so actually became the basis of her obsessional neurosis. In her case, as in many others, the course of the analysis made it probable that this origin of the doubt had deeper roots than that uncertainty, with which we are familiar, about the subject's own sex.[4]

In the patient X., who used to revel in numerous recollections of that earliest period of her life which she called her childhood's paradise, this disappointment was closely connected in her memory with an unjust punishment inflicted on her by her father when she was five or six years old. It transpired that at this time a sister had been born and that she had felt herself supplanted by this sister in her father's affections. As deeper strata were revealed it became clear that behind the jealousy of her sister there lay a furious jealousy of her mother which related in the first instance to her mother's many pregnancies. "Mother *always* had the babies", she once said indignantly. More strongly repressed were two further roots (by no means equally important) of her feeling that her father was faithless to her. The one was sexual jealousy of her mother dating from her witnessing parental coitus at a time when her sense of reality was sufficiently awakened for it to be impossible for her any longer completely to incorporate all that she saw in her phantasy of an experience undergone by herself. It was a mishearing on her part which put me on the track of this last source of her feeling: once as I was speaking of a time "*nach* der Enttäuschung" (after the disappointment), she understood me to say "*Nacht* der Enttäuschung" (the night of the disappointment) and gave the association of Brangäne keeping vigil during Tristan and Isolde's love-night.

A repetition-compulsion in this patient spoke in language no less clear: the typical experience of her love-life was that she first of all fell in love with a father-substitute and then found him faithless. In connection with occurrences of this sort the final root of the complex became plainly evident: I allude to her feelings of guilt. Certainly a great part of these feelings was to be construed as reproaches originally directed against the father and then turned upon herself. But it was possible to trace very clearly the way in which the feelings of guilt, especially those which resulted from strong impulses to do away with her mother (to the patient this identification had the special significance of "doing away with her" and "replacing her') had produced in her an expectation of calamity, which of course referred above all to the relation with her father.[5]

I wish especially to emphasize the strong impression I received in this case of the importance of *the desire to have a child* (from the father).[6] My reason for laying stress upon it is that I think we are inclined to underestimate the unconscious power of this wish and in particular its libidinal character, because it is a wish to which the ego can later more easily assent than to many other sexual impulses. Its relation to the "penis-envy" complex is twofold. On the one hand it is well known that the maternal instinct receives an "unconscious libidinal reinforcement"[7] from the desire for a penis, a desire which comes earlier in point of time because it belongs to the auto-erotic period. Then when the little girl experiences the disappointment described in relation to her father she renounces not only her claim upon him but also the desire for a child. This is regressively succeeded (in accordance with the familiar equation) by ideas belonging to the anal phase and by the old demand for the penis. When this takes place that demand is not simply revived, but is reinforced with all the energy of the girl-child's desire for a child.

I could see this connection particularly clearly in the case of the patient Z., who, after several symptoms of the obsessional neurosis had vanished, retained as the final and most obstinate symptom a lively dread of pregnancy and childbirth. The experience which had determined this symptom proved to be her mother's pregnancy and the birth of a brother when the patient was two years old, while observations of parental coitus, continued after she was no longer an infant, contributed to the same result. For a long time it seemed that this case was singularly well calculated to illustrate the central importance of the "penis-envy" complex. Her coveting of the penis (her brother's) and her violent anger against him as the intruder who had ousted her from her position of only child, when once revealed by analysis, entered consciousness heavily charged with affect. The envy was, moreover, accompanied by all the manifestations which we are accustomed to trace to it: first and foremost the attitude of revenge against men, with very intense castration phantasies; repudiation of feminine tasks and functions, especially that of pregnancy; and further, a strong unconscious homosexual tendency. It was only when the analysis penetrated into deeper strata under the greatest resistances imaginable that it became evident that the source of the "penis-envy" was her envy on account of the child which her mother and not she had received from her father, whereupon by a process of displacement the penis had become the object of envy in place of the child. In the same way

her vehement anger against her brother proved really to have reference to her father, who she felt had deceived her, and to her mother
who, instead of the patient herself, had received the child. Only
when this displacement was cancelled did she really become free
from "penis-envy" and from the longing to be a man, and was she
able to be a true woman and even to wish to have children herself.

Now what process had taken place? Quite roughly it may be
outlined as follows: (1) the envy relating to the child was displaced
to the brother and his genital; (2) there clearly ensued the mechanism discovered by Freud, by which the father as love-object is
given up and the object-relation to him is regressively replaced by
an identification with him.

The latter process manifested itself in those pretensions to
manhood on her part of which I have already spoken. It was easy
to prove that her desire to be a man was by no means to be understood in a general sense, but that the real meaning of her claims was
to act her father's part. Thus she adopted the same profession as her
father, and after his death her attitude to her mother was that of a
husband who makes demands upon his wife and issues orders.
Once when a noisy eructation escaped her she could not help thinking with satisfaction: "Just like Papa". Yet she did not reach the
point of a completely homosexual object-choice; the development
of the object-libido seemed rather to be altogether disturbed, and
the result was an obvious regression to an auto-erotic narcissistic
stage. To sum up: displacement of the envy which had reference to
children on to the brother and his penis, identification with the
father, and regression to a pregenital phase all operated in the same
direction—to stir up a powerful "penis-envy" which then remained
in the foreground and seemed to dominate the whole picture.

Now in my opinion this kind of development of the Oedipus
complex is typical of those cases in which the castration complex is
predominant. What happens is that a phase of identification with
the mother gives way to a very large extent to one of identification
with the father, and at the same time there is regression to a pregenital stage. This process of identification with the father I believe to
be one root of the castration complex in women.

At this point I should like to answer at once two possible objections. One of them might run like this: such an oscillation between
father and mother is surely nothing peculiar. On the contrary, it is

to be seen in every child, and we know that, according to Freud, the libido of each one of us oscillates throughout life between male and female objects. The second objection relates to the connection with homosexuality, and may be expressed thus: in his paper on the psychogenesis of a case of homosexuality in a woman Freud has convinced us that such a development in the direction of identification with the father is one of the bases of manifest homosexuality; yet now I am depicting the same process as resulting in the castration complex. In answer I would emphasize the fact that it was just this paper of Freud's which helped me to understand the castration complex in women. It is exactly in these cases that, on the one hand, the extent to which the libido normally oscillates is considerably exceeded from a quantitative point of view, whilst, on the other hand, the repression of the love-attitude towards the father and the identification with him are not so completely successful as in cases of homosexuality. And so the similarity in the two courses of development is no argument against its significance for the castration complex in women; on the contrary, this view makes homosexuality much less of an isolated phenomenon.

We know that in every case in which the castration complex predominates there is without exception a more or less marked tendency to homosexuality. To play the father's part always amounts also to desiring the mother in some sense. There may be every possible degree of closeness in the relation between narcissistic regression and homosexual object-cathexis, so that we have an unbroken series culminating in manifest homosexuality.

A third criticism which suggests itself here relates to the temporal and causal connection with "penis-envy" and runs as follows: Is not the relation of the "penis-envy" complex to the process of identification with the father just the opposite of that depicted here? May it not be that in order to establish this sort of permanent identification with the father there has first to be an unusually strong "penis-envy"? I think we cannot fail to recognize that a specially powerful "penis-envy" (whether it is constitutional or the result of personal experience) does help to prepare the way for the changeover by which the patient identifies herself with the father; nevertheless, the history of the cases I have described, and of other cases as well, shows that notwithstanding the "penis-envy" a strong and wholly womanly love-relation to the father had been formed, and that it was only when this love was disappointed that the feminine role was abandoned. This abandonment and the consequent identification with the father then revives the "penis-envy", and only when it derives nourishment from such powerful sources as these can that feeling operate in its full strength.

For this revulsion to an identification with the father to take place it is essential that the sense of reality should be at least to some extent awakened; hence it is inevitable that the little girl should no longer be able to content herself, as she formerly did, simply with a phantasied fulfilment of her desire for the penis, but should now begin to brood upon her lack of that organ or ponder over its possible existence. The trend of these speculations is determined by the girl's whole affective disposition; it is characterized by the following typical attitudes: a feminine love-attachment, not yet wholly subdued, to her father, feelings of vehement anger and of revenge directed against him because of the disappointment suffered through him, and last but not least, feelings of guilt (relating to incestuous phantasies concerning him) which are violently aroused under the pressure of the privation. Thus it is that these broodings invariably have reference to the father.

I saw this very clearly in the patient Y., whom I have already mentioned more than once. I told you that this patient produced phantasies of rape—phantasies which she regarded as fact—and that ultimately these related to her father. She too had reached the point of identifying herself to a very great extent with him; for instance, her attitude to her mother was exactly that of a son. Thus she had dreams in which her father was attacked by a snake or wild beasts, whereupon she rescued him.

Her castration phantasies took the familiar form of imagining that she was not normally made in the genital region, and besides this she had a feeling as though she had suffered some injury to the genitals. On both these points she had evolved many ideas, chiefly to the effect that these peculiarities were the result of acts of rape. Indeed, it became plain that her obstinate insistence upon these sensations and ideas in connection with her genital organs was actually designed to prove the reality of these acts of violence, and so, ultimately, the reality of her love-relation with her father. The clearest light is thrown upon the importance of this phantasy and the strength of the repetition-compulsion under which she laboured, by the fact that before analysis she had insisted on undergoing six laparotomy operations, several of which had been performed simply on account of her pains. In another patient, whose coveting of the penis took an absolutely grotesque form, this feeling of having sustained a wound was displaced on to other organs, so that when her obsessional symptoms had been resolved the clinical picture was markedly hypochondriacal. At this point her resistance took the following form: "It is obviously absurd for me to be analysed, seeing that my heart, my lungs, my stomach, and my intestines are evidently organically diseased." Here again the insistence on the reality of her phantasies was so strong that on one occasion she had almost compelled performance of an intestinal operation. Her associations constantly brought the idea that she had been struck down (*geschlagen*) with illness by her father. As a matter of fact, when these hypochondriacal symptoms cleared up, phantasies of being *struck* (*Schlagephantasien*) became the most prominent feature in her neurosis. It seems to me quite impossible to account satisfactorily for these manifestations simply by the "penis-envy" complex. But their main features become perfectly clear if we regard them as an effect of the impulse to experience anew after a compulsive fashion the suffering undergone at the hands of the father and to prove to herself the reality of the painful experience.

This array of material might be multiplied indefinitely, but it would only repeatedly go to show that we encounter under totally different guises this basic phantasy of having suffered castration through the love-relation with the father. My observations have led me to believe that this phantasy, whose existence has indeed long been familiar to us in individual cases, is of such typical and fundamental importance that I am inclined to call it the second root of the whole castration complex in women.

The great significance of this combination is that a highly important piece of repressed womanhood is most intimately bound up with the castration phantasies. Or, to look at it from the point of view of succession in time, that it is wounded womanhood which gives rise to the castration complex, and that it is this complex which injures (not *primarily*, however) feminine development.

Here we probably have the most fundamental basis of the revengeful attitude towards men which is so often a prominent feature in women in whom the castration complex is marked; attempts to explain this attitude as resulting from "penis-envy" and the disappointment of the little girl's expectation that her father would give her the penis as a present, do not satisfactorily account for the mass of facts brought to light by an analysis of deeper strata of the mind. Of course in psycho-analysis the "penis-envy" is more readily exposed than is the far more deeply repressed phantasy which ascribes the loss of the male genital to a sexual act with the father as partner. That this is so follows from the fact that no feelings of guilt at all are attached to "penis-envy" in itself.

It is specially frequent for this attitude of revenge against men to be directed with particular vehemence against the man who performs the act of defloration. The explanation is natural, namely, that it is precisely the father with whom, according to the phantasy, the patient mated for the first time. Hence in the subsequent actual love-life the first mate stands in a quite peculiar way for the father. This idea is expressed in the customs described by Freud in his essay on the taboo of virginity; according to these the performance of the act of defloration is actually entrusted to a father-substitute. To the unconscious mind, defloration is the repetition of the phantasied sexual act performed with the father, and therefore when defloration takes place all those affects which belong to the phantasied act are reproduced—strong feelings of attachment combined with the abhorrence of incest, and finally the attitude described above of revenge on account of disappointed love and of the castration supposedly suffered through this act.

This brings me to the end of my remarks. My problem was the question whether that dissatisfaction with the female sexual role which results from "penis-envy" is really the alpha and omega of the castration complex in women. We have seen that the anatomical structure of the female genitals is indeed of great significance in the mental development of women. Also, it is indisputable that "penis-envy" does essentially condition the *forms* in which the castration complex manifests itself in them. But the deduction that therefore their repudiation of their womanhood is based on that envy seems inadmissible. On the contrary we can see that "penis-envy" by no means precludes a deep and wholly womanly love-attachment to the father and that it is only when this relation comes to grief over the Oedipus complex (exactly as in the corresponding male neuroses) that the envy leads to a revulsion from the subject's own sexual role.

The male neurotic who identifies himself with the mother and the female who identifies herself with the father repudiate, both in the same way, their respective sexual roles. And from this point of view the castration fear of the male neurotic (behind which there lurks a castration wish upon which, to my mind, sufficient stress is never laid) corresponds exactly to the female neurotic's desire for the penis. This symmetry would be much more striking were it not that the man's inner attitude towards identification with the mother is diametrically opposed to that of the woman towards identification with the father. And this in two respects: in a man this wish to be a woman is not merely at variance with his conscious narcissism, but is rejected for a second reason, namely, because the notion of being a woman implies at the same time the realization of all his fears of punishment, centred as they are in the genital region; in a woman, on the other hand, the identification with the father is confirmed by old wishes tending in the same direction, and it does not carry with it any sort of feelings of guilt but rather a sense of acquittal. For there ensues, from the connection I have described as existing between the ideas of castration and the incest-phantasies relating to the father, the fateful result, opposite to that in men, that being a woman is in itself felt to be culpable.

In his papers entitled "Trauer und Melancholie"[8] ("Grief and melancholia") and "The psychogenesis of a case of female homosexuality",[9] and in his *Group Psychology and Analysis of the Ego*, Freud has shown more and more fully how largely the process of identification bulks in human mentality. It is just this identification with the parent of the opposite sex which seems to me to be the point from which in either sex both homosexuality and the castration complex are evolved.

Notes

1. Cf. in particular Abraham, "Manifestations of the female castration complex" (1921), *International Journal of Psychoanalysis*, Vol. III, p. 1.
2. Cf. Freud, "Tabu der Virginität", *Sammlung kleiner Schriften*, Vierte Folge.

3. Cf. Abraham, "Zur narzisstischen berwertung der Excretions-vorgänge in Traum und Neurose", *Internationale Zeitschrift*, 1920.
4. Cf. the explanation Freud gives of doubt as doubt of the subject's capacity for love (hate).
5. [While revising the translation of this paragraph I wrote *competition-repulsion* instead of repetition-compulsion!—Trans. Ed.]
6. Cf. O. Rank's paper "Perversion und neurosis", published in *International Journal of Psychoanalysis*, Vol. IV, Part 3.
7. Cf. Freud, "Über Triebumsetzungen insbesondere der Analerotik", *Sammlung kleiner Schriften*. Vierte Folge.
8. *Sammlung kleiner Schriften*. Vierte Folge.
9. *International Journal of Psychoanalysis*, Vol. I, p. 125.

Womanliness as a masquerade*

Joan Riviere

Every direction in which psycho-analytic research has pointed seems in its turn to have attracted the interest of Ernest Jones, and now that of recent years' investigation has slowly spread to the development of the sexual life of women, we find as a matter of course one by him among the most important contributions to the subject. As always, he throws great light on his material, with his peculiar gift both clarifying the knowledge we had already and also adding to it fresh observations of his own.

In his paper on "The early development of female sexuality"[1] he sketches out a rough scheme of types of female development, which he first divides into heterosexual and homosexual, subsequently subdividing the latter homosexual group into two types. He acknowledges the roughly schematic nature of his classification and postulates a number of intermediate types. It is with one of these intermediate types that I am to-day concerned. In daily life types of men and women are constantly met with who, while

*Article citation:
Riviere, J. (1929). Womanliness as a masquerade. *International Journal of Psychoanalysis, 10*: 303–313.

mainly heterosexual in their development, plainly display strong features of the other sex. This has been judged to be an expression of the bisexuality inherent in us all; and analysis has shown that what appears as homosexual or heterosexual character-traits, or sexual manifestations, is the end-result of the interplay of conflicts and not necessarily evidence of a radical or fundamental tendency. The difference between homosexual and heterosexual development results from differences in the degree of anxiety, with the corresponding effect this has on development. Ferenczi pointed out a similar reaction in behaviour,[2] namely, that homosexual men exaggerate their heterosexuality as a "defence" against their homosexuality. I shall attempt to show that women who wish for masculinity may put on a mask of womanliness to avert anxiety and the retribution feared from men.

It is with a particular type of intellectual woman that I have to deal. Not long ago intellectual pursuits for women were associated almost exclusively with an overtly masculine type of woman, who in pronounced cases made no secret of her wish or claim to be a man. This has now changed. Of all the women engaged in professional work to-day, it would be hard to say whether the greater number are more feminine than masculine in their mode of life and character. In University life, in scientific professions and in business, one constantly meets women who seem to fulfil every criterion of complete feminine development. They are excellent wives and mothers, capable housewives; they maintain social life and assist culture; they have no lack of feminine interests, e.g. in their personal appearance, and when called upon they can still find time to play the part of devoted and disinterested mother-substitutes among a wide circle of relatives and friends. At the same time they fulfil the duties of their profession at least as well as the average man. It is really a puzzle to know how to classify this type psychologically.

Some time ago, in the course of an analysis of a woman of this kind, I came upon some interesting discoveries. She conformed in almost every particular to the description just given; her excellent relations with her husband included a very intimate affectionate attachment between them and full and frequent sexual enjoyment; she prided herself on her proficiency as a housewife. She had followed her profession with marked success all her life. She had a high degree of adaptation to reality, and managed to sustain good and appropriate relations with almost everyone with whom she came in contact.

Certain reactions in her life showed, however, that her stability was not as flawless as it appeared; one of these will illustrate my theme. She was an American woman engaged in work of a propagandist nature, which consisted principally in speaking and writing. All her life a certain degree of anxiety, sometimes very severe, was experienced after every public performance, such as speaking to an audience. In spite of her unquestionable success and ability, both intellectual and practical, and her capacity for managing an audience and dealing with discussions, etc., she would be excited and apprehensive all night after, with misgivings whether she had done anything inappropriate, and obsessed by a need for reassurance. This need for reassurance led her compulsively on any such occasion to seek some attention or complimentary notice from a man or men at the close of the proceedings in which she had taken part or been the principal figure; and it soon became evident that the men chosen for the purpose were always unmistakeable father-figures, although often not persons whose judgement on her performance would in reality carry much weight. There were clearly two types of reassurance sought from these father-figures: first, direct reassurance of the nature of compliments about her performance; secondly, and more important, indirect reassurance of the nature of sexual attentions from these men. To speak broadly, analysis of her behaviour after her performance showed that she was attempting to obtain sexual advances from the particular type of men by means of flirting and coquetting with them in a more or less veiled manner. The extraordinary incongruity of this attitude with her highly impersonal and objective attitude during her intellectual performance, which it succeeded so rapidly in time, was a problem.

Analysis showed that the Oedipus situation of rivalry with the mother was extremely acute and had never been satisfactorily solved. I shall come back to this later. But beside the conflict in regard to the mother, the rivalry with the father was also very great. Her intellectual work, which took the form of speaking and writing, was based on an evident identification with her father, who had first been a literary man and later had taken to political life; her adolescence had been characterized by conscious revolt against him, with rivalry and contempt of him. Dreams and phantasies of this nature, castrating the husband, were frequently uncovered by analysis. She had quite conscious feelings of rivalry and claims to superiority over many of the "father-figures" whose favour she would then woo after her own performances! She bitterly resented any assumption that she was not equal to them, and (in private) would reject the idea of being subject to their judgement or criticism. In this she corresponded clearly to one type Ernest Jones has sketched: his first group of homosexual women who, while taking no interest in other women, wish for "recognition" of their masculinity from men and claim to be the equals of men, or in other words, to be men themselves. Her resentment, however, was not openly expressed; publicly she acknowledged her condition of womanhood.

Analysis then revealed that the explanation of her compulsive ogling and coquetting—which actually she was herself hardly aware of till analysis made it manifest—was as follows: it was an unconscious attempt to ward off the anxiety which would ensue on account of the reprisals she anticipated from the father-figures after her intellectual performance. The exhibition in public of her intellectual proficiency, which was in itself carried through successfully, signified an exhibition of herself in possession of the father's penis, having castrated him. The display once over, she was seized by horrible dread of the retribution the father would then exact. Obviously it was a step towards propitiating the avenger to endeavour to offer herself to him sexually. This phantasy, it then appeared, had been very common in her childhood and youth, which had been spent in the Southern States of America; if a negro came to attack her, she planned to defend herself by making him kiss her and make love to her (ultimately so that she could then deliver him over to justice). But there was a further determinant of the obsessive behaviour. In a dream which had a rather similar content to this childhood phantasy, she was in terror alone in the house; then a negro came in and found her washing clothes, with her sleeves rolled up and arms exposed. She resisted him, with the secret intention of attracting him sexually, and he began to admire her arms and to caress them and her breasts. The meaning was that she had killed father and mother and obtained everything for herself (alone in the house), became terrified of their retribution (expected shots through the window), and defended herself by taking on a menial role (washing clothes) and by *washing off* dirt and sweat, guilt and blood, everything she had obtained by the deed, and "disguising herself" as merely a castrated woman. In that guise the man found no stolen property on her which he need attack her to recover and, further, found her attractive as an object of love. Thus the aim of the compulsion was not merely to secure reassurance by evoking friendly feelings towards her in the man; it was chiefly to make sure of safety by masquerading as guiltless and innocent. It was a compulsive reversal of her intellectual performance; and the two together formed the "double-action" of an obsessive act, just as her life as a whole consisted alternately of masculine and feminine activities.

Before this dream she had had dreams of people putting masks on their faces in order to avert disaster. One of these dreams was of a high tower on a hill being pushed over and falling down on the inhabitants of a village below, but the people put on masks and escaped injury!

Womanliness therefore could be assumed and worn as a mask, both to hide the possession of masculinity and to avert the reprisals expected if she was found to possess it—much as a thief will turn out his pockets and ask to be searched to prove that he has not the stolen goods. The reader may now ask how I define womanliness or where I draw the line between genuine womanliness and the "masquerade". My suggestion is not, however, that there is any such difference; whether radical or superficial, they are the same thing. The capacity for womanliness was there in this woman—and one might even say it exists in the most completely homosexual woman—but owing to her conflicts it did not represent her main development, and was used far more as a device for avoiding anxiety than as a primary mode of sexual enjoyment.

I will give some brief particulars to illustrate this. She had married late, at twenty-nine; she had had great anxiety about defloration, and had had the hymen stretched or slit before the wedding by a woman doctor. Her attitude to sexual intercourse before marriage was a set determination to obtain and experience the enjoyment and pleasure which she knew some women have in it, and the orgasm. She was afraid of impotence in exactly the same way as a man. This was partly a determination to surpass certain mother-figures who were frigid, but on deeper levels it was a determination not to be beaten by the man.[3] In effect, sexual enjoyment was full and frequent, with complete orgasm; but the fact emerged that the gratification it brought was of the nature of a reassurance and restitution of something lost, and not ultimately pure enjoyment. The man's love gave her back her self-esteem. During analysis, while the hostile castrating impulses towards the husband were in process of coming to light, the desire for intercourse very much abated, and she became for periods relatively frigid. The mask of womanliness was being peeled away, and she was revealed either as castrated (lifeless, incapable of pleasure), or as wishing to castrate (therefore afraid to receive the penis or welcome it by gratification). Once, while for a period her husband had had a love-affair with another woman, she had detected a very intense identification with him in regard to the rival woman. It is striking that she had had no homosexual experiences (since before puberty with a younger sister); but it appeared during analysis that this lack was compensated for by frequent homosexual dreams with intense orgasm.

In every-day life one may observe the mask of femininity taking curious forms. One capable housewife of my acquaintance is a woman of great ability, and can herself attend to typically masculine matters. But when, e.g. any builder or upholsterer is called in, she has a compulsion to hide all her technical knowledge from him and show deference to the workman, making her suggestions in an innocent and artless manner, as if they were "lucky guesses". She has confessed to me that even with the butcher and baker, whom she rules in reality with a rod of iron, she cannot openly take up a firm straightforward stand; she feels herself as it were "acting a part", she puts on the semblance of a rather uneducated, foolish and bewildered woman, yet in the end always making her point. In all other relations in life this woman is a gracious, cultured lady, competent and well-informed, and can manage her affairs by sensible rational behaviour without any subterfuges. This woman is now aged fifty, but she tells me that as a young woman she had great anxiety in dealings with men such as porters, waiters, cabmen, tradesmen, or any other potentially hostile father-figures, such as doctors, builders and lawyers; moreover, she often quarrelled with such men and had altercations with them, accusing them of defrauding her and so forth.

Another case from every-day observation is that of a clever woman, wife and mother, a University lecturer in an abstruse subject which seldom attracts women. When lecturing, not to students but to colleagues, she chooses particularly feminine clothes. Her behaviour on these occasions is also marked by an inappropriate feature: she becomes flippant and joking, so much so that it has caused comment and rebuke. She has to treat the situation of displaying her masculinity to men as a "game", as something *not real*, as a "joke". She cannot treat herself and her subject seriously, cannot seriously contemplate herself as on equal terms with men; moreover, the flippant attitude enables some of her sadism to escape, hence the offence it causes.

Many other instances could be quoted, and I have met with a similar mechanism in the analysis of manifest homosexual men. In one such man with severe inhibition and anxiety, homosexual activities really took second place, the source of greatest sexual gratification being actually masturbation under special conditions, namely, while looking at himself in a mirror dressed in a particular way. The excitation was produced by the sight of himself with hair parted in the centre, wearing a bow tie. These extraordinary "fetishes" turned out to represent a *disguise of himself* as his sister; the hair and bow were taken from her. His conscious attitude was a desire to be a woman, but his manifest relations with men had never been stable. Unconsciously the homosexual relation proved to be entirely sadistic and based on masculine rivalry. Phantasies of sadism and *"possession of a penis"* could be indulged only while reassurance against anxiety was being obtained from the mirror that he was safely "disguised as a woman".

To return to the case I first described. Underneath her apparently satisfactory heterosexuality it is clear that this woman displayed well-known manifestations of the castration complex. Horney was the first among others to point out the sources of that complex in the Oedipus situation; my belief is that the fact that womanliness may be assumed as a mask may contribute further in this direction to the analysis of female development. With that in view I will now sketch the early libido-development in this case.

But before this I must give some account of her relations with women. She was conscious of rivalry of almost any woman who had either good looks or intellectual pretensions. She was conscious of flashes of hatred against almost any woman with whom she had much to do, but where permanent or close relations with women

were concerned she was none the less able to establish a very satisfactory footing. Unconsciously she did this almost entirely by
means of feeling herself superior in some way to them (her relations
with her inferiors were uniformly excellent). Her proficiency as a
housewife largely had its root in this. By it she surpassed her
mother, won her approval and proved her superiority among rival
"feminine" women. Her intellectual attainments undoubtedly had
in part the same object. They too proved her superiority to her
mother; it seemed probable that since she reached womanhood her
rivalry with women had been more acute in regard to intellectual
things than in regard to beauty, since she could usually take refuge
in her superior brains where beauty was concerned.

The analysis showed that the origin of all these reactions, both
to men and to women, lay in the reaction to the parents during the
oral-biting sadistic phase. These reactions took the form of the
phantasies sketched by Melanie Klein[4] in her Congress paper, 1927.
In consequence of disappointment or frustration during sucking or
weaning, coupled with experiences during the primal scene which
is interpreted in oral terms, extremely intense sadism develops
towards both parents.[5] The desire to bite off the nipple shifts, and
desires to destroy, penetrate and disembowel the mother and
devour her and the contents of her body succeed it. These contents
include the father's penis, her fæces and her children—all her
possessions and love-objects, imagined as within her body.[6] The
desire to bite off the nipple is also shifted, as we know, on to the
desire to castrate the father by biting off his penis. Both parents are
rivals in this stage, both possess desired objects; the sadism is
directed against both and the revenge of both is feared. But, as
always with girls, the mother is the more hated, and consequently
the more feared. She will execute the punishment that fits the
crime—destroy the girl's body, her beauty, her children, her capacity for having children, mutilate her, devour her, torture her and kill
her. In this appalling predicament the girl's only safety lies in
placating the mother and atoning for her crime. She must retire
from rivalry with the mother, and if she can, endeavour to restore
to her what she has stolen. As we know, she identifies herself
with the father; and then she uses the masculinity she thus obtains
by *putting it at the service of the mother*. She becomes the father,
and takes his place; so she can "restore" him to the mother. This

position was very clear in many typical situations in my patient's life. She delighted in using her great practical ability to aid or assist weaker and more helpless women, and could maintain this attitude successfully so long as rivalry did not emerge too strongly. But this restitution could be made on one condition only; it must procure her a lavish return in the form of gratitude and "recognition". The recognition desired was supposed by her to be owing for her self-sacrifices; more unconsciously what she claimed was recognition of her *supremacy* in *having* the penis to give back. If her supremacy were not acknowledged, then rivalry became at once acute; if gratitude and recognition were withheld, her sadism broke out in full force and she would be subject (in private) to paroxysms of oral-sadistic fury, exactly like a raging infant.

In regard to the father, resentment against him arose in two ways: (1) during the primal scene he took from the mother the milk, etc., which the child missed; (2) at the same time he gave to the mother the penis or children instead of to her. Therefore all that he had or took should be taken from him by her; he was castrated and reduced to nothingness, like the mother. Fear of him, though never so acute as of the mother, remained; partly, too, because his vengeance for the death and destruction of the mother was expected. So he too must be placated and appeased. This was done by masquerading in a feminine guise for him, thus showing him her "love" and guiltlessness towards him. It is significant that this woman's mask, though transparent to other women, was successful with men, and served its purpose very well. Many men were attracted in this way, and gave her reassurance by showing her favour. Closer examination showed that these men were of the type who themselves fear the ultra-womanly woman. They prefer a woman who herself has male attributes, for to them her claims on them are less.

At the primal scene the talisman which both parents possess and which she lacks is the father's penis; hence her rage, also her dread and helplessness.[7] By depriving the father of it and possessing it herself she obtains the talisman—the invincible sword, the "organ of sadism"; he becomes powerless and helpless (her gentle husband), but she still guards herself from attack by wearing towards him the mask of womanly subservience, and under that screen, performing many of his masculine functions herself—"for him"—(her practical ability and management). Likewise with the mother: having robbed her of the penis, destroyed her and reduced her to pitiful inferiority, she triumphs over her, but again secretly; outwardly she acknowledges and admires the virtues of "feminine" women. But the task of guarding herself against the woman's retribution is harder than with the man; her efforts to placate and make reparation by restoring and using the penis in the mother's service were never enough; this device was worked to death, and sometimes it almost worked her to death.

It appeared, therefore, that this woman had saved herself from the intolerable anxiety resulting from her sadistic fury against both parents by creating in phantasy a situation in which she became supreme and no harm could be done to her. The essence of the phantasy was her *supremacy* over the parent-objects; by it her sadism was gratified, she triumphed over them. By this same supremacy she also succeeded in averting their revenges; the means she adopted for this were reaction-formations and concealment of her hostility. Thus she could gratify her id-impulses, her narcissistic ego and her super-ego at one and the same time. The phantasy was the main-spring of her whole life and character, and she came within a narrow margin of carrying it through to complete perfection. But its weak point was the megalomanic character, under all the disguises, of the necessity for supremacy. When this supremacy was seriously disturbed during analysis, she fell into an abyss of anxiety, rage and abject depression; before the analysis, into illness.

I should like to say a word about Ernest Jones's type of homosexual woman whose aim is to obtain "recognition" of her masculinity from men. The question arises whether the need for recognition in this type is connected with the mechanism of the same need, operating differently (recognition for services performed), in the case I have described. In my case direct recognition of the possession of the penis was not claimed openly; it was claimed for the reaction-formations, though only the possession of the penis made them possible. Indirectly, therefore, recognition was none the less claimed for the penis. This indirectness was due to apprehension lest her possession of a penis *should be* "recognized", in other words "found out". One can see that with less anxiety my patient too would have openly claimed recognition from men for her possession of a penis, and in private she did in fact, like Ernest Jones's cases, bitterly resent any lack of this direct recognition. It is clear that in his cases the primary sadism obtains more gratification; the father has been castrated, and shall even acknowledge his defeat. But how then is the anxiety averted by these women? In regard to the mother, this is done of course by denying her existence. To judge from indications in analyses I have carried out, I conclude that, first, as Jones implies, this claim is simply a displacement of the original sadistic claim that the desired object, nipple, milk, penis, should be instantly surrendered; secondarily, the need for recognition is largely a need for absolution. Now the mother has been relegated to limbo; no relations with her are possible. Her existence appears to be denied, though in truth it is only too much feared. So the guilt of having triumphed over both can only be absolved by the father; if he sanctions her possession of the penis by acknowledging it, she is safe. By *giving* her recognition, he *gives* her the penis and to her instead of to the mother; then she has it, and she may have it, and all is well. "Recognition" is always in part reassurance, sanction, love; further, it renders her supreme again. Little as he may know it, to her the man has admitted his defeat. Thus in its content such a woman's phantasy-relation to the father is similar to the normal Oedipus one; the difference is that it rests on a basis of sadism. The mother she has indeed killed, but she is thereby excluded from enjoying much that the mother had, and what she does obtain from the father she has still in great measure to extort and extract.

These conclusions compel one once more to face the question: what is the essential nature of fully-developed femininity? What is *das ewig Weibliche*? The conception of womanliness as a mask, behind which man suspects some hidden danger, throws a little light on the enigma. Fully-developed heterosexual womanhood is founded, as Helene Deutsch and Ernest Jones have stated, on the oral-sucking stage. The sole gratification of a primary order in it is that of receiving the (nipple, milk) penis, semen, child from the father. For the rest it depends upon reaction-formations. The acceptance of "castration", the humility, the admiration of men, come partly from the overestimation of the object on the oral-sucking plane; but chiefly from the renunciation (lesser intensity) of sadistic castration-wishes deriving from the later oral-biting level. "I must not take, I must not even ask; it must be *given* me." The capacity for self-sacrifice, devotion, self-abnegation expresses efforts to restore and make good, whether to mother or to father figures, what has been taken from them. It is also what Radó has called a "narcissistic insurance" of the highest value.

It becomes clear how the attainment of full heterosexuality coincides with that of genitality. And once more we see, as Abraham first stated, that genitality implies attainment of a *post-ambivalent* state. Both the "normal" woman and the homosexual desire the father's penis and rebel against frustration (or castration); but one of the differences between them lies in the difference in the degree of sadism and of the power of dealing both with it and with the anxiety it gives rise to in the two types of women.

Notes

1. *The International Journal of Psychoanalysis*, Vol. VIII, 1927.
2. "The nosology of male homosexuality", *Contributions to Psychoanalysis*, 1916.
3. I have found this attitude in several women analysands and the self-ordained defloration in nearly all of them (five cases). In the light of Freud's "Taboo of virginity", this latter symptomatic act is instructive.
4. "Early stages of the Oedipus conflict", *International Journal of Psychoanalysis*, Vol. IX, 1928.
5. Ernest Jones, "Early stages of the Oedipus conflict", p. 469, regards an intensification of the oral-sadistic stage as the central feature of homosexual development in women.
6. As it was not essential to my argument, I have omitted all reference to the further development of the relation to children.
7. Cf. M. N. Searl, "Danger situations of the immature ego", Oxford Congress, 1929.

CHAPTER FOUR

Active technique

Glover, Edward (1924). "Active therapy" and psychoanalysis—a critical review. *International Journal of Psychoanalysis*, 5: 269–311.

In 1919 Freud gave his keynote paper to the Congress in Budapest, where the psychoanalytic world was reunited after the war. Freud's paper concluded with optimism and the sweeping statement that "the large scale application of our therapy will compel us to alloy the pure gold of analysis with the copper of direct suggestion" (Freud, 1919a, p. 168). The time was one of hope and renewal.

In that year, Ferenczi's views focused initially on a therapeutic problem that arose when affect was very separate from the intellect and its representations. He reported experiments with an active technique. In 1922, at Freud's instigation, an essay prize was offered, in the journal and the *Zeitschrift*, on the topic "The relation of psycho-analytic technique to psycho-analytic theory". In response, Ferenczi produced a book with Otto Rank, *The Development of Psychoanalysis* (1925) (originally published in German, *Entwicklungsziele der Psychoanalyse*, in 1923). Ferenczi took this opportunity to elaborate his methods further.

Ferenczi and Rank's book acknowledged Freud's distinction between remembering and repeating (Freud, 1914g). Many have critiqued the book which led to Ferenczi becoming somewhat estranged from mainstream psychoanalysis. Freud, who had at first supported Ferenczi's "active technique", later caustically commented, "The best way to shorten treatment, is to carry it out correctly" (quoted in Glover, 1928, p. 185). Alexander's concern about the technique centred around the responsibility for id impulses which the analyst risks taking from the patient in the active technique:

> Every time that we resort to commands and prohibitions (including the setting of a term) we are yielding to [the patient's] unconscious tendencies, even though a skilful application of this method may often advance the analysis for the time being. The main resistance is directed against accepting responsibility for the instinctual life, against independent judgment and the task of dealing with the infantile relations to the parents, which have been revived in analysis. [Alexander, 1925, p. 494]

Edward Glover's long paper, republished here, is a meticulously argued appraisal of the place of Ferenczi's "new"'method in the development of psychoanalytic technique. First of all, the "active therapy" is merely a technique to adopt in certain intractable cases, where the gratification aroused by the analysis itself undermines the motivation to learn from the analysis. As Glover states, the intervention may be to prohibit a masturbatory satisfaction, like crossing the legs on the couch—or it might be to order certain libidinal satisfactions, like the use of obscene words. There is, as Sachs (1925) said, a deliberate attempt to alter the relation between ego and id, rather than to interpret it.

Despite Freud's vision of a psychoanalysis alloyed with other methods, a constant suspicion has remained that non-interpretive intervention means a pollution of the pure gold, not a useful alloying. At the same time, work with difficult patients has attracted a constant interest in non-interpretive interventions. Ironically, in 1946 Alexander introduced his "corrective emotional experience" (Alexander & French, 1946), which proved just as contentious as the book he had reviewed. In addition, developments in self-psychology (Kohut, 1971) and certain analysts of the object-relations (Rayner, 1992) and inter-subjectivist (Renik, 1995) schools experiment with the analyst's disclosure of his or her counter-transference. This debate has been influenced and stimulated by the re-reading of Ferenczi in the last ten years (Berman, 1996).

Glover's paper is valuable as it presents the innovations of active technique against the backdrop of an exposition of psychoanalytic therapy as it was understood then. In the course of his very extensive argument he covered a great deal of the theory of interpretation. Glover developed from this point a general interest in defining and describing analytic technique. He became more authoritative in a number of works he later published (Glover, 1927–1928, 1931). In a book (Glover, 1955), he reported the results of a questionnaire researching other analysts' methods. The paper here republished sets out the criteria by which we could assess even current arguments for non-interpretive interventions.

References

Alexander, F. (1925). Review of *Developments in Psychoanalysis* (*Entwicklungsziele der Psychoanalyse*) by Sandor Ferenczi and Otto Rank. *International Journal of Psychoanalysis, 6*: 484–496.

Alexander, F., & French, T. M. (1946). *Psychoanalytic Therapy*. New York: Ronald Press.

Berman, E. (1996). The Ferenczi renaissance. *Psychoanalytic Dialogues, 6*: 391–411.

Ferenczi, S. (1919). Technical difficulties in the analysis of a case of hysteria. *Zeitschrift für Psychanalyse, 5*: 34–40.

Ferenczi, S., & Rank, O. (1925). *The Development of Psychoanalysis* (*Entwicklungsziele der Psychoanalyse*). New York: Nervous and Mental Disease Publishing.

Freud, S. (1914). Remembering, repeating and working-through. *S.E., 12*: 145–156. London: Hogarth Press.

Freud, S. (1919). Lines of advance in psychoanalysis. *S.E., 17*: 157–168. London: Hogarth Press

Glover E. (1927–1928). Lectures on technique in psycho-analysis. *International Journal of Psychoanalysis, 8*: 311–338; 486–520; *9*: 7–46; 181–218.

Glover, E. (1931). The therapeutic effect of inexact interpretation: a contribution to the theory of suggestion. *International Journal of Psychoanalysis, 12*: 397–411.

Glover, E. (1955). *The Technique of Psychoanalysis*. London: Balliere, Tindall and Cox.

Kohut, H. (1971). *The Analysis of the Self*. New York: International Universities Press.

Rayner, E. (1992). Matching, attunement and the psychoanalytic dialogue. *International Journal of Psychoanalysis, 73*: 39–54.

Renik, O. (1995). The role of an analyst's expectations in clinical technique: reflections on the concept of resistance. *International Journal of Psychoanalysis, 43*: 83–94.

Sachs, H. (1925). Metapsychological points of view in technique and theory. *International Journal of Psychoanalysis, 6*: 5–12.

"Active therapy" and psycho-analysis—a critical review*†

Edward Glover

PART I

Introductory

To limit a review of work on active technique to a consideration of the technical suggestions made by Ferenczi would be, as Ferenczi himself suggests, to misunderstand the use of the word "active" and in reality to leave out of account important stages in the history of psycho-analytic therapy.

As he points out, the Breuer–Freud cathartic method was essentially one of great activity. A vigorous attempt was made, under hypnosis if necessary, to awaken memories, i.e. not only was the attitude of the physician an active one, but the patient was called upon to make definite strenuous efforts. Further, the present method is passive only by contrast. It is true that the patient

---

* Read before the British Psycho-Analytical Society, Feb. 21, 1923.

† Article citation:
Glover, E. (1924). "Active therapy" and psycho-analysis—a critical review. *International Journal of Psychoanalysis*, 5: 269–311.

remains passive, but the physician cannot permit the patient's phantasies to continue indefinitely and, when the material is ready to crystallize, the former must abandon his passivity and interpret in order to make easier the associative paths otherwise barred by resistance. During this "obstetrical thought-assistance", as Ferenczi calls it, the patient remains, as before, passive.

If one follows the development of technique from the time of the cathartic method onwards, it is clear that, not only in stating the aims of psycho-analysis, but in the working out of the dynamics of transference, resistance, etc., most contributions to psycho-analytic literature (and especially those of Freud himself) are contributions to the problem of activity in technique. One might refer, for instance, to Freud's working out of the stages in psycho-analytic therapy where he distinguishes a first phase, during which libido is detached from the symptoms and crowded on to the transference, from the second when the battle rages round this new object, libido is freed, and to prevent withdrawal of this libido to the unconscious, the ego is educated by the interpretative suggestions of the analyst to the point of reconciliation of the two.[1]

In his work on the dynamics of the transference,[2] too, Freud lays down conceptions of regression and re-activation with corresponding resistance which are fundamental for the theoretical consideration of active technique and his description of the plasticity of libido and its capacity for collateral circulation is one which Ferenczi uses freely and with effect. Indeed, Freud's early paper on dream-interpretation in analysis is a contribution to the subject of activity in so far as he deprecates the use of interpretation as an art *per se* (i.e. what might be called an arbitrary or active use of interpretation), and lays down that it must be subject to the same rules as treatment in general, with the rider that active interpretation can be occasionally followed as a concession to scientific interest.[3]

More directly concerned with the transference situation are Freud's remarks on the dangers of "repetition" and the function of "working through", in which he points out that the aim of the physician must be the remembering and reproduction in the psychic plane. The physician, he says, must enter into a long-drawn-out fight to prevent the patient discharging impulses in action which should be limited to mental expression. Successful prevention of this nature can be regarded as a triumph and the physician should see to it that the patient does not carry significant repetitions into action.[4]

In 1910 Freud laid down that in anxiety-hysteria the patient cannot produce the necessary material as long as he is protected by the condition of the phobia and that, although it is not possible for him to give up these precautionary measures from the outset, one must assist by translation of the unconscious until such time as he can bring himself (*sich entschliessen*) to give up the protection of the phobia and lay himself open to a now much reduced anxiety.[5]

After an interval of eight years, and shortly after the publication of Ferenczi's paper on active treatment in hysteria, he returns to the same point with a significant change in the verb. "One will hardly ever overcome a phobia", he says, "by waiting until the patient is induced to give it up as the result of analysis. Treated in this way he will never bring up the material so necessary for a convincing solution of the problem. One must adopt other measures. Take, e.g. the case of agoraphobia of which two types are recognized, one slight, the other more severe. The former suffer from anxiety when they walk in the street unaccompanied but they have not altogether given up going by themselves: the latter protect themselves by giving up the attempt. In these latter cases success can only be attained by inducing the patient under the influence of analysis to behave like cases of the slighter type, i.e. to go about alone and to fight down the resultant anxiety. In this way the phobia is slightly weakened and only then will the patient produce associations which will lead to its solution."[6]

In the same paper he says that the principle of activity lies in the carrying out of treatment in a state of abstinence; substitute-satisfactions must be denied, especially the most cherished of satisfactions. Not every one, of course, and not necessarily sexual intercourse. The sufferings of the patient should not come to an end too quickly, and when we have alleviated them by breaking up and reduction of symptoms, we must induce sensitiveness at some other point by means of privation. At the same time we must be on the look-out for substitute-formations. Unhappy marriages and bodily ill-health are the most common forms of relief from neurosis. Abstinence originally led to symptom-formation, and it must be the mainspring of the will to health. Again in reference to the obsessional neurosis, "I have no doubt that in these cases the proper technique lies in waiting until the treatment has itself become a compulsion, and in forcibly restraining the compulsion to disease with this counter-compulsion". The use of the term "induce" (*bewegen*) in the case of anxiety-hysteria and of "forcibly restrain" (*gewaltsam unterdrücken*) in the case of the obsessional neurosis is of significance.

Other writers have worked on the same theme from much the same point of view, as, for example, where Reik[7] likens psychoanalysis to the work of a machine for the running of which some degree of friction is indispensable; on the whole, the previous quotations may be taken as representing the general point of view. Now, whilst these observations seem to have been dictated by a combination of clinical expediency and widening of theoretical insight, in Ferenczi's case there seems in addition to run throughout a consistent train of thought, given increasing consideration in an attempt to make the technique more effective in exceptional cases and generally to shorten, if possible, a lengthy procedure.

Referring in a reminiscential vein to his pre-analytic days, Ferenczi tells how a peasant suffering from attacks of loss of consciousness came to consult him. While his history was being noted, which elicited a story of conflict with the father, the patient broke off in a faint in the middle of a sentence, namely, "I must work like a scavenger whilst—" At this point Ferenczi seized the patient, shook him vigorously, and shouted to him to complete the sentence, which then ran—"whilst my younger brother stays at the home farm." The loss of consciousness proved to be a flight from reality, and the patient was amazed to find himself completely and immediately cured.[8]

Passing over intervening stages, we find Ferenczi, in his paper on transitory symptom-formations (1912), regarding such miniature neuroses as points of attack for dealing with the patient's strongest resistances.[9] Such symptoms being affectively experienced in the patient's own person lead, after suitable analysis, to that conviction of the correctness of interpretation which cannot be attained by logical insight alone. They are representations of unconscious feeling stirred up by analysis and forced back, which, no longer capable of complete suppression, are converted into somatic symptoms, an explanation the quantitative factor of which has recently been emphasized by Alexander.[10]

In order not to disturb the case-illustration of Ferenczi's development in technique, his general paper on technique[11] may be considered here, although really it follows that on the analysis of hysteria. It contains many excellent suggestions of a general kind, from which the following, more active, may be selected. The patient can defeat the analyst with the latter's own weapons. Asked to produce associations without regard to content, the former will produce only nonsensical associations and try to reduce both analysis and analyst to absurdity. This must be stopped by interpretation of the underlying intent, the patient's triumphant counter, namely, "I'm only doing what you ask", being met with the explanation that to produce solely nonsensical associations is in itself a form of thought selection. Sudden silence is a transitory symptom which, if persisting after interpretation, must be met with silence. In some cases a patient breaking off with an "*à propos*" can be asked to finish his sentence, since this involves not connected thinking, but connected saying of what is already thought. Obscene words must be spoken, and the compromise of writing them down should be avoided. Do not be content with generalities: concrete representations rather than philosophical speculations constitute the real association form, an interjected "for example" often getting nearer to the unconscious content. On the question of influencing the patient's decisions his views may be summed up briefly; first find whether the decision is really urgent or whether it is being thrown at the analyst as a gas-bomb to cause confusion. If real and the patient has any capacity for decision, let him decide; if real but the patient is incapable of decision from reality-testing reasons, he may be helped; if real but the incapacity for decision is of the form of a phobia, make the patient come to *some* decision.

Although there is nothing new in the way of theoretical consideration in this paper, or in a short note on influencing the patient during treatment which appeared in the previous *Zeitschrift*, still the general tendency to active interference once ordinary interpretation seems to fail is quite outstanding.

The logical development of these tendencies is to be found in Ferenczi's method of dealing with the analysis of some cases of hysteria.[12] On one occasion, observing that a patient's analysis approached a condition of stalemate, he prescribed a certain period within which treatment must be finished. The patient, however, hid

her resistance behind a positive transference which was characterized by passionate love declarations; treatment was ended at the
stated time, leaving the former quite satisfied with the result.
Renewed after an exacerbation of symptoms, analysis again brought
about improvement, but just up to the previous stage; beyond that
the love-defence was again brought into play and again treatment
was ended (this time owing to extrinsic causes). A third attempt was
made with an identical result, but now Ferenczi observed that in the
perpetual love-phantasies connected with the physician the patient
remarked on certain genital sensations. In addition she lay always
with the legs crossed. This led to a discussion on masturbation, the
performance of which she denied. Finally Ferenczi forbade her to
cross the legs, explaining that she thus discharged unconscious
excitations in a larval form of masturbation, and the result of this
prohibition was immediate increase of bodily and mental restlessness, accompanied by phantasies similar to those of delirium.
Infantile experiences and circumstances conducing to illness were
remembered in fragments. But again the analysis lingered, and the
transference-love masked resistance. Then Ferenczi made the
discovery that she eroticized her household activities, as in unconsciously working with the legs pressed together. Prohibition of these
extra-mural gratifications led merely to a slight improvement, but
also to the performance of various plucking movements during the
hour. These were carried out on, so to speak, "indifferent" parts of
the body, but became masturbation equivalents capable of producing orgasm. They had been carried out in childhood, and now, after
due suppression, sexuality found its way back to the genital zone,
the immediate result of which was the return of an infantile obsessional neurosis. After solution of the latter, an irritation of the
bladder made its appearance, usually at times unsuitable for relief.
This relief was in turn forbidden, and the patient finally reported an
act of genital masturbation, a regressive stage which did not last
long and led gradually to pleasure in normal intercourse.

Ferenczi then formulated his new rule, namely, watchfulness for
larval forms of masturbation giving cover to libido and possibly
displacing the whole sexual activity, i.e. a short way for the discharge in motility of pathogenic phantasies, a short-circuiting of
consciousness. These forms must be forbidden when noticed, and
in reply to criticism Ferenczi points out that this is a provisional

measure. Sometimes the completed treatment renders this form of gratification superfluous, but not always. Masturbation for the first time in a patient's life during treatment is a favourable turn in events, but only if manifest masturbation with conscious erotic phantasies. Larval forms must be analysed, but must first be forbidden, to prevent short-circuiting, and only when the patient can endure these conscious phantasies may he be given freedom to masturbate.

Many larval forms are not neurotic, many are neurasthenic, and many are unconsciously gratified throughout life, as in the case of persons who, preoccupied in business or metaphysical speculation, with hands deep in the pockets, touch, press, or rub the penis. Similarly, clonic contraction of calf-muscles, and, in women engaged in housework, pressing together of the limbs. The danger is that lack of orgasm leads to anxiety states or that the small discharges obtained disturb potency in a way not occurring in ordinary conscious masturbation. There may be, too, a transference from symptomatic actions to *tics convulsif*, many of which are stereotyped masturbation equivalents.

Ferenczi then sets about a detailed consideration of the rationale of active technique which is available in his paper given at the Hague Congress,[8] but in the meanwhile he has added to, systematised and differentiated stages in the process.

We have seen that he regards the cathartic method as above all active and the passive technique as containing an active component in the form of interpretation, which is permissible by actual authority of the transference, the patient remaining meanwhile passive. But this activity or passivity is practically limited to mental functions, and apart from the rules about punctual attendance, and the making of decisions without guidance or alternately the shelving of decisions, the *actions* of the patient are not directly interfered with. The experience with anxiety-hysteria, where phobias are brought into actual play with resultant accessibility of new material, is the one exception which demands a category by itself. Here the active interference is not so much on the part of the physician as on the part of the patient; a task is laid upon him which leads to the *doing* of unpleasant things.

Fortified by Freud's declaration of the necessity for carrying out treatment in a state of abstinence, Ferenczi finds occasion for a new variety of task, in cases with masturbatory touching of the genitals, stereotypies, tic-like movements, namely, the giving up of pleasurable activities. Here is his first illustration.

The patient, a musician with phobias and obsessive fears, amongst other inhibitions suffers from stage-fright and attacks of deep blushing. Although able to practise complicated finger exercises when alone, she cannot do so in public, and more, although really gifted, has the obsessive thought that she *must* blame herself for incapacity. Her breasts are large, and thinking herself to be observed much in the street, she is at a loss to know how to conceal her bust, sometimes crossing her arms to press in the breasts. Yet doubt follows all attempts. She is sometimes shy in manner, sometimes bold, unhappy if not noticed, alarmed if any real attention is paid to her. Her mouth smells, she thinks, yet a visit to the dentist can show no abnormality whatever.

After some analysis with Ferenczi she understands her main constructions, yet her condition does not satisfy him. One day she remembers a vulgar street "catch", which her elder sister, who, by the way, was rather tyrannical towards her, used to sing. She repeats the *double entendre* and remains silent, whereupon Ferenczi asks her to *sing* the air, which after a prolonged delay (two hours in all) she does, hesitatingly at first, but later with a full soprano. The resistance continues, but on hearing that her sister was in the habit of accompanying the song with suggestive gestures, he asks her to reproduce these gestures exactly. Having done so once, she begins to show a taste for repetition, which leads to a countermand. Then for the first time come memories of her brother's birth, singing and dancing before parents who dote on her. An order to conduct part of a symphony leads to the discovery of penis-envy (the baton) and the compulsory playing of a difficult piano part sheds light on her dread of examinations. Her self-blame is on account of the masturbation represented by the finger exercises. Similarly a request to go to the public swimming-bath uncovers the exhibitionistic motive behind her breast-ceremonial, and the discovery that she was passing flatus during the analytic hour in a kind of play, retaining and letting go, led, on the countermanding of this activity, to the tracing of the anal-erotic motive in the mouth-smelling fancy. Finally, treatment was greatly helped by the interpretation of certain movements and gestures whilst on the piano stool: these were carried out and stopped to order, and an unconscious masturbatory practice was revealed.

The technique applies not only in the activation and control of erotic tendencies, but also in the case of highly subliminated activities. A patient whose interest in versification was only partly gratified in puberty is asked to write poetry and displays distinct poetic gift, behind which is the desire for masculine productivity, clitoris-fixation and anæsthesia. When forbidden the new activity, it transpires that really a misuse of talent is in question, the masculine attitude is secondary, a genital trauma having led to displacement to auto-erotism and homosexuality. She only takes to the pen when she fears non-fulfilment of her female functions. The result is a re-established capacity for normal female activity.

Here we have the two stages—"painful" tasks, then "painful" abstinences, commands and prohibitions. The former render repressed instinct-components into conscious wish-formations and the latter force the awakened excitations back to infantile situations and repetitions. Since these have been subjectively experienced by the patient and objectively observed *in flagrante delicto*, they cannot be denied. In both stages the mechanism is that of producing a situation of privation.

When of course the patient is already active, masturbates, produces symptomatic acts and transitory neuroses, there is no need for the first stage, forbidding alone is necessary, although sometimes it is advisable to encourage first the full acting out of such situations. Urinary habits, flatus activities, sphincter play in general, various gestures, handling of the face, movements of the legs, shaking of the body, are suitable *points d'appui*. Even apparent contradictions in theoretical technique are sometimes permissible, as when a patient threatens to cheat in analysis and is encouraged to do so, or when he seems to be associating beside the point and is arbitrarily brought back to connect and complete the broken thread of thought.

Then as to indications: the technique must be used as little as possible, since the passive attitude is best, not only for the patient, but—and this deserves italicizing—also for the physician. It is a therapeutic adjuvant, to be used sparingly like the forceps in midwifery.

1.   Beginners are advised against using it. They may easily go wrong or be led into error, and in any case will tend to lose insight into the dynamics of the neurosis.

2.   At all events never employ the technique in the early stages of treatment. The transference must be permitted to develop to a sufficient degree of durability—in other words, to a compulsion—otherwise premature action against the pleasure mechanism will lead to the breaking off of treatment.

3.   At the end it is often necessary and frequently induces the characteristic last "present" of unconscious material from certain cases.

4.   It can be used in all forms of neurosis, but it is more often indispensable in obsessions and in anxiety-hysteria; in pure conversion-hysteria it is seldom needed.

     In this grouping two dangers are present: *a*. the cure may be too rapid, as where an inhibited woman suddenly becomes bold, is surrounded by admirers, and breaks off treatment at the end of the first stage; *b*. the resistances encountered may lead to the premature termination of treatment.

     Masturbation has already been considered, but Ferenczi adds to this a note on forbidding unsuccessful attempts at satisfaction on the part of impotent persons, although this, he says, is by no means an axiom.

5.   Active therapy finds a suitable field in character analysis. Here, as with the psychotic, insight is absent, and we have a private psychosis narcissistically tolerated by the ego. If these characteristics cannot be melted down in the boiling heat of the transference love-situation (to use Freud's phrase), active technique can be tried; but the resistance is great, the narcissism defending the infantile memories can interfere with the aim of psycho-analysis, and there is always a risk that the patient may break off treatment.

Ferenczi then asks: Can the attitude of the physician be made use of in a more active sense; can the interpretative suggestion which influences the ego in analysis be carried over in some cases in a kind of pedagogic guidance in which some form of praise or blame can be made use of? Leaving this question unanswered, he makes the suggestion that, as the neurotic has something of the child in him, child methods are to a certain extent applicable, more especially in the maintaining of an optimum temperature in the transference situation by a shade of coolness in the heated stages, and of friendliness in the reserved phases.

In the earlier part of his paper Ferenczi differentiated psycho-analytic suggestion from the popular variety, in so far as psycho-analytic suggestion does not say to the patient, "There is nothing the matter with you", and also in that the psycho-analytic interpretations are based on memories or repetitions, and not explanatory conversion, as by Dubois.

He now anticipates possible retaliatory criticisms from Bjerre, Jung and Adler. But Bjerre neglects pathogenic causes, and contents himself with taking the patient's mental and ethical guidance in hand. Jung detaches the patient from the past and links his attention to the tasks of life, whilst Adler concerns himself not with the analysis of libido, but with the nervous character.

Ferenczi, on the other hand, deals with individual or isolated activities, and even then not as an *a priori* moral influence, but merely to counter the pleasure principle, to dam up eroticism (*die "Unmoral"*), and to remove obstacles to the progress of an analysis of causes. He may, however, in some stages not only tolerate the erotic tendency, but encourage it.

Returning to suggestion, he insists that in active technique certain measures only are presented, apart altogether from the idea of successful outcome, and, indeed, without any certainty of knowing what the outcome will be. No improvement is promised: rather the contrary. The stimulation of a new distribution of psychic energy promises discomfort, and often disturbs the placid torpor of the stagnant analysis.

Catharsis again hoped to awaken memories and thus release affect; active therapy stimulates activities and inhibitions in the hope of attaining secondary unconscious material. Analysis begins where catharsis ends. Catharsis is an aim and end in itself; active therapy is a means to an end. It increases resistances by stimulating the sensitiveness of the ego, and increases the symptoms by increasing conflict; the new condition of tension or increase in tension disturbs hitherto untouched areas. Like the counter-irritant treatment, it not only discovers hidden foci, but increases immunity; the great vessels are tied and circulation flows through the smaller arteries lying deep in the tissues.

PART II

I. Consideration of the Ferenczi technique

In so far as the phrase "active technique" is associated with the name of Ferenczi, it is necessary to be guided strictly by the indications laid down by Ferenczi himself. From these it will be seen that this technique is by no means to be regarded as a therapy in itself, but rather as a special procedure devised to meet a special analytical situation, namely, where the substitute-gratification of libido-impulses forms a barrier to examination of the underlying unconscious formations. This gratification may be present with comparatively little qualification in numerous larval forms of masturbation, or directly in the form of neurotic character-traits; or, again, it may be qualified by the compromise-formation of the symptom. Hence the application of the procedure may be merely occasional during some analyses or much more constant in others, as, for example, some cases of anxiety-hysteria and in obsessional neurosis. In either instance a prerequisite of its application is the establishment of a durable transference situation where the analyst's active interference is supported by the authority of the imago he represents.

Considering the question merely from this point of view, two criticisms occur, one of general principle, and the other of detail, both of which have been made by Van Ophuijsen.[13] First as to the principle. Van Ophuijsen considers that active technique is really an important alteration in so far as the analyst makes use of the transference-situation instead of immediately analysing it. Secondly, that as these resistance states, which necessitate active therapy, may be regarded as "repetition" phenomena, Ferenczi should have limited his rule in the case of larval masturbation by prohibiting this only when it is the source of resistance *at the time*. In reality, Van Ophuijsen's criticism of detail involves yet another principle, that of the therapeutic part played by the compulsion to repeat and the working through of traumata in the transference-situation, and on these points I should like to offer the following observations:

Transference.—As far as transference is concerned, the situation might be put as follows: In psycho-analysis a "transference neurosis" gradually replaces the original neurosis, and this former must be dealt with in turn by repeated analytical interpretation of the repetition-compulsion, as manifested in the transference-resistances. One must ask, therefore: Do not active interferences on the part of the analyst disturb the transference picture as a spontaneous repetition, since the recognition by the patient of transference material *as such* is greatly facilitated by the passive role of the analyst and his impersonality? In other words, when the father-imago is revived by a figure that does not advise, persuade, convert, or command, it is more easily recognized *as such* than when it is anchored to the present by a *real* situation in which a physician actually does advise, persuade, convert or command a patient. From this point of view, too, the possibility of blunders present even in an orthodox analysis is heightened by the hazard of piling up even stronger resistances. Again, since the patient is in a "transference" neurosis, i.e. an affective relation to the analyst repeating the infantile fixation, he is *"sensitized"* to even ordinarily trivial behaviour on the part of the analyst and reacts to it with massive affect, i.e. with a psychical anaphylactic reaction.

In ordinary analysis, however, the recognizable triviality of the occasion conjoined with a prompt analysis of its significance usually prevents a "second fixation" occurring. Now since the final stage of analysis is agreed to be arrived at through the analytic dissolution of the "transference neurosis" anything in the nature of a "second fixation" must surely constitute a difficulty.

The answer of the "activist" to this criticism is in effect that he is throwing a sprat to catch a mackerel, that the most important repetition is wanting, being more or less actively satisfied elsewhere, and in such cases, and in such cases only, the durability of the transference can be put to the hazard. If he fails, and the analysis is broken off, he is in no worse case than the protagonist of passive methods who has merely attained stalemate.

This is still open to the counter that it is unnecessary to make a rule of involving the direct authority of the imago in such situations, and that repeated analysis of the gain through illness, of the gain through larval acts, or of the gain from indulging character-traits, can be made to focus the patient's attention on the *performance* or *non-performance* of such traits or acts. In so far as this focusing is arbitrarily determined it is an active step, but it avoids the necessity of the physician, so to speak, entering the arena clad in the mantle of the imago.

As a matter of fact, although Ferenczi frequently mentions the danger of losing a patient inherent in the application of active technique, at only one point does he mention the opposite risk; speaking of influencing the outside life of patients incapable of coming to a decision, he says: "Here the physician should be aware that he is no longer behaving as a psycho-analyst, that indeed his interference may cause positive difficulty as regards duration of treatment, e.g. an unwished-for strengthening of the transference-relationship."

Repetition phenomena.—We know from Freud that the transference is in itself a repetition phenomenon, and that the greater the resistance the more does repetition replace memory-work. The main fight then is to prevent repetition obtaining motor discharge and to use the transference when serviceable as a playground in which the patient is given almost complete freedom to expand. This leads to the establishment of an artificial illness, the "transference-neurosis", a provisional state having the characteristic of real experience. But the interpretation of this experience does not immediately overcome resistance; the patient must be allowed time to work through the compulsion. At this stage, says Freud, "the physician can only wait and permit a course which can neither be avoided nor indeed hastened".[14] He summarizes the position later[15] by saying that this transference neurosis must be allowed as little repetition as possible, but notes that the relationship between memory and reproduction varies in every case. The patient as a rule cannot be spared this part of the treatment, part of his forgotten existence must be re-experienced. It would seem then that the conditions under which varying degrees of play can be allowed to this repetition-compulsion ought to be accurately studied before any conclusions can be drawn as to the point at which active interference might be permissible.

We are now familiar with the general economic function of the biological repetition-compulsion in binding traumatic stimuli, and so in working through traumata. There is, however, a natural tendency to regard transference phenomena (involving, as they do, relations with an imago) as *in themselves* the *complete* representation of this economic function.

The extension of libido to the object by means of primary identification, the ultimate mode of object-choice and the vicissitudes which this choice undergoes provide a series of situations during the repetition of which the analyst plays a repertory part. The role is mainly that of an object, but even where narcissistic choice has prevailed developmentally over the anaclitic type and the analyst is made to play from time to time the part of subject by identification, the situation in both cases represents an extension of libido from ego to object. Since this series of situations has developed gradually from early stages of primary narcissism, it is small wonder that the subject-object polarity should occupy the foreground of the analytic picture, and that the part played by narcissistic libido in repetition should tend to be minimized. Repetition can, however, make use of the analytic technique itself for the working through of auto-erotic vicissitudes, i.e. unconnected with the object, or more correctly, connected with the self as object. This represents the primary narcissistic stage in the modification of instinct before the impulse is turned towards the object.[16] Now, although both auto-erotic and subject-object activities might be included under the common heading of ontogenetic vicissitudes, or individual modifications, of the compulsion to repeat, they are clearly distinguishable from each other as regards amenability to transference influence. It is, of course, true that auto-erotic manifestations are capable of influence through the transference in two ways: first, that historically the subject was induced to abandon conscious manifestations either through the direct influence of the object, or by the influence of the object indirectly as introjected ego-ideal; secondly, that where auto-erotic manifestations are regressively activated, the regression has taken a path which is still associatively linked to the object. It retraces the steps taken in the first limitation of auto-erotic impulses under object influence, and a situation arises which is somewhat loosely analogous to that of regressive hate which really continues love at the anal level.[17]

But whilst this degree of modification of auto-erotic impulses through the object exists, we know that many of the component-impulses continue from the primary stage to the point of serving the interests of genital primacy without direct modification;[16]

indeed, that they continue to serve pleasure interests apart from object-choice and genital primacy, just as narcissism runs a course apart from the contributions made by narcissism to object-choice. In this sense, then, they differ from the sadism and exhibitionism "pairs" by being unmodified, and are autonomic by permission of the pleasure-principle;[18] repetitions are therefore found not in the transference situation, but in the patient's own aberrations in following the analytic rule, his traits and mannerisms, i.e. not in his relations to the analyst, but to the technique of the analysis. Again, however much the ego may be influenced by the object or by the ego-ideal, it is arguable that the abandonment of narcissistic enjoyment may, under certain conditions, such as ego-sensitiveness, or perhaps a time factor, constitute in itself a trauma comparable with and even stronger than the traumata which lead later to the abandonment of the parental Oedipus relation (or which are caused by this abandonment). I am indebted here to a suggestion of Mrs Isaacs in reference to suckling, that there may be an optimum psychic duration of this process, curtailing or lengthening of which may prove a trauma in itself. Here then would be an additional source of "pain", likely to be worked through by auto-erotic repetition and less amenable to the transference.

Now, although these ontogenetic or individual modifications of the compulsion to repeat comprise the larger part of analytic repetition phenomena, and even so with "subject–object" repetitions forming, as it were, a screen behind which auto-erotic repetitions are more difficult to distinguish, we cannot afford to jettison entirely what might be called the phylogenetic aspects of the compulsion. These will consist mainly of two manifestations: first, the primary economic biological function of any organism to use repetition as a "binding" mechanism;[19] and secondly, the repetitions of racial traumata not yet racially worked through. Some hint of the latter is given in the so-called archaic reactions, as in some female types of castration reaction, and in the incompleteness with which in certain archaic types active impulses have undergone passive changes; of course, the idea of psychic phlogeny is in keeping with this assumption.

At this point we reach the delicate question of the hereditary factors operating on ego-development, not only phylogenetically, but individually. In particular one would have to consider whether the history of racial libido-development can work or has wrought any permanent change in ego-structure, and secondly how far, in any individual, permanent ego-injury can be wrought by massive libido disorder.

However this may be, a point arises in the consideration of active technique calling for careful decision; how far, that is, repetitions should be merely interpreted, or, assuming that they may be actively interfered with, what interval should be allowed for working through? This problem, interestingly enough, is not necessarily solved even when acting is converted into memory work, since the function of repetition may still be operative auto-erotically when ontogenetic libido-fixation has been loosened, and is probably in any case a permanent factor in the sense of biological function. Not only so; the conversion of acting into memory-work may reach a stage in working back at which early experiences, e.g. primal scenes, etc., cease to be capable of direct reproduction in adult recollection, and may quite conceivably be only capable of reproduction as repetitions. Perhaps the best example of this class of experience would be the cumulative engrams connected with the gratification of the oral libido.

The question of determining the optimum amount of repetition in analysis is obviously one requiring the nicest judgment; a rather outstanding example of the difficulty exists in cases such as[20] one treated consecutively by two analysts for over two years, in which daily one-half of the time was spent in the working through of rage affect. Of an opposite type are cases of extreme transference passion where insight is obscured by greater or lesser degrees of projection; here some limitation of analytical repetition is called for it the ultimate success of the analysis is not to be jeopardized. Again, where the technique is adapted by the patient to satisfy mainly urethral, anal and onanistic impulses, the procedure must vary greatly; some hint as to the proper procedure might probably be gained by estimating the amount of modification such impulses seem to have undergone in the history of the individual. Where the larval formations are in the nature of regressions, or where they are adapted to the expression of guilt consciousness or object-defiance, it is probable that active prohibition can be employed effectively. Again, where the larval expression in "association" form of anal or urethral activities plays into the hands of the latent exhibitionist, active interference will probably have fruitful result. On the other hand, one might go so far as to say that, where narcissistic fixation is strong or where the links originally binding the ego to the object have been weakly forged, active technique is bound to fail in that the transference does not hold the key to the situation. It is possible that in the cases described by Ferenczi regression or guilt factors largely determined the persistence of larval traits, but it is clear from a consideration of the second stage of his active technique (when, after interpretation, the newly encouraged or demanded activity is prohibited) that there is a danger of allowing too short a repetition interval to elapse.

Aetiological Factors.—Here, again, a decision would depend on numerous factors, of which the condition of falling ill would seem to be the most important. We know from Freud[21] that, apart from that evolution of illness represented in the series privation, introversion and phantasy investment, regression, conflict and compromise-formation in the symptom, a second type exists which falls ill in an attempt to fulfil the demands of reality, i.e. not because of a privation imposed by the outer world, but because, in an attempt to exchange from an older gratification to a later sanctioned gratification, the patient wrecks himself against inner difficulties. An exaggeration of this latter type is seen in the third type, where, owing to developmental inhibitions, the patient turns ill as soon as he passes childhood and has, outside childhood, never reached a normal phase of health. The fourth type exists where, at certain ages and for certain biological reasons, the libido is suddenly increased, and consequently a relative privation occurs. Of course, none of these types are pure, but it would seem that only in the first and last (where absolute or relative libido frustration occurs) is the application of active technique at all promising, and that in the second and third types (where ego-development is faulty) active interference, if any, should be more of the pedagogic type. The criterion is in the last event the condition of the ego. A similar condition is seen in the analysis of young people and of those of rather advanced years. Hug-Hellmuth[22] shows how in the adolescent the technique is altered in an active direction, but more as a strengthening under educational guidance. As regards Ferenczi's type of activity, she thinks that the setting of tasks to children, especially those with inferiority-feeling, is certainly indicated in the later stages, but she is none too enthusiastic, and says later, "A careful avoidance of *direct* prohibition is more important, and taking counsel with the child is better than both".

Again, Abraham[23] has shown us that in advanced years cases are not necessarily refractory to psycho-analysis, that the age of the neurosis is of more importance than the age of the patient. He definitely alters his technique, however, by treating such cases more like children, encouraging more and explaining more, and often providing stimuli by spontaneous reference to previous work.

Alterations in the usual passive technique such as those of Hug-Hellmuth and Abraham, based as they were on mature consideration of empirical data, go far to confirm the suggestion that no active step should be taken in the usual analysis until something definite is known of the patient's ego-structure. To say this is, in one sense, merely to repeat one of Ferenczi's pre-requisites, viz. a serviceable transference; but, on the other hand, it is important to distinguish the disorders of the whole ego induced by libido disturbance from more serious permanent impairments of ego-function. Finally, the possibility that a neurosis may itself be a kind of defensive screen protecting underlying ego-disorder adds a degree of urgency to the suggestion.

A Special Difficulty.—During the theoretical consideration of the transference situation it was suggested that one of the dangers of applying active technique was the production of a "second fixation", in that the analyst's injunctions would lend colour in reality to the unconscious identifications of the patient. A practical instance of this, by no means uncommon in routine analysis, may give rise to especial difficulty, and justifies being singled out for emphasis. It is found in those persons who see in the analytical situation a substitute for coitus, where the bearing of the analyst is summed up by the patient in terms of sexual aggression and is interpreted in accordance with heterosexual or homosexual identifications.

The converse situation, in which the physician himself regards the analytic situation in terms of aggression, finds an interesting and, from the point of view of active therapy, a telling illustration in a paper delivered at the Berlin Congress (1922), where von Hattingberg[24] considered the significance of the analytical situation itself, paying meticulous attention to the relation of physician and patient, and the state of aggression represented by the supine position of the latter relative to the analyst. It might be argued, of course, that the deeper one carries the analysis either preliminary to or as the result of active technique, the less likelihood there is of such confusion. This, however, would scarcely apply in the case of masochistic impulses which are so deeply rooted. The use of orders and prohibitions with their avowed intention of causing "pain" is surely calculated to play into the hands of the masochist and possibly strengthen the guilt feeling, which, as Freud has pointed out, is responsible for so many of the cases which remain refractory after a long and seemingly complete analysis.[25] In such cases active therapy would defeat its own ends by providing another displacement in place of the one attacked.

It might be added here that, although Ferenczi has wisely emphasized the inherent dangers of the method, and the risks of failure, he has not yet published a detailed account of the mechanisms leading to failure; this would have been a valuable supplement to a most valuable contribution.

Summary.—The application of active technique tends to increase the difficulties of transference solution by inducing a "second fixation", especially where the patient exhibits strong masochistic trends. It affects transference repetitions (involving object-choice), and these have to be distinguished from auto-erotic vicissitudes of the repetition-function. The latter, especially those adapted to unmodified narcissistic gratification, are less accessible to transference influence. Further, there are various phylogenetic manifestations of the compulsion to repeat which operate functionally or in response to ego-defect. Hence the determining of an optimum period for "working through" must vary widely. The valuation of developmental or secondary injuries (of whatever source) to ego-structure is an essential preliminary to the tentative application of active technique.

2. Other "active" methods

It remains to consider what methods of approach other than those described by Ferenczi might be included under the more general term of active forms of therapy, and to inquire on what theoretical grounds they are based. In one instance a question of expediency determined the use of a hybrid active technique, where Simmel[26] employed a kind of modified catharsis in the treatment of war-neurosis. He laid great stress on abreaction during hypnosis, but found dream-interpretation of invaluable assistance, and made use of hypnosis to make the patient dream in his presence. Special difficulties and the limitations under which this work was carried out rendered full analysis impossible, and in any case no new point in theory is concerned. It is perhaps interesting to remember in this connection that Freud[6] in one paper anticipated a state of affairs where, in response to growing demand, a modification of psycho-analytic technique involving suggestion and hypnosis methods might be inevitable.

Work by Nunberg, Hollos, Ferenczi and others on active measures in the treatment of psychotic conditions cannot be conveniently dealt with here. Although exceedingly important, forming in fact the last of four possible main divisions of technique, viz. the technique in childhood, in the neuroses, in old age, and in the psychoses, and although a necessary complement to the full understanding of the technique in the transference-neuroses, it can be excluded from discussion mainly on the grounds that the use of active technique in the sense of the papers already abstracted has, with the possible exception of the neurotic character-trait, centred round libido analysis and presumed a large degree of ego-integrity.

In the same way special technique in childhood is also excluded, since the methods of Hug-Hellmuth are not devised for specially resistant cases, but empirically to meet a special pedagogic-analytical situation, though even here the paper of Sokolnicka[27] suggests that with children also the question of active pedagogic interference guided by analytical judgement is not quite settled as against the claims of methodic analysis.

Passing these over, we find that, in general, work on this subject is connected intimately with a study of resistance manifestations.

Resistance.—An early paper by Reik[7] considers the factors here as three-fold. The main component is narcissism. The physician becomes identified with the conscience (the ego-ideal being built up from primary narcissism) and therefore bears the full brunt of resistance. The second component is the hostile feeling once attached to the father, later developing as a reaction to the endopsychic perception of the patient's own homosexual tendencies towards the father. A third is the anal-erotic component. Reik also emphasizes the role

of the physician as castrator and the part played by exhibitionism. He then describes many of the more common manifestations
of resistance-compromise occurring outside as well as during
analysis, recommending careful analysis of, amongst other forms,
dumbness (a combination of shame and hostility together with
punishment for the hostility: dumb = dead), loquacity, and premature unsuccessful attempts at intercourse on the part of impotent
persons. Abraham's paper[28] is confined to the study of a special
group of neurotics who produce more or less permanent resistance.
The most important characteristic is narcissism and an attitude of
stubbornness against the father. The transference is poor, and the
patients grudge the analyst his father-role; they wish to do things
themselves, and alone, and an identification with the physician
takes place, like a child *playing* the father and wishing to do it better.
Auto-analysis is a narcissistic self-enjoyment in defiance of the
father, and is really an onanistic equivalent. The patients were
chiefly obsessional neurotics.

Abraham calls attention to the connection between "association" and defæcation and between "association" and flatus, the
patient's problem being "if, when and how much". In such anal
cases the cost of treatment even prolonged makes no appeal, since
these patients are more parsimonious with unconscious material
than with money; nothing is too dear for them to preserve their
narcissism. Abraham suggests an alteration in the usual technique
in these cases, having discovered that a surprising amount of
material may be obtained if the patient is instructed in the narcissistic and hostile nature of his resistance right at the beginning
of the analysis. This however, is as far as he goes in suggesting
active interference. At this point the interesting paper by Reich[29]
is relevant in so far as he deals with the analysis of two special
narcissistic types and suggests some alterations in technique.

In considering factors conducing to the neurotic character-trait,
Reich differs from Alexander, who was inclined to regard such
traits as the result either of libido-pressure not in itself strong
enough to force its way to symptom-formation or of repression
too weak to prevent some degree of gratification in reality. Reich
thinks the "trait" is an expression of damaged integrity of the whole
or part personality. Behind the castration feeling common to all
cases exists a strong narcissistic constellation, itself the result of

overstress of erogenicity in oral, anal and urethral zones. This increases ego-libido, and sets up irritability of the whole personality. The more ego-libido is disturbed, the more diffuse the symptom. That hysterical symptoms can be circumscribed is due to their concern with object-libido. The neurotic character-trait is therefore due to a predominance of disturbance in ego-libido; it does not lie between health and neurosis, but is more serious than neurosis. Reich then describes two narcissistic types, one with manifest inferiority-feeling but strong latent narcissism, the other with latent inferiority and manifest compensating narcissism; both are of anal-urethral disposition, both present great difficulty in treatment and in both cases Reich has adopted at certain stages of the treatment an "active" modification of technique. Briefly, there comes a point in analysis of types with manifest inferiority-feeling, when the analyst does not attempt to reassure the patient during his self-depreciation; on the contrary, he agrees with the patient's self-criticism, pointing out, however, the latent basis of superiority. In the opposite type, with latent castration-inferiority, Reich found that in the midst of self-laudation, it often advanced the analysis to get the patient to rise from the couch and sit opposite.

Two facts emerge from consideration of the literature on resistance. It would seem that apart from the active technique practised by Ferenczi there is no organised method of active interference, and that if there is to be any substitute for active invocation of the imago's authority it can only be effected by a more thorough application of a rigorous deterministic attitude during analysis of such cases, to be continually brought into play during periods of resistance, whether of positive, negative or narcissistic origin. On the other hand, it is to be noted that in examining the causes of resistance to treatment all three writers have paid considerable attention to phenomena which have been described earlier in this paper as narcissistic or auto-erotic modifications of the repetition-compulsion.

To discuss therefore at what stages the application of stricter analytic determinism is indicated, it is necessary to familarise oneself with the various forms of narcissistic "analytical" gratification, and especially with the numerous character-traits and their classification.

Analytical Auto-Erotism.—The outstanding features of the history of transference-dynamics are the division of transference into positive and negative, the operation of ambivalence, the fact that positive as well as negative can cloak a vigorous resistance, and that working through infantile experience can cover equally intense resistance. That the analysis itself can be made use of to exploit auto-erotic stages and characteristics, i.e. repetitions in which the necessity for imago-co-operation is only secondary, has not received the same systematic study. Not only then can coitus and pregnancy situations be gratified in movement and spoken word during the analysis, but, as Ferenczi, Reik and Abraham show, associations can be exploited in the interests of anal-erotic activities (flatus and defæcation), whilst onanistic satisfaction can be displaced not only to association, but to innumerable symptomatic acts and mannerisms. The intense satisfaction of urethral erotism in association, e.g. the continuous or interrupted flow (as where one of my patients identified his free associations and urination in the common phrase, "a flow of golden sovereigns") is probably not sufficiently recognized. Further, although exhibitionistic and scoptophilic impulses and their reaction-formations are easily recognized and interpreted as such, the persistence of this trait as a possible libido leakage in an "association" form requires constant handling. Ferenczi has recognized this in insisting on the use of obscene words without euphemistic alteration and in the exact detailing of all phantasies. In the writer's opinion the same applies to the defensive use of *adult obscenity* to cover infantile experience. Just as inhibition in the use of obscene words current in adult life is a measure of the repression of direct exhibitionistic or viewing activities, so a glib use of the same words may be a measure of the strength of reaction-formations, i.e. obscenity may be employed as a defence against obscenity. Moreover, sadistic and masochistic impulses in addition to more obvious forms of gratification can obtain satisfaction in choice of word and speech forms during analysis, as for example where another of my patients played frequently with clang-associations based on the "hard C" or "K"; this was found to gratify oral, anal and urethral impulses and to provide onanistic satisfaction, the effort necessary to sound "K" being at once defæcation and orgasm. Castration was also represented and the series "coruscating", "kak", "cock", "cunt", "catsmeat" and "cough" was a tabloid version of the patient's complex activities. Urethral erotics on the other hand usually dwell on the sibilants.

We are again indebted to Ferenczi[30] for suggestions on this very point. In an early paper he calls attention to the use of simile in analysis and regards the interpretation of such as a not unimportant part of technique. The concentration on seeking the comparison leads to a lessening of censorship, so that we get in the simile memory-traces from the life-history of the individual. One patient, for example, likens psycho-analysis to a cure for tapeworms, which continues unsuccessful so long as the head remains in, and subsequent analysis of the simile sheds valuable light on his identifications.

Important as are these auto-erotic gratifications in words, phrases and modes of speech, it would be a mistake to neglect the object-relationship which can be represented in individual words and phrases. We have here an interesting contrast to transference-repetitions, which, as we have seen, tend to obscure auto-erotic repetitions. Further, the manipulation is in both instances peculiarly calculated to foster analytic resistance. We know from Freud[31] that the first real investment of objects is a "thing"-investment which is contained in the unconscious, and that the possibility of any object-presentation becoming conscious depends upon a union of the "thing"-presentation with the corresponding "word"-presentation which over-invests the former. He explains how in the transference-neurosis repression of presentations consists in denying to this "thing"-investment translation in words directly connected with the object. Hence the schizophrenic having withdrawn instinctual investment from object-presentations attempts to regain the object by hypercathexis of the word presentation. Now whilst these word-manipulations in the schizophrenic are subject to the "primary process" in a very marked degree, and the neologisms are seemingly quite without meaning, we have reason to assume from the mistakes, neologisms and word-plays so frequently met with in everyday analysis that a similar process is at work with perhaps a different aim. The schizophrenic attempts to heal himself, the neurotic in all probability to retain gratification of unconscious wishes by displacement of investment from thing to word-presentations. However that may be, the necessity of distinguishing auto-erotic from object word-play remains.

The Character-Trait.—In the use of words, either during analysis or in everyday life, we have something which is exceedingly characteristic of the individual, and the question arises whether the general term "neurotic character-trait" is not capable of subdivision. The character-trait is considered by Alexander[10] as standing midway between neurosis and health, by Reich as being ultra-neurotic, by Ferenczi as a private psychosis. Its characteristic is that the patient gets more *real* satisfaction for libido-formations and, in so far as its repetition leads to injury of his own interests, substitutes a real punishment for a symbolic punishment. The patient adopts a stereotyped relationship to life, and makes this a medium of expression. Alexander has suggested that either a relative damming up of libido or inefficient repression is the main factor in its production; Reich, as we have seen, attributes the trait to a narcissistic regression which is necessary for toleration of it. Alexander's suggestions can both be reduced to a quantitative factor, and in this connection Freud's[32] recent pronouncement is of importance, viz. that neurotic formations are not in themselves so important as the amount of attention (i.e. libido-cathexis) they receive. This would suggest that Reich's regression factor is only important in so far as it determines the amount of ego and object libido respectively contributed to the character "formation".

Adopting the term "neurotic" trait without prejudice, it would seem possible to separate traits in which the "word"-presentation is mainly affected from traits where relationship of the self to actual objects (including the self) is concerned. In both groups, too, a main subdivision is possible, viz. traits concerning the subject and traits concerning the object. This subdivision is, perhaps, more difficult in the case of "word"-traits, but in the other instance a line can be drawn more easily between object character-traits and auto-erotic character-traits. The former are then neuroses of action with play and gratification in the real outer world, the latter are neuroses of action with play and gratification on the real self. Gratification of oral libido again provides numerous examples of the auto-erotic trait (sucking and chewing pencils, chewing pieces of paper, smoking, etc.), whilst nose-picking, ear-boring, kneading bread, etc., exemplify anal traits. It is true that in these activities a regressional object-relationship is also found, and without question a "mixed" (over-determined) trait is the rule. Just how mixed it is can be gathered from the parallel instance of onanism (not in itself a trait); here one can trace in operation at the same time direct organ pleasure, narcissistic phantasy-formations and object phantasy-formations. This is probably true of the "smoking" trait. Now it is generally agreed that in the neurotic character-trait we find one of the most potent factors in continued resistance. Further, it is likely that such traits as gratify unmodified narcissistic libido are much less calculated to give rise to unconscious guilt feeling (apart, of course, from racial manifestations of this), can operate independently of the transference situation, and in so far as they are bound up with imago-representations are less amenable to influence and more adapted to the defiance aspect of the negative transference. In short, there is every reason to believe that in the patient's own use of analytical material and situations there is wide scope for substitute-gratification; possibly here takes place that leakage of libido which, if unobserved, might lead ultimately to the necessity for positive imago-interference.

Analytical Applications.—It has been suggested that the only substitute for "active" technique would be a deliberate focusing of attention to manifestations of resistance, but it does not follow that it is either practicable or politic to examine all such manifestations arbitrarily. Indeed, if we classify the unconscious manifestations of the analytical hour in a somewhat rough way, it will be seen that each of these requires different handling. It is agreed, for example, that direct attack on *symptom-formations* is inadvisable for the excellent reason that it is hoped to recreate them in a fresh neurosis within the transference. The *transitory symptoms*, however, are more amenable to direct attack, and it is generally agreed that the *symptomatic act*, verbal slips, etc., make excellent material for immediate analysis, often uncovering intense resistances.

Practice in the handling of *dream-material* seems to vary considerably, but whilst on the whole it is to be regarded more as a "theme", it is still available on special occasions for deliberate analysis, as distinguished from running elucidation in the course of free association. Finally, as we have seen, the *character-trait* covers numerous manifestations not only in everyday speech and conduct, but in analytical speech and conduct; these provide ample cover for the strongest resistance, and would require not only continuous analysis, but at times of crisis deliberate survey and analytical scrutiny.

It is at any rate a legitimate suggestion that before applying the direct active technique of Ferenczi, a persistent analysis should be made, in order of accessibility, of the symptomatic act, the transitory symptom, repetitive transference-phenomena, auto-erotic repetitions, and finally the neurotic trait.

On a properly constructed couch, every alteration from the supine attitude no matter how slight, every sound, no matter how inarticulate, has to be regarded as strictly determined and during resistance periods as material for unwearied analysis. Failing any advance by this method, the next justifiable step would be the deliberate focusing of analytical attention, whenever possible, on the performance or non-performance of certain substitute-formations, together with a rather arbitrary consideration of narcissistic factors in resistance after the manner of Abraham. If this again failed, the analyst would then take into account the type of falling ill, the quantitative investment of symptoms and—a factor which Jones[33] emphasizes on resistance—the existence of gravely defective harmony in the environment, before proceeding to exploit his imago authority by the issue of prohibitions.

Terminology.—It is probable that the use of the term "active" is responsible for some of the difficulties in considering "active technique", and the word is certainly calculated to give rise to confusion of thought in the minds of enthusiastic psychotherapists. On the other hand, Ferenczi has rightly queried the accuracy of the term "passive" as a description of current therapy. It would, perhaps, be advisable to adopt some terminology which would give a hint as to the psychological mechanisms implied. From this point of view, the "active technique" of Ferenczi is essentially "object" therapy, inasmuch as it depends for its success on the links formed at the earliest stages between the ego and the object.

Regarded from the point of view of libido-investment, it is "quantitative", a therapy alternately of "expansion" and "deprivation", of "flooding" and "damming up". It implies a temporary "displacement" along "regressional" paths; it is not so much "active" as "reactivating".

"Passive" therapy, on the other hand, whilst in the main an "object" therapy, probably owes some of its success to the play given by the technique to auto-erotic impulses, not only in the production of associations, but, as often occurs, by spontaneous attempts at interpretation.

In the latter instance this "auto-analysis" is frequently a cover for strong resistance, although, like other resistance-repetitions, a certain amount of play must be given it. The pride in producing associations is in a somewhat different case, and might be regarded in one sense as a kind of temporary sanctioned sublimation of auto-erotic impulses, albeit one which lends itself in a unique way to repetition interests. In a sense, too, it could be said that "passive" therapy is of the most advanced type possible, in that it implies an artificial stabilizing of the authority of the ego-ideal, and "active" therapy would seem to be an intermediate stage between passive therapy and analytical suggestion. The deliberate focusing of attention on performance or non-performance of substitutive acts or speech is less a reinforcing of the ego-ideal than the providing of a stimulus-situation with which the ideal must deal. The series would then run: passive interpretative technique, active interpretative technique, and, lastly, the Ferenczi technique based on transference authority, for which some such term as "reactivation (or congestive) technique" would seem more applicable than the one at present used.

3. The position of the analyst

Assuming that direct imago-interference is justifiable, there are certain implications consideration of which cannot be avoided. First, what are the logical or expedient limits to laying injunctions on the patient? If, for example, a patient practises larval forms of narcissistic gratification or exhibits auto-erotic traits which, if carried out in their original direct form, would give rise to conscious inhibitions, there does not seem to be any reason, from the purely theoretical point of view, why he should not be asked to reproduce on the couch any one or all of these direct forms.

Ferenczi, it will be remembered, was not content with a performance of his injunctions during non-analytic periods, but insisted on the inhibited act being performed in his presence. And if there are no theoretical limitations to the scope of active technique, at least the empirically expedient limitations should be understood thoroughly.

Then as to the bearing of the analyst. If the latter may stimulate analysis by means of injunctions and prohibitions, should be not be permitted in the last resort to make use of a kind of imago pantomime by actually imitating before the patient what he considers to be a significant imago-detail? The case reported by Groddeck,[34] where he stimulates his patient by getting up and imitating before her a certain limping gait, suggests numerous possibilities, which become even more relevant when we consider the training of analysts themselves. It is perhaps a moot point whether all persons being analysed for training would present resistances necessitating the application to themselves of active technique, although, regarding this matter from the point of view of quantitative libido-investment, it is theoretically presumable that they do. In any event, it would seem a prerequisite for the application of active methods that the analyst should have experienced the tension produced by imago-interference—in short, that active therapy should begin at home. It has, of course, been frequently argued that self-analysis is doomed to superficiality, and theoretically it can be understood that the transference-repetition of infantile situations, except in the purely primary narcissistic stages, cannot be attained in the absence of an imago (as Freud puts it, "In the long run, no one can be slain *in absentia* or *in effigie*"). Clearly Freud's definition of resistance as anything that interferes with the course of analysis applies excellently to counter-resistance. Now, since counter-resistance, like resistance, has a sadistic component, the situation of causing "tension-pain" in the patients is obviously calculated to play into the hands of this component.

Studying works on technique with the aid of Ferenczi's simile-analysis, we find much food for reflection. From a recent book on technique can be taken the following phrases, e.g. "penetrating", "cause no pain", "touch lightly with your probe", "use of force", "with a steel fist", "violence, short and sharp".

It was probably his own reaction against a similar situation, together with an increased sensitiveness to it, which led v. Hattingberg to criticize the analytical supine position as affording, both in actual arrangement and in interpretative technique, opportunity for satisfaction of the analyst's unconscious aggression. His criticism missed the mark because he read his own conflicts into a theoretical consideration of technique, but it is an excellent example of that same sensitiveness which has already been advanced as one of the reaction difficulties of applying active technique to the patient;

indeed, the criticism would be actually justified if an analyst were unaware of an unconscious temptation to indulge aggressive components. It must be granted, of course, that, *cœteris paribus*, the opposite risk exists in passive technique, namely, where the analyst, by masochistic identification, refrains from exploiting fully the possibilities of passive technique, but this again is a criticism of the analyst's training, and not of analytic method.

Appendix[35]

Since the foregoing paper was written there has appeared, as one of a new series of psycho-analytical publications, an essay on the "Developmental aims of psycho-analysis", by Ferenczi and Rank.[36] In a footnote to the introduction the authors state that previous work by one of them on "active" methods has been either ignored or misunderstood by the majority of analysts. That the work has been ignored in periodical literature may perhaps be due to increasing pressure of contributions on other important matters; in this sense the criticism is perhaps justified, but in this sense only. Indeed, one might go so far as to say that the interest aroused by Ferenczi's work has been reflected not only in animated discussions among groups, but in a constant and increasing stream of private discussion and debate. That it has been misunderstood is a possibility not to be excluded; indeed, the footnote goes on to suggest that misunderstanding may be due to the fact that the papers in question did not deal sufficiently with the orientation of the method in respect to other technical procedure. We must remember, however, that many other generalizations about technique (transference, resistance, repetition, etc.) have been put before, and have been accepted by, the same psycho-analytical audience which is now credited with misunderstanding this latest expedient. This is a psychological phenomenon which can scarcely be explained away on the score of lack of proper orientation. Quite apart from motivations of unconscious resistance, there are two equally feasible explanations: either that satisfactory empirical data were not yet available, or that there existed some general recognition of a change in the dynamic point of view involved.

However that may be, the authors have at any rate compensated for any "lethargic" reaction on the part of their readers by official canonization of "active" methods in a definitely, though perhaps too briefly formulated, scheme of therapeutic procedure. Now it must be noted that in the same periodical literature during the same time no supplementary clinical evidence on "active" methods has been adduced. On the other hand, one of the authors has published a paper[37] on libido-processes in treatment and later a more ambitious treatise[38] in which all life-processes, including psychological healing-processes, have been regarded from one refracting angle. Hence it is, perhaps, not unfair to suggest that this recent authorization of "active" methods is to some extent at least the result of a happy conjunction of forces, whereby a tendency to give fixed form to treatment at the same time countenances and supports a previously isolated series of important observations. This collaboration adds greatly to the authority of the writers' pronouncements, an authority to which their previous distinguished contributions would in any case render them entitled, but it has nevertheless some of the disadvantages of composite presentation.

Very briefly then, since one assumes that the essay itself will be carefully studied, the position is as follows:

Freud put the main accent on "remembering" during analysis and regarded the substitution of remembering by a tendency to "re-experience" as a resistance. Ferenczi and Rank regard repetition not only as unavoidable, but in certain instances as the only way of reproducing the actual unconscious. Reproduction therefore is not to be limited, but provided one knows how to control the phenomena, to be insisted upon. When, on account of anxiety and guilt-feeling, repetition is hindered by resistance, this in some instances can only be overcome by active interference, by insisting on repetition. Repetition is therefore the main agent in technique.

For the analyst, psycho-analysis of the patient represents a process within the libido-development of the latter having individual form and definite duration. This process takes an automatic course and the physician's duty is merely to interfere when resistance disturbances require correction. Analysis permits libido expansion which is often inhibited in real life; it must at certain points insist on this expansion. In general the analyst behaves rather passively towards repetition, as an object or rather phantom object; where correction is necessary he behaves "actively".

In analysis we have to deal with phases of resistance and of transference, the overcoming of which goes on during the main analytical work, which one might describe as a treatment by libido-withdrawal (a "lowering" cure). In the resistances of the ego we meet with mainly preconscious memory-material or manifest character-peculiarities and ideal-formations. These are overcome gradually. The narcissistic resistances are met with early and often give rise to the greatest difficulty, sometimes necessitating narcissistic injury or temporary suspension of the old ego-ideal.

From the transference there can be reproduced portions of disturbed infantile development; this takes place by translation of unconscious manifestations into the language of consciousness, also by the tendency to repeat old libido-situations. In contradistinction to the manifestations of the resistance-phase, we find here a reproduction of situations which for the most part have never been conscious. These are intensively experienced for the first time through analysis of the transference. The main resistance here is infantile anxiety (guilt-feeling in relation to the parents), which arises from the conflict of ego (ideal) with libidinal tendencies. The neurotic has an excess of guilt-feeling, the reduction of which by partial analytic resolution and abreaction enables libido-tendencies to appear in the form of transference, to be made conscious and to be worked out (*verarbeiten*).

If infantile libido has thus been freed from repression, if the patient has with the "active" assistance of the analysis found courage to recognize his libidinal tendencies, we have then to separate from the analytic situation the infantile libido reproduced in the transference. This is a special phase of libido "weaning" or, in analytic terminology, it constitutes the correct analysis of the transference. The artificial transference-situation with its now actual tendencies towards fixation must, after suitable working-through, be resolved by demolition of the transference. This must take place gradually as did the automatic libido-development of the first phase under ego-inhibitions. At the point when libido-development is completely unravelled and transfered to analytic fixation, interference on the part of the analyst is directed towards the duration in that "he sets an appointed time by which the unwinding of threads from the analytic reel to the spool of reality must be complete". This must be adhered to apart from any seeming "progress" made by the patient in the meantime. New ego-resistances appear; the patient wants real libido-gratification in analysis. This must be renounced and the results of analysis accepted.

In the first phase of analysis the patient calls in investments from the advanced ego-positions (personality, neurosis) and guides them back to the Oedipus situation and its fore-stages. The real resistances that are aroused here do not disturb analytic work; they act like a watch-spring in regulating and dosing libido-processes. But they are also more than functional; they reproduce in themselves, hence their analysis is of the utmost importance. If this is successful, the transference in the full unconscious sense is now established. The nature of transference and of resistances show in each case what has happened to the Oedipus libido. In this sense the castration complex represents in analysis the negative Oedipus complex; it is a neurotic means of defence making use of normal infantile bisexuality. With this investigation the disease is now rendered superfluous. Activation and resolution of the primary neurosis in analysis correspond to the chronological sequence in disease; infantile neurosis, clinical neurosis. The first phase represents ego-education in so far as the ego is taught to tolerate ideas running counter to its requirements. In a later phase, after transference is developed, infantile libido-development is completely expanded. The stage of libido-weaning is carried on by ego-energies from the new ideal, plus a component of natural egoism. These ego-energies are, of course, like the capacity for transference, present in all cases which are not insane. On them depends the healing process, i.e. a *further* transference from analyst to reality. The patient turns to what life offers; sublimation is compressed into a short space.

The creation of the analytic situation reproduces the infantile trauma. The patient shows that it is the ideal parent-imago he wants. We cannot give this in the form he wishes, and even if we did, "*as is often the case*",[39] we should only apparently "cure" him by making him happy in love. We must bring him up to a painful experience, i.e. the conflict between libido-tendencies and the ego-ideal. Transference establishes a provisory ideal against which the old ideal defends by resistances. These frequently take the form of father-identification with exhibition of obstinacy. Even in this first phase of analysis active interference is required which "need not go beyond that degree of parental authority existing in the transference". When these ego-resistances are overcome and the transference is widely established, reproduction continues until libido-resistances arise; these fight against recognizing that libido wishes are unattainable in analysis. At this point the nature of the transference is first explained. All explanations and translations are here merely a first resource. In general, the analyst only ceases to be passive when resistances demand some regulation of libido-processes, and here mere translation is less important than understanding the tendency of associations. Every expression of the patient must be understood and interpreted as first and foremost a reaction to the present analytic situation.

Abreaction of affect is still the important therapeutic agent, but with this difference, that in the original catharsis affect was connected with the original experiences, whereas in analysis affect is discharged through and by means of the analyst and analysis. It is the difference between seeking memories to reach affect, and provoking affect to uncover the unconscious. This creates, so to speak, "new actual memories". The state of privation represented by analysis constitutes a trauma-repetition which is essential to bring about therapeutic conviction.

Later, in a historical review of technique in which certain previous tendencies are criticized, the authors warn against adopting "wild activity" as a substitute for overcoming technical difficulties. They state specifically: "The moderate but, if need be, energetic activity required in analysis is as follows: the physician to a certain extent actually fills the role thrust upon him by the unconscious of the patient and his flight tendencies." This encourages inhibited repetition-tendencies. "Where the repetition comes about spontaneously, provocation is unnecessary." In describing the relations of theory to practice, the authors recall how wider application of the new "activity" followed from experiences in dealing with anxiety-hysteria when the patient was made to face certain painful situations.

One of the chief results of the scientific insight attained by analytic observation was the discovery that the Oedipus complex was the root complex and the significance of its repetition in the analytic situation. Nevertheless the most important part of real analytic interference consists neither in the demonstration of an "Oedipus complex" nor simply in its repetition in analysis, but in the loosening or separation of infantile libido from its fixation on the first object. This implies a complete living through in the relation of patient to physician and the latter must occasionally take suitable measures (activity) to uncover traces. The knowledge by means of which we are in a position to interfere at the correct moment and with appropriate dosing, consists in a conviction of the universal significance of certain fundamental early experiences ("as for example the Oedipus conflict").

It is one of the drawbacks of a short theoretical essay such as that of Rank and Ferenczi that the meaning of certain passages tends to be rather obscure. This difficulty is not in any way lessened in the present instance by almost total absence of clinical illustrative material whereby the exact implications of terminology might be controlled. We know, for example, from Ferenczi's earlier work that the customary interpretative interference is, in his view, active; moreover, it may be said that his special "activity" as then described has not been in any way modified. Nevertheless, in describing active interference "which need not go beyond that degree of parental authority existing in the transference," it is clear that the licence permitted must, in the absence of exact definition, vary in accordance with the analyst's predilections. This is the more important in that the statement in question applies to interference in the first stage of analysis, i.e. before the transference situation has been unfolded.

Another drawback has been appreciated by the authors themselves when they suggest that the idea of hard and fast stages should not be taken too literally. This is a welcome reassurance, not merely for the reason advanced that these stages are not found so schematically in practice, but because a fixed demarcation of stages implies a much more complete knowledge of ego-processes than we are at present entitled to claim. But, although the authors are ready to make allowance for the merging of one phase into the other, no such allowance is hinted at in the application of active steps in technique. Whatever doubt there may be as to the nature of interference in the first stage, there is none as to the use of activity in the unfolding of transference-situations, nor, again, when the time is ripe to commence the last phase of libido-weaning. Whilst this latter seems to cover the process usually known as analysing and dissolving the transference, an additional active step is taken, viz. setting a term to the analysis itself. On theoretical grounds it is difficult to say whether this is merely the climax to a series of deprivation situations or whether it is not merely a completion in the last phase of what is supposed by the authors to have been already completed, viz. the activation and re-experience of infantile libido-situations in the transference. It might be said that, if the transference had been effectively uncovered, this would include complete emotional investigation of the most important privation occurring at the Oedipus stage; in that case the necessity for this final jog during dissolution of the transference would not be too apparent. But perhaps the difficulty is an artificial one, due to thinking too rigidly in stages; in this sense the current elastic handling of cases, whilst seemingly an indication of ineffectively applied knowledge, may prove to be more in keeping with the actual dynamics of the situation. At any rate, it will be interesting to compare in future the results of this manoeuvre as applied by active therapists in all cases with the results occasionally noted by "passive" analysts when, for some reason or other, the stage of transference-dissolution has been of fixed duration. Theoretically, of course, all such comparisons will be beside the point, but as empirical data they will meet on common ground.

In the meanwhile three questions arise: 1. How far has the case for universal application of "active" methods been satisfactorily established? 2. How far does the division into stages together with the process of libido-weaning meet with the exigencies of analytic practice? 3. And how far does our present knowledge of ego-psychology permit us to adopt an attitude of finality on therapeutic procedure?

In the first place, since no additional clinical evidence has been adduced, we are entitled to say that the question is still open to investigation and discussion. A fresh pronouncement of some importance has, however, to be chronicled: the active therapist definitely shoulders the responsibility of actually playing to some extent the imago-role thrust upon him by the patient. There is no need to recapitulate here the considerations already brought forward in the foregoing paper on this point, but, since ego-mechanisms have recently been more widely discussed, it may well be to single out two special aspects of the question. The "active" therapist would discount the dangers of a second fixation on the grounds not only that he really wishes to bring about a second fixation, but that, provided he knows how to dissolve it later, there is no danger. His point seems to be that without this imago-play it may be impossible to secure that toleration of infantile ego-counter impulses which is admittedly the preliminary to analytic success. The natural question arises: Does he, after playing this part, really succeed in dissolving the second fixation, or has he, like the *hypnotiseur*, gained immediate progress at an ultimate sacrifice? The answer would seem to lie in the part played by the ego-ideal in analysis and, going further back, in the degree to which "Es"-excitations have really been subordinated to control during ideal-formation.

Freud[40] has shown that the climax in the series of object-formations (partial to complete), subject-object identifications, and choice of complete love-object, is reached in overcoming the complete Oedipus relation, and that a process of identification on the oral pattern takes place whereby a special stamp is left on the ego. The main point about this early ideal-formation is that, by introjecting the parent, the child has *ipso facto* built up in himself an active repressing force; obstacles to sexual gratification existing outside the ego are now erected within the ego, and exercise a repressing function, the energy for which is supplied from narcissism *via* the aim-inhibited impulses and the narcissistic ideal-ego. At the same time there exist in a state of repression allo-erotic relations with parental images, which vary in accordance with identification and the form of the Oedipus complex. Now the parental introjected ego-ideal brings about a denial not only of sexual impulses towards the parents, but, in addition, of erotic phantasy and auto-erotic activities of a direct nature. There is here a striking difference from the new introjection taking place during analysis. To appreciate this we have only to compare the parental attitude with the attitude of "passive" analysts. Whilst the latter clearly indicate the *unattainability* of direct erotic strivings towards the new object, they entirely suspend "criticism" or "judgment" of the wish-formations and phantasy-activities, or, again, of actual activities outside analysis of a direct auto-erotic or object type. They may interpret, explain or, in the event of libido-leakage, continue to emphasize the nature of these resistance-defences, but they avoid playing the parental role as far as that is possible. This is an extraordinary difference, and to it as well as to the uncovering of anxiety-formations is due the fact that the patient is able to tolerate (hence to uncover) in conscious- ness the phantasy products of infantile sexuality.

The usual passive therapy thus slowly modifies the old ego- ideal, and even when interpretation pursues a more arbitrary course, as in calling attention repeatedly to the existence of libido- leakages, a stimulus-situation is provided for an increasingly stable system (i.e. adapted to reality). In Ferenczi's congestive therapy, whilst the authority present in the ideal is invoked, the libidinal imagines are also activated. To these latter situations the patient is already sensitized. "Do this", "Don't do that" (*Gebot und Verbot*) are, after all, the battle-cries of the nursery, and, however laudable their intent, are calculated to reactivate, this time in reality, the associated ideas of parental tyranny and judgment. The analyst who uses them has, moreover, legitimately aroused old phantasy hopes and anticipations. Whoever says "Don't" may also smack. It is easy to imagine that where the patient has a tendency to self-punishment, especially in the inverted Oedipus situation, the issue of a prohibi- tion provides a real gratification of castration-phantasies, ultimately a symbolic gratification of "passive" technique that entire suspen- sion of criticism, either actual or implied (as in prohibition), permits and assists the gradual introjection of the new ideal without acti- vating in reality a direct infantile libidinal relation to the analyst, that the toleration of ego-counter achieved. It might be argued, indeed, that the prerequisite for any justifiable application of congestive methods is not so much the usual "durable transfer- ence", but what one might call a serviceable alteration of the ego- ideal. It should be noted in passing that, whilst the authors do not see any risk in a second fixation if properly handled, they do call attention (p. 23) to the frequency with which "cure" is effected by allowing the patient some success in his analytical love.

The second point has already been elaborated in the foregoing paper; it concerns the degree to which auto-erotic activities have in the first instance been rendered amenable to object influence. This is again a matter of the stability and over- or under-strictness of the ego-ideal. Where original "Es"-excitations have not been deeply affected by object influence or where component-impulses have only been slightly modified, it would seem that "activity" must defeat its own ends, that we must be even more passive, give more scope to repetition, i.e. to working through, rather than merely to re-experience. It is on some such score that doubts as to the wisdom of a standardised technique become most insistent; one misses in particular any reference to the varying conditions of ego-development or capacity for reality-testing such as are constantly present in analytic practice.

This brings us to consider the advisability of giving a fixed form to the process of analysis. The preliminary criticism might be advanced that in giving this form, and especially in defining the duration of the so-called weaning stage, we run the risk of using methods of treatment which presume a fuller knowledge of ego and libido processes than we at present possess. It is true that the authors appeal against a too rigid demarcation of stages; we must note, however, that the demarcation is effected mainly on a libidinal basis. Perhaps some of the more obvious overlapping of their stages in practice is due to the fact that analysis is regarded mainly as an automatic libido-process within the individual's history having individual form and duration. The phrase "individual form" is surely another way of saying that ego dispositions and development vary in each case. Indeed it is conceivable that analysis might be divided into phases from the point of view solely of ego-development (e.g. introjection and projection phases, subject-object relations, ideal-formation, etc.); but this would be merely an exercise in ingenuity. The authors certainly attempt to correlate ego and libido processes, but it is perhaps not unfair to say that they seem to take up an attitude of slight impatience with the ego, e.g. in the last phase of analysis we find them still making coercive gestures. It must be added that in putting the accent entirely on a successful "weaning", a tendency is established which would make analysis less an elastic and adaptable therapeutic process than a rigid discipline based on one general formula. We are bound to recall the point of view of one of the authors in another book, *Das Trauma der Geburt*, where the application of a formula to instinctual activities and mechanisms is very rigorously carried out. There is, indeed, some indication of this attitude in the significant

parenthesis concerning the universality of certain early experiences—"*for example*, the Oedipus conflict."[41]

It is, perhaps, unfair to press comparisons too closely, but the
authors on more than one occasion appeal to the practice of general
medicine in support of their thesis. It is always a good disciplinary
exercise for analysts to study the therapeutic canons of general
medicine. But at the same time we must not forget the reluctance of
scientifically-minded clinicians to standardize phenomena either in
diagnosis or treatment. Standardization in general medicine is
usually a preliminary to making new standards to cover exceptions
to the previous rule. As for limiting the duration of a phase of treatment, this it is true is sometimes illustrated by the use of transference authority at the bedside, but a rigid application of the parallel
would confront us with many perplexing situations, e.g. the limitation of treatment during convalescent or resolution stages of
organic disease.

It cannot be too frequently emphasized that the importance of a
book of this kind lies mainly in its fundamental *tendencies*. The
problem of "active" therapy still remains a problem to be solved in
due course as the result of additional experience and insight. The
comments made here are not intended to imply that active steps are
empirically unsound. It may well be that in certain cases at certain
times the empirical advantages may outweigh any drawbacks
inherent in the application of active technique. On the other hand,
we are entitled to enter a plea for more prolonged consideration of
phenomena and against too rapid a crystallization of set principles.
The founder of psycho-analysis has set us an example of patient
and penetrating research which cannot be bettered. Doubtless we
shall in the future be indebted to the creator of "active" methods for
further illuminating observations on the subject; the present essay
indeed is full of very cogent criticisms such as we are accustomed
to expect from his pen. And here the matter might well rest, were it
not that the last chapter of the essay contains speculations of great
importance from the point of view of "tendency". The gist of these
speculations is as follows:

The authors suggest that displacement of accent in treatment to
"knowing" and "managing" (*handeln*) will lead in course of time to
increasing resemblance between analytical methods and those of
general medicine; with this exception, that the timing and "dosage"

of interference will be more accurate in the former instance. Hypnosis was not radical because its use concealed psychic motivations; nevertheless it owed its undeniable results to the elimination of intellectual resistances. "It would be an enormous advance in therapeutic efficiency if we could, for example, combine this invaluable advantage of the hypnotic technique with the advantage of possible analytical solution of the hypnotic affect-situation." So far, psycho-analysis has shown us that the crux of the hypnotic affective relationship is the Oedipus complex, but we do not yet understand the specific conditions of the hypnotic state. If we did, the analyst might again include hypnosis in his technique without fear of producing permanent fixation. Exclusion of intellectual resistances is more necessary since we now penetrate more deeply into the layers of consciousness, thereby making this knowledge itself a means of resistance. The immediate tendency is towards simplification of analytical technique which may possibly bring about a semblance of monotony and formality in analytic methods.

It is clear from this that the authors have taken the wise precaution of hedging round these speculations with conditional clauses; hence the matter cannot be regarded from the point of view of immediate policy requiring immediate consideration. Nevertheless the tendency is noteworthy, and is frankly characterized as such in the last chapter. Reference to the foregoing review (see p. 297) will perhaps indicate that this ultimate tendency had then been in part anticipated. It was originally the present writer's intention to add to his classification of therapeutic procedure by including a group of "activation methods reinforced by hypnotic technique", and it may be permissible now to amplify the statement that current "passive" methods are theoretically the most "advanced" methods possible. Then it was suggested that the distinction between methods lay in the physician's attitude to the patient's ego-ideal. In the meantime Jones has published a contribution to the nature of auto-suggestion in which is set out with the utmost clearness the essential difference between analytic processes and suggestion or hypnotic processes.[42] This paper deserves the closest study, and we can only refer here to his view that the suspension of ego-ideal criticism involved in the latter is effected at the price of repression of allo-erotic impulses, which regress towards auto-erotism. This regression-process runs counter to the raising of assimilative capacity on the part of the ego-ideal. Our attention is thus drawn to an incompatibility in principle, and if analysis is to be combined with suggestion and hypnotic methods, we must be alive to the possibility that the analytic process is much less likely to be completed. It would be an interesting subject for discussion whether in the active (Ferenczi) position we have not already reached a theoretical "debateable land", in so far as a general passive attitude leading to increased assimilative capacity on the part of the ego-ideal is combined with an active attitude which, whilst intended to increase still further this assimilative capacity, permits regressive identifications by making use of infantile libidinal technique (*Gebot, Verbot*). Certainly, as Jones remarks,[42] one of the strongest resistances exists when the patient projects on to the analyst his own repressed mental processes, identifying him with his own real ego; and we must consider how far actually playing the part ascribed by the patient's unconscious tends to reinforce this resistance projection.

Returning to the question of hypnotism, we have to note that the advantage anticipated by the writers is that of eliminating intellectual resistances, which, they hold, is the more called for since analysis now penetrates more deeply or widely into conscious layers. This argument is at any rate not quite one-sided. Quite apart from the fact that earlier in the essay the authors associate their more active expedients with libido-resistances, we must ask whether it is not precisely by deeper investigations of action-mechanisms that we may provide that damming-up of the libido, the escape of which in their view necessitated activation methods.[43]

Notes

1. *Vorlesungen zur Einführung in die Psychoanalyse*, Leipzig, 1917. English translation: *Introductory Lectures on Psychoanalysis*, International Psycho-Analytical Press, 1922. Lecture XXVIII.
2. "Zur Dynamik der Übertragung", *Zentralblatt für Psychoanalyse*, Bd. II, 1912. Republished in *Sammlung kleiner Schriften*, Vierte Folge.
3. "Die Handhabung der Traumdeutung in der Psychoanalyse", *Zentralblatt für Psychoanalyse*, Bd. II, 1912. Republished in *Sammlung kleiner Schriften*, Vierte Folge.

4. "Weitere Ratschläge zur Technik der Psychoanalyse", *Zeitschrift für Psychoanalyse*, Bd. II, 1914. Republished in *Sammlung kleiner Schriften*, Vierte Folge.
5. "Die Zukünftigen Chancen der psychoanalytischen Therapie", *Zentralblatt für Psychoanalyse*, Bd. I, 1910. Republished in *Sammlung kleiner Schriften*, Vierte Folge.
6. "Wege der psychoanalytischen Therapie", *Zeitschrift für Psychoanalyse*, Bd. V, 1919.
7. "Einige Bemerkungen zur Lehre vom Widerstande", *Zeitschrift für Psychoanalyse*, Bd. III, 1915. Translated in *International Journal of Psychoanalysis*, Vol. V, 1924, p. 141.
8. "Weiterer Ausbau der 'aktiven Technik'", *Zeitschrift für Psychoanalyse*, Bd. VII, 1921.
9. Translated in S. Ferenczi, *Contributions to Psychoanalysis*, Boston, 1916.
10. "The castration complex in the formation of character", *International Journal of Psychoanalysis*, Vol. IV, 1923.
11. "Zur psychoanalytischen Technik", *Zeitschrift für Psychoanalyse*, Bd. V, 1919.
12. "Technische Schwierigkeiten einer Hysterieanalyse", *Zeitschrift für Psychoanalyse*, Bd. V, 1919.
13. *Bericht über die Fortschritte der Psychoanalyse 1914–19*, p. 131, 1921.
14. "Weitere Ratschläge zur Technik der Psychoanalyse", *Sammlung kleiner Schriften*, Vierte Folge, p. 452.
15. *Jenseits des Lustprinzips*, Wien, 1920. English translation: *Beyond the Pleasure Principle*, 1922.
16. Cf. Freud, "Triebe und Triebschicksale", *Sammlung kleiner Schriften*, Vierte Folge.
17. The various tissue changes induced under hypnosis might be brought forward in support of the complete accessibility of narcissistic libido to object influence. Without going deeply into theoretical consideration of this point (on which much light is shed by Ferenczi in his paper on hysterical materialisation-phenomena), it may be said that such alterations presuppose not only a strong transference capacity (and therefore strong object-modification of subject-impulses), but, as Ferenczi suggests, an advanced state of modification in which the body is "genitalized". The induction of such changes, themselves in the nature of a transference "conversion", does not preclude the co-existence of a stream of auto-erotic activity more or less inaccessible to transference influence.

18. It seems probable that even in the case of modified "component" pairs, especially the exhibitionism-scoptophilia pair, the primary narcissistic stage has still continuous gratification throughout life. This is less capable of direct proof owing to the fact that in the second stage of modification, namely, the turning of the impulse from the object against the self, a pseudo-narcissistic phase is attained. In the case of the erotogenic zones the continuance of primary organ-pleasure apart from any modification is more easily demonstrable.

19. Cf. *Jenseits des Lustprinzips*.

20. Personally communicated by Abraham.

21. "Über neurotische Erkrankungstypen", *Sammlung kleiner Schriften*, Dritte Folge, 1921, p. 306.

22. "Zur Technik der Kinderanalyse", *Zeitschrift für Psychoanalyse*, Bd. VII, 1921.

23. "Zur Prognose psychoanalytischer Behandlungen in vorgeschrittenem Lebensalter", *Zeitschrift für Psychoanalyse*, Bd. VI, 1920.

24. "Zur Analyse der analytischen Situation", *Zeitschrift für Psychoanalyse*, Bd. X, 1924.

25. *Das Ich und das Es*, 1923.

26. *Kriegsneurosen und psychisches Trauma*, Leipzig, 1918.

27. "Analysis of an obsessional neurosis in a child", *International Journal of Psychoanalysis*, Vol. III, 1922.

28. "Über eine besondere Form des neurotischen Widerstandes", *Zeitschrift für Psychoanalyse*, Bd. V, 1919.

29. "Zwei narzisstische Typen", *Zeitschrift für Psychoanalyse*, Bd. VIII, 1922.

30. "Die Analyse von Gleichnissen", *Zeitschrift für Psychoanalyse*, Bd. III, 1915.

31. "Das Unbewusste", *Sammlung kleiner Schriften*, Vierte Folge, p. 329 ff.

32. "Certain neurotic mechanisms in jealousy, paranoia and homosexuality", *International Journal of Psychoanalysis*, Vol. IV, 1923.

33. *Papers on Psycho-Analysis*, p. 376, London, 1923.

34. "Eine Symptomanalyse", *Zeitschrift für Psychoanalyse*, Bd. VI, 1920.

35. Added in April, 1924.

36. *Entwicklungsziele der Psychoanalyse*, Internationaler Psychoanalytischer Verlag, 1924.

37. Rank: "Zum Verständnis der Libidoentwicklung im Heilungsvorgang", *Internationale Zeitschrift für Psychoanalyse*, 1923.

38. *Das Trauma der Geburt*, Internationaler Psychoanalytischer Verlag, 1924.

39. Reviewer's italics.

40. *Das Ich und das Es*, Internationaler Psychoanalytischer Verlag, 1923.

41. Reviewer's italics.

42. "The nature of auto-suggestion", *International Journal of Psychoanalysis*, Vol. IV, 1923.

43. In the literature of active therapy, reference is frequently made to the remarks of Freud in his "Wege der psychoanalytischen Therapie" (1919), concerning simplification of technique. It may be well to consider the context of these remarks. Freud first refers to the possibility of meeting a demand for wider application of the benefits of psycho-analysis especially among the people. He thinks it possible that poor people will be less ready to abandon their neuroses, since their conditions of life are not so attractive and to be ill is to have some claim on social support. He then goes on: "In all probability the application of our therapy to numbers will compel us to alloy the pure gold of analysis with a plentiful admixture of the copper of direct suggestion: indeed, just as in the treatment of war-neuroses, hypnotic influence might be included. But, however this psychotherapy for the people (*fürs Volk*) may take shape, out of whichever elements it is constituted, the most effective and most important part thereof will assuredly remain that which is borrowed from strict, non-tendencious psycho-analysis."

CHAPTER FIVE

Character formation

Abraham, Karl (1925). The influence of oral erotism on character-formation. *International Journal of Psychoanalysis*, 6: 247–258.

Abraham, Karl (1926). Character-formation on the genital level of libido-development. *International Journal of Psychoanalysis*, 7: 214–222.

In his paper on the anal character, Freud (1908b) moved on from interpreting symptoms to make a determined attempt to understand character and its development. Typically, he took his well-tried model: a character trait like a dream symbol or a symptom has a hidden, unconscious meaning which can be discovered by the psychoanalytic method, and is to be understood in terms of libidinal restriction. His bright idea, aroused probably by the Ratman case (according to Strachey's introduction to the paper in the *Standard Edition*), was that certain character traits had a special relation to anal impulses—in particular, orderliness, parsimony, and obstinacy. Freud was claiming that character traits could be laid down by fixation points, just like neurotic symptoms. Character traits resulted from the libido hanging on to a particular level of development, as opposed to a regression to the fixation point under stress, which is more typical of neurotic symptoms. At this pre-genital level, certain impulses, anal ones, become settled in the personality, and typically what the personality expresses is traits opposed to the impulses, that is, institutionalized reaction formations.

This idea, that character itself could be analysed, caught on slowly. But Jones (1918)[1] and Abraham (1923) contributed loyally to this understanding of the anal character. Abraham then became interested in how other libidinal phases of development could be manifested in character rather than in symptoms. The two papers republished here expanded this general theme by dealing with the oral and genital characters.

In particular he described certain traits which might express oral impulses. He discerned two kinds of oral trait connected to two sub-phases of orality—the pre-ambivalent and the oral-sadistic sub-phases—and thus arise two forms of the oral character. These were the optimistic, acquisitive character and the ambivalently hostile or envious character. Like the anal traits, these result from the distur-bance to libidinal gratification, but this time at the oral level.[2] However, Abraham was concerned that the picture is not as clear as the anal one. He attributed this to the fact that the lasting oral char-acter traits invariably underlie anal traits as well, resulting in a mixed picture. There is, therefore, a need to unravel the complex interaction between the oral and anal levels of character formation. The same is true of the genital stage. At the genital level he described processes by which aspects of previous levels are incor-porated. So, he claims, there is the beginning of an experience of others as whole persons, and relations with them combine affec-tionate interests with the simple desire for erotic satisfaction. There is a gradual movement away from narcissism, ambivalent feelings come to be resolved and, finally, character is derived from charac-teristic objects that are introjected.

These ideas may now be outdated in the sense that the progres-sion through the libidinal phases is no longer stressed. However, the understanding of character formation as the prominence of traits that derive from the urgent repression of a libidinal impulse point towards the defensiveness which these fixated characters exhibit and institutionalize within their personalities. When Freud described his structural model, in 1923, the emphasis on the characteristic libidinal impulses was superseded by the analysis of the ego.[3] Under the influence of Anna Freud's *Ego and Mechanisms of Defence* (Anna Freud, 1936), the attention to character moved from an emphasis on the stages of libido to the way the ego handles the libido at the various stages. With the development of ego-psychology, and especially the characteristic combinations of defences, character came to be understood in terms of the characteristic defences and reaction formations against the most troubling of the components of libido. Character came thus to be a formation of the defences, as Reich proposed (Reich, 1931).

Notes

1. In the meantime Freud (1916d) had discussed the role of guilt in shaping certain characters, including the criminal.
2. In a discursive paper that covers many interesting points about character analysis based on phases of libidinal development, Glover (1925) links oral characters to the phase of omnipotence in the development of the sense of reality that is described in the paper by Ferenczi (1926), discussed later.
3. Ferenczi (1920) pointed out the change from a libido psychology to an ego-psychology was enabled by Freud's theory of narcissism.

References

Abraham, K. (1923). Contributions to the theory of the anal character (Ergänzung zur Lehre vom Analcharakter). *International Journal of Psychoanalysis*, 4: 400–418.

Ferenczi, S. (1920). General theory of the neuroses. *International Journal of Psychoanalysis*, 1: 294–296.

Ferenczi, S. (1926). The acceptance of unpleasant ideas: advance in knowledge of the sense of reality. *International Journal of Psychoanalysis*, 7: 312–323.

Freud, A. (1936). *Ego and Mechanisms of Defence*. London: Hogarth.

Freud, S. (1908b). Character and anal erotism. *S.E., 9*: 169–175. London: Hogarth Press.

Freud, S. (1916d). Some character-types met with in psychoanalytic work. *S.E., 14*: 311–333. London: Hogarth Press.

Glover, E. (1925). Notes on oral character formation. *International Journal of Psychoanalysis, 6*: 131–154.

Jones, E. (1918). Anal erotic character traits. *Journal of Abnormal Psychology, 13*: 261–284.

Reich, W. (1931). The characterological mastery of the Oedipus complex. *International Journal of Psychoanalysis, 12*: 452–467.

The influence of oral erotism on character-formation*†

Karl Abraham

According to the usual view the formation of character is to be traced back partly to inherited dispositions, and partly to the effect of environment, under which a particular significance is ascribed to up-bringing. Psycho-analytical investigation, however, has drawn attention to sources of character-formation which had not previously been sufficiently considered. On the basis of psycho-analytical experience we conclude that those elements of the infantile sexuality which are excluded from participation in the sexual life of the adult individual undergo transformation to some extent into certain character-traits. Freud, as is well known, was the first to show that certain elements of infantile anal erotism suffer this fate. Some part of the anal erotism enters into the final organization of mature sexual life, part of it undergoes sublimation, and the rest finds an outlet in character-formation. These contributions to

---

* Read before the Eighth Congress of the International Psycho-Analytical Association, Salzburg, 1924.

† Article citation:
Abraham, K. (1925). The influence of oral erotism on character-formation. *International Journal of Psychoanalysis*, 6: 247–258.

character from anal sources are to be regarded as normal. They render it possible for the individual to adapt himself to the demands of his environment as regards cleanliness, love of order, and so on. Besides this, however, we have learnt to recognize an "anal character" in the clinical sense, which is distinguished by an extreme accentuation of certain character-traits; but it is to be noted that excessive addiction to cleanliness, parsimony and similar tendencies never succeeds completely. We invariably find the opposite extreme more or less strongly developed.

Now experience teaches us that not all the deviations from the final character-formation of the genital stage of development originate in the anal sources just mentioned. On the contrary, oral erotism has been recognized as a source of character-formation as well. Here, too, we can perceive that a certain amount of this falls within normal bounds, and that outside this there are distinctly abnormal degrees of accentuation of it. If our observations are correct, then we can speak of oral, anal, and genital sources of character-formation; in doing so, however, we quite consciously neglect one aspect of the problem, because we are only taking into consideration those contributions to the formation of character derived from the erotogenic zones, and not those coming from the component-instincts. This neglect is, however, more apparent than real; for example, the close connection of the component of cruelty in infantile instinctual life with oral erotism makes itself evident in character-formation, so that it is hardly necessary to draw special attention to it.

What my investigations lead me to say about character-traits of oral origin will perhaps be disappointing in some respects, because I cannot offer a picture comparable in completeness to that of the anal character. I shall point, therefore, to certain differences between them which should not be lost sight of, and which will be calculated to reduce expectations to more appropriate proportions.

First of all, it should be remembered that of the pleasurable tendencies that are connected with intestinal processes only a small part can come to form part of normal erotism in an *unrepressed* form. In contrast to this, an incomparably greater part of the libidinal cathexis of the mouth which characterizes infancy can still find application in later life. Thus the oral elements in infantile sexuality do not need to be absorbed by character-formation or sublimation to the same extent as the anal ones.

Further, it should be emphasized that a retrograde transformation of character such as is connected with the outbreak of certain nervous disturbances may to a great extent come to a stop at the anal stage. If it proceeds further and a pathological intensification of oral traits, which will be described later, ensues, then this latter will show an admixture of others belonging to the anal stage. We should always, therefore, expect to find combinations of the two kinds of traits rather than a pure culture of oral characteristics.

If we now proceed more deeply into the study of such mixed products of two different sources of character-formation we are enabled to recognize something new. We learn that the origin of the anal character is interwoven in the closest manner with the fate of the oral erotism, and cannot be completely understood without reference to this connection.

Clinical experience led Freud to the view that in many people the particular libidinal emphasis on the intestinal processes is constitutionally founded. There can be no doubt about the correctness of this view. We need only call to mind how in certain families positive phenomena of anal erotism as well as anal character-traits infallibly reveal themselves in the most different members. Nevertheless, however well-founded this view may be, we have another to put beside it; it arises from the following considerations founded on psycho-analytic experience.

An intense pleasure in the act of sucking is a feature of infancy. We have familiarized ourselves with the view that this pleasure is not to be ascribed entirely to the process of taking food, but that it is conditioned in a high degree by the significance of the mouth as an erotogenic zone.

This primitive way of obtaining pleasure is never completely abandoned by human beings; on the contrary, it persists under all kinds of disguises during the whole of life, and even experiences a reinforcement at times in particular circumstances. Nevertheless, the growth of the child, both physically and mentally, involves a far-reaching renunciation of the original pleasure in sucking. Now observation shows that every such renunciation of pleasure only takes place by way of an exchange. It is just this process of renunciation and the course it takes under different conditions which merits our attention.

Reference must first be made to the process of the irruption of teeth which, as is well known, replaces a considerable part of the pleasure in sucking by pleasure in biting. It is sufficient to call to mind how during this stage of development the child puts every object it can into its mouth and tries with all its strength to bite it to bits.

In the same period of development ambivalence in the relations of the child to objects of the outer world is set up. It is to be noted that the friendly as well as the hostile aspect of this attitude is connected with pleasure. At about the same period a further displacement of pleasurable sensation to other bodily functions and areas occurs.

A particularly significant fact is that the pleasure in sucking makes a kind of journey. At about the time that the child is being weaned it is being trained in habits of bodily cleanliness. An important pre-requisite for the success of this process lies in the gradually developing function of the anal and urethral sphincters. The action of these muscles is the same as that of the lips in sucking, and is obviously imitated from the latter. At first the unchecked voiding of bodily excretions was accompanied by stimulation of the apertures of the body which was undoubtedly pleasurable. When the child adapts itself to the demands of training and learns to retain its excretions this new activity also is at once accompanied by pleasure. The pleasurable sensations in the organ connected with this process form the foundation upon which the mental pleasure in retention of every kind of possession is gradually built up. More recent investigations have shown that the possession of an object originally signified to the infantile mind the same thing as the result of incorporation of it into the body. There was to begin with only the one kind of pleasure, that connected with taking in something coming from without or with expelling bodily contents; henceforth there is added to this the pleasure in retaining bodily contents, which leads to pleasure in all forms of property. The relation in which these three sources of physical and mental gratification stand to one another is of the greatest practical significance for the later social conduct of the individual. If the pleasure in getting or taking is brought into the most favourable relation with the pleasure in possession, as well as with that of rendering up the possession, then an exceedingly important step is made in laying the foundations of

the individual's social relations. When the most favourable relationship between these three tendencies has been established it
constitutes the most important preliminary condition for overcoming the ambivalence of the emotional life.

In the preceding remarks attention has been called only to single
traits out of a multiform developmental process. For the purpose of
our investigation it is sufficient to make clear that the first and
perhaps most important step towards a later normal conduct in
social as well as sexual relationships consists in dealing successfully
with oral erotism. But there are numerous possibilities that this
important process of development may suffer disturbance.

If we wish to understand these disturbances we need only again
call to mind that the pleasure of the sucking period is to a great
extent a pleasure in taking in, in getting something. It then becomes
apparent that any quantitative divergence from the usual degree of
pleasure gained can give occasion for a disturbance.

The sucking period can be rich in "pain" and poor in pleasure for
the child to an unusual degree, and this will depend on the particular circumstances in which the child was fed. In such circumstances
the child's earliest pleasurable craving is gratified imperfectly,
the blissfulness of the sucking stage is not sufficiently enjoyed.
Freud made it clear long ago that stomach and bowel troubles in
infancy can have a harmful effect on the mental development of the
child.

In other cases the same period is abnormally rich in pleasure. It
is well known how some mothers indulge the craving for pleasure
in their infants by granting them every wish. The result then is an
extraordinary difficulty in weaning the child, which sometimes
cannot be successfully accomplished until two or three years have
elapsed. In rare cases the child persists in taking food by sucking
from a bottle almost up to adult age.

Whether the child in this early period of life had to go without
pleasure or was indulged with an excess of pleasure, the effect is the
same. The child takes leave of the sucking stage under difficulties.
Because its need for pleasure was either not sufficiently gratified or
had become too insistent, its craving fastens with particular intensity on the possibilities of pleasure during the next stage. In doing
this it finds itself in constant danger of a new disappointment, to
which it will react with an increased tendency to regression to the

earlier stage. In other words: In the child who was disappointed or over-indulged in the sucking period the pleasure in biting, which is also the most primitive form of sadism, will be especially emphasized. Thus the commencement of the formation of character in such a child takes place under the influence of an abnormally pronounced ambivalence. In practice such a disturbance of the development of character expresses itself in pronounced hostile and jealous traits. Abnormally overdeveloped envy, which is so common, finds its explanation here. The origin of this character-trait in an oral source has already been alluded to by Eisler;[1] I fully agree with his view, but would like to emphasize its relation to the later oral stage. In many cases an elder child, who is already at the stage of taking food by biting and chewing, has the opportunity of observing a younger child being suckled. In such cases its envy is reinforced by this special circumstance. Sometimes this character-trait is incompletely surmounted by being turned into the opposite; the original envy, however, comes to light again without any difficulty from under various disguises.

If the child evades the Scylla of this danger, it is threatened by the Charybdis of another. The child attempts to resume the abandoned act of sucking in an altered form and take it up again in another locality. The sucking activity of the sphincters at the excretory apertures of the body has already been mentioned. We have recognized that an inordinate desire to possess, especially in the form of abnormal parsimony and avarice, stands in close relation to this process. These traits, belonging to the clinical phenomena of the anal character, are built up on the ruins of an oral erotism that has miscarried in development. Here only one path of this defective development will be described. The preceding description will suffice to show how dependent is our understanding of the anal character on adequate knowledge of the preceding stages of development.

We will pass on to consider the direct contributions rendered by oral erotism to the formation of character; an example from daily psycho-analytical observation will furnish an illustration.

Neurotic parsimony, which may be developed to the point of avarice, is often met with in people who are inhibited from properly earning a livelihood; the anal sources of character-formation provide no explanation of this. What we find here is an inhibition of the craving for objects, which indicates that the libido has under-gone some special vicissitude. The pleasure in acquiring desired objects seems here repressed in favour of pleasure in holding fast to existing posessions. People in whom we find this inhibition are regularly burdened with a pronounced anxiety lest they should lose the most trifling of their possessions. Anxiety regarding such losses prevents them from devoting themselves to the earning of money, and renders them in many ways helpless towards practical life. We shall understand such a type of character-formation better if we take related phenomena for comparison.

In certain other cases the *entire* character-formation is under oral influence, but this can only be proved after a penetrating analysis. According to my experience in these cases we are here concerned with persons in whom the sucking period was undisturbed and highly pleasurable. They have brought with them from this happy period a deeply rooted conviction that it will always be well with them. They face life with an imperturbable optimism which often helps them to actual attainment of practical aims. There are also less favourable types of development here. Some people are dominated by an expectation that there must be a good person caring for them, a representative of the mother, of course, from whom they will receive everything necessary in life. This optimistic belief in fate actually condemns them to inactivity. We again recognize them as people who were overindulged in the sucking period. Their whole conduct in life shows that they expect the mother's breast to flow for them eternally, so to speak. These people expect to make no kind of effort, in some cases they actually disdain undertaking any bread-winning occupation.

This optimism, whether it occurs in connection with energetic conduct in life or as in the last-mentioned aberration with indiffer-ence to worldly matters, stands in noteworthy contrast to a phenomenon of the anal character that has not been sufficiently appreciated up to the present. I refer to a melancholic seriousness which passes over into marked pessimism. I have to point out, however, that this trait is for the most part not directly of anal origin, but originates in the disappointment of oral desires in the earliest years. Here the optimistic belief described above in the benevolence of fate is completely absent. On the contrary, these persons perpetually show an apprehensive attitude towards life, and, moreover, have a tendency to make the worst of everything and find undue difficulties in the simplest undertakings.

The influence of character-formation which is thus rooted in oral erotism shows itself in the entire conduct of the individual, and makes itself felt in his choice of profession, his predilections, and his hobbies. The type of neurotic official who is only able to exist when all the circumstances of his life have been prescribed for him once and for all may be mentioned as an example. To him the necessary condition of life is that his means of sustenance should be guaranteed to him up to the day of his death. He renounces any possibility of improving his position in favour of a secure and regularly flowing source of income.

So far we have dealt with certain people whose entire character-formation is explained by the gratified state of their libido in the oral stage of development in infancy. In psycho-analytic work, however, we observe other individuals who are burdened throughout their whole life with the after-effects of an ungratified sucking period. In the character of these people there is not the least trace of any such development.

In their social conduct these people always seem to be asking for something, in which they vary between making modest requests and assertive demands. The manner in which they bring forward their wishes has something in the nature of persistent sucking about it; they are as little to be put off by hard facts as by reasoned arguments, but continue to plead and to insist. One might say that they incline to suck "like leeches". They are particularly sensitive to being alone, even for a short time. Impatience is a marked characteristic with them. In certain persons psycho-analytic investigation reveals a regression from the oral-sadistic to the sucking stage; in them the conduct described is found intermixed with a cruel trait which makes them something like vampires in their attitude to other people.

In the same people we meet certain traits of character which we have to trace back to a peculiar displacement within the oral sphere. The longing to experience gratification by way of sucking has changed in them to a need to *give* by way of the mouth. We find here beside the persistent longing to obtain everything a constant urge to communicate orally to other people. An obstinate urge to talk thus results, and in most cases a feeling of overflowing is connected with it; these persons have the impression that their flow of thought is inexhaustible, and they ascribe to their utterances in speech either a special influence or an unusual value. In such cases the principal relation to other people is effected by the way of oral discharge. The obstinate insistence described above naturally occurs chiefly by means of speech; the same function serves at the same time for the act of giving, however. I could regularly establish that these people were unable to keep a curb on other activities just as they were on their speaking. Thus one frequently finds in them a neurotically exaggerated need to urinate, which often becomes noticeable simultaneously with an outburst of talking or directly after it.

In those phenomena of character-formation which belong to the oral-sadistic stage, too, speaking takes over representation of repressed impulses from another quarter. In certain neurotics the hostile tendency in speech is especially striking; in this instance it serves the unconscious purpose of killing the adversary. Psycho-analysis has demonstrated in such cases that in place of a violent attack by way of biting and devouring a milder form of aggression has appeared, though the mouth is still utilized as the organ of it. In certain neurotics speaking is used to express the entire range of instinctual trends, whether friendly or hostile, social or asocial, and irrespective of the sphere of impulse to which they originally belonged. In these people the impulsion to talk signifies desiring as well as attacking, killing, or annihilating, and at the same time every kind of bodily evacuation, including the act of fertilization. Speaking, in the phantasies of such people, is subject to the narcis-sistic valuation which the unconscious applies to all physical and psychical productions. The entire conduct here described puts such persons in a particularly striking contrast to reticent people with anal character-formation.

Such observations most emphatically draw our attention to the varieties and differences existing in the realm of oral character-formation. The field which we are investigating is anything but strictly limited or poor in variations. The most important differ-ences are, however, dependent on whether a phenomenon of character has developed on the basis of the erlier or the later oral stage, whether, in other words, it is the expression of an uncon-scious tendency to suck or to bite. In the latter case we shall find in connection with such a character-trait the most marked phenomena of ambivalence, positive and negative cravings of instinct, hostile and friendly tendencies, while we may assume on the basis of our experience that the character-traits derived from the stage of sucking are still not subjected to ambivalence. This fundamental difference, according to my observations, extends to the most trifling peculiarities in the conduct of life. At a meeting of the British Psychological Society (Medical Section) Dr Edward Glover recently read a paper in which he took these contrasts into particular consideration.[2]

Very significant contrasts in the character-formation of different individuals are to be traced psycho-analytically from the decisive influences on the process of formation of character exercised in one case by oral, in the other case by anal, impulses. Similarly, the connection of sadistic elements with the discharge of libido pertaining to the erotogenic zones is of considerable significance. A few examples which serve only for illustration, but do not aim at completeness, may verify this. In our psycho-analyses we are able to trace manifestations of very intense craving and effort back to the primary oral stage; it need hardly be mentioned that the participation of other sources of impulse in this should by no means be overlooked. But the desires derived from that earliest stage are still free from the tendency towards destruction of objects which is characteristic of the impulses of the next stage.

The covetous impulses which are derived from the second oral stage are the antithesis of the modesty in demands which we meet so frequently as a phenomenon of the anal character. It is true here that the weakness of the inclination to get and acquire is made up for by the obstinacy in holding fast to possessions which has been mentioned already.

Characteristic, too, are the differences in the inclination to share one's own possessions with others. Generosity is frequently found as an oral character-trait; the orally gratified person is here identifying himself with the lavish mother. It is different at the next oral-sadistic stage, where envy, hostility and jealousy make such behaviour impossible. If, therefore, in many cases generous or envious behaviour is derived from one of the two oral stages of development, the tendency to covetousness, known already to us, corresponds to the following anal-sadistic stage of development of character.

There are noteworthy differences in social conduct, too, according to the stage of development of the libido from which the formation of character is derived. People who were gratified in the earliest stage are bright and sociable; persons fixated at the oral-sadistic stage are hostile and snappy, while moroseness, inaccessibility and reticence go with the anal character.

Further, persons with oral character are accessible to new ideas, in a favourable as well as an unfavourable sense, while conservative behaviour opposed to all innovations belongs to the anal character; though this certainly also prevents hasty abandonment of what has proved good.

A similar contrast exists between the impatient importunity, haste and restlessness of people with oral character-formation, and the perseverance and persistence of the anal character, which, on the other hand, certainly also tends to procrastination and hesitation.

The character-trait of ambition, which we meet with so frequently in our psycho-analyses, Freud[3] derived long ago from urethral erotism. This explanation, however, does not seem to have penetrated to its deepest sources. According to my experience, and also to that of Dr Edward Glover, this is rather a character-trait of oral origin which is later reinforced from other sources, among which the urethral should be particularly mentioned.

Further, it has to be noted that certain contributions to character-formation originating in the earliest oral stages coincide in important respects with some derived from the final genital stages, which is probably to be explained from the fact that at these two stages there is less danger of disturbance to the libido by ambivalence.

In many people we find, beside the oral character-traits described, other psychological manifestations which we have to derive from the same instinctual sources, namely, impulses which have escaped any social transformation. As examples a morbidly intense appetite for food and the inclination to various kinds of oral perversion are especially to be mentioned. Further, we meet many kinds of neurotic symptoms which are determined orally, and finally also phenomena which have come into being by the path of sublimation. These latter products deserve a separate investigation, which, however, would exceed the limits of this paper; hence a single example only can be briefly mentioned.

The displacement of the infantile pleasure in sucking to the intellectual sphere is of great practical significance. Curiosity, the pleasure in observing, receives important reinforcements from this source, and this not only in childhood, but also during the whole of life. In persons with a special inclination towards observing nature, and towards many branches of scientific investigation, psycho-analysis proves a close connection between these impulses and repressed oral craving.

A glance into the workshop of scientific investigation enables us to recognize how impulses pertaining to the different erotogenic zones must support and supplement one another, if the most favourable results possible are to be achieved. The optimum is reached when an intensive imbibing of observations is combined with ample tenacity, ability to "digest" the collected facts, and a sufficiently strong impulse to give them back to the world provided this does not occur with undue haste. Psycho-analytical practice enables us to recognize various kinds of divergences from this opti-mum. Thus there are people with an intense mental capacity for absorbing, who, however, are inhibited in production. Others again produce in too much of a hurry. It is no exaggeration to say of such people that what they have scarcely taken in comes out of their mouths again immediately. When they are analysed it often proves that these same persons tend to vomit food that has just been taken. They are people who show the most extreme neurotic impatience; a satisfactory combination of forward-pushing oral impulses with retarding anal ones is lacking in their character-formation.

It seems to me particularly important, in conclusion, to allude once more to the significance of such combinations. In the normal formation of character we invariably find derivatives from all the original sources happily combined with one another.

It is important, moreover, to consider the numerous possibilities of such combinations because it prevents us from overestimating some one particular point of view, although this may be an impor-tant one. If we consider the problems of character-formation from the one large unifying point of view which psycho-analysis affords us, from that of infantile sexuality, then it is obvious "how every-thing weaves itself into a whole" in the characterological sphere. The realm of infantile sexuality extends over and includes entirely opposite aspects. It involves the entire unconscious instinctual life of the mature human being. Likewise it is the scene of the very important mental impressions of the earliest years, among which we also have to reckon prenatal influences. Sometimes we may feel dismayed in face of the mass of phenomena which meets us in the wide field of human mental life, from the play of children and other typical products of the early activity of phantasy, from the development of interests and talents, up to the most highly valued achievements of mature human beings and the most extreme differences in single individuals. But then let us remember the man who has given us the instrument for this investigation, psycho-analysis, and thereby opened to us the way to infantile sexuality, this living source of life.

Notes

1. *Internationale Zeitschrift für Psychoanalyse*, Bd. VII, 1921, S. 171.
2. "The significance of the mouth in psycho-analysis", *British Journal of Medical Psychology*, Vol. IV, Part 2, 1924.
3. "Character and anal erotism" (1908), *Collected Papers*, Vol. II, 1924.

Character-formation on the genital level of libido-development*[1]

Karl Abraham

In the two phases of development already discussed[2] we were able to recognize *archaic types of character-formation*. They represent in the life of the individual recapitulations of primitive states which the human race has passed through at certain stages of its development. Here, as in general in biology, we find the rule holding good that the individual repeats in an abbreviated form the history of his ancestors. Accordingly, in normal circumstances the individual will traverse those early stages of character-formation in a relatively short space of time. In this chapter I shall give in very rough outline an idea of the way in which the character of men and women in its definitive form is built up on those early foundations.

According to the traditional view, character is defined as the direction habitually taken by a person's voluntary impulses. It is not part of the intention of this paper to spend much time

* Article citation:
Abraham, K. (1926). Character-formation on the genital level of libido-development. *International Journal of Psychoanalysis*, 7: 214–222.

in finding an exact definition of character. We shall, however, find it advisable not to be too much influenced by the "habit" of attributing great importance to the direction usually taken by these impulses of the will. For our previous discussions have already made it clear that character is a changeable thing. We shall therefore do better not to make their duration and permanence an essential criterion of character-traits. It will be sufficient for our purposes to say that we consider the character of a person to be the sum of his instinctive reactions towards his social environment.

We have already seen that in early life the child reacts to the external world purely on the basis of its instincts. It is only by degrees that it overcomes to some extent its egoistic impulses and its narcissism and takes the step towards object-love. And, as we know, attainment of this stage of development coincides with another important event, namely, attainment of the highest level of libidinal organization—the genital level, as it is called. Believing as we do that the character-traits of men and women have their origin in definite instinctual sources, we should naturally expect that the development of a person's character would only be complete when his libido has reached its highest stage of organization and has achieved the capacity for object-love. And in fact Freud's view, that a person's sexual attitude is reflected in the whole trend of his mental attitude in general, finds complete confirmation by all the facts observed in this field as well.

In the first of these three essays it has been shown in detail that the individual is able to fill his place and exercise his powers fully and satisfactorily in his social environment only if his libido has attained the genital stage. But we have not as yet given special attention to that process which consists in the transition from the second stage of character-formation to the third and final one.

The first function of this third stage in the formation of character is of course to get rid of the remaining traces of the more primitive stages of development, in so far as they are unfavourable to the social behaviour of the individual. For he will not, for instance, be able to achieve a tolerant and fair-minded attitude to other people and to interests outside his own, until he has got the better of his destructive and hostile impulses springing from sadistic sources, or of his avarice and mistrust derived from anal ones.

We shall therefore examine with great interest the process by means of which such a transformation takes place.

An overwhelming abundance of material connected with the processes we have grouped under the general heading of the Oedipus complex presents itself to us, and draws our attention to this class of mental events. If we confine ourselves to the case of the male child, we find that the most powerful sources of affect in early years consist in his erotic desire for his mother and his wish to put his father out of the way. And closely allied to them are his ideas about castration. If he can successfully master the emotions centred round this subject it will have a decisive effect on the form taken by his character. I shall content myself with a very brief survey of this question, since I can refer the reader to the paper by Alexander, already published,[3] on the relations between character and the castration-complex. Generally speaking, we may say that when the child has been able to subdue his Oedipus complex with all its constituents he has made the most important step towards overcoming his original narcissism and his hostile tendencies; and at the same time he has broken the power of the pleasure-principle to dominate the conduct of his life.

At this point I will dwell in greater detail on a particular aspect of this process of change, since its significance for the formation of character has as yet received hardly any attention. This is the extensive alteration which takes place in the boy's attitude towards the body of persons of the opposite sex, i.e. in the first instance towards that of his mother. Originally her body was to him an object of mingled curiosity and fear; in other words, it aroused ambivalent feelings in him; but gradually he achieves a libidinal cathexis of his love-object as a whole, that is, with the inclusion of those parts of it which had formerly aroused these contrary feelings in him. If this has been achieved there arise in him expressions of his libidinal relation to his object that are inhibited in their aim—feelings of fondness, devotion and so on—and these co-exist with his directly erotic desires for it. And indeed, during the boy's latency period, these "aim-inhibited" sentiments predominate over his sensual feelings. If the child's development continues to be normal, these new sentiments that have been established towards his mother next become carried over to his father. They gradually extend their field and the child adopts a friendly and well-wishing attitude, first to persons of his near environment, and then to the community at large. This process seems to me to be a very important basis for the final and definitive formation of a person's character. It occurs at the time at which the individual passes out of that phase of his libidinal development which Freud has called the phallic stage. It implies that he has attained a point in his object-relations where he no longer has an ambivalent attitude towards the genital organ of his heterosexual object, but recognizes it as a part of that object whom he loves as an entire person.

Whereas on the earlier levels of character-development the interests of the individual and those of the community ran counter to one another, on the genital level the interests of both coincide to a great extent.

We are thus led to the conclusion that the definitive character developed in each individual is dependent upon the history of his Oedipus complex and particularly on the capacity he has developed for transferring his friendly feelings on to other people or on to his whole environment. If he has failed in this, if he has not succeeded in sufficiently developing his social feelings, a marked disturbance of his character will be the direct consequence. Among our patients, with every aspect of whose mental life we become acquainted in psycho-analytic treatment, there are a great number who are suffering in a greater or less degree from disturbances of this kind. The history of their early childhood never fails to show that certain circumstances occurred to prevent the development of these social feelings. We always find that the sexual impulses of such people are unaccompanied by any desire for affectionate relations. And, similarly, in their daily life they have difficulties in getting a proper contact of feeling with other people. How greatly such a favourable development of character from a social point of view depends upon the degree to which these "affectionate" instinctual components develop is most clearly seen in a class of persons whose childhood has been in especial stamped by the circumstances of their birth. I refer to illegitimate children. From the very beginning these have suffered from a want of sympathy and affection from the people about them. If a child has no examples of love before it, it will have difficulty in entertaining any such feelings itself, and it will besides be incapable of discarding those primitive impulses which are originally directed *against* the external world. And thus it will readily succumb to an unsocial attitude. We see the same thing happen with the neurotic patient who, though born and educated in the usual circumstances, feels that he is not loved, that he is the "Cinderella" of the family.

Since we are on the topic of the definitive stage of character-formation, it may be as well to obviate a possible misunderstanding. It is not the intention of this discussion to say what exactly a "normal" character is. Psycho-analysis has never set up norms of this sort, but contents itself with ascertaining psychological facts. It simply ascertains how far an individual or a group of persons has managed to travel along the line of development from the earliest stage to the latest in the structure of their character. It is precisely analytic experience which teaches us that even the most complete characterological development in a social sense merely represents a *relative* success in overcoming the more primitive types of formation, and that individual circumstances of an internal and external nature determine how completely the final aim will be achieved or how far that achievement will be a lasting one.

In 1913 Freud drew attention to the case of a female patient in whom at the time of the menopause there appeared, side by side with neurotic symptoms, certain phenomena of involution of character.[4] This was the first time that such an observation had been made. We look upon neurotic symptoms as products of a regression in the psychosexual sphere. By uniting both processes under the general heading of regression, Freud was able to explain why a change in character takes place at the same time as neurotic symptoms are formed. This observation of Freud's has since been often confirmed. But it is not only at one particular period of life that a person's character is denpendent upon the general position of his libido; that dependence exists at every age. The proverb which says "Youth knows not virtue" (*"Jugend kennt keine Tugend"*) is expressing the truth that in early life character is still without definite form or stability. Nevertheless, we should not overestimate the fixity of character even in later years, but ought rather to bear in mind certain psychological facts which I shall briefly touch upon now.

It was Freud who first pointed out that important changes can take place at any time in the mental make-up of the individual through the process of introjection. Women in particular tend to assimilate their character to that of the man with whom they are living. And when they change their love-object it can happen that they change their character accordingly. It is, moreover, worth noticing that husband and wife who have lived long together tend to resemble one another in character.

Psycho-analysts are familiar with the fact that when a neurosis sets in it can bring with it a regressive change of character; conversely, that an improvement in the neurosis can be accompanied by a change of character in a progressive direction. Some time ago[5] I was able to point out that in the intervals between the periodical return of symptoms persons suffering from cyclical disorders exhibit a character similar to that of obsessional neurotics, so that according to our view they progress from the oral to the anal-sadistic level.

But there are other reasons why we cannot set up a norm for character. As we know, individuals show extraordinarily wide variations in character, according to their social class, nationality and race. We need only consider how widely nations or groups of people differ from one another in their sense of order, love of truth, industry, and other mental qualities. But, besides this, each group of people will vary in its behaviour at different times. A single nation, for instance, has changed its conceptions of cleanliness, economy, justice, etc., more than once in the course of its history. Observation has shown, furthermore, that alterations in the external circumstances of a people, a social class and so on, can entail radical changes in its dominating characteristics. The effect of the Great War in this respect is still fresh in our memory. Thus we see that, as soon as suitable alterations take place in their internal or external relations, a group of people shows the same mutability of character as an individual.

In the two preceding papers I have shown how the final stage of character-formation is built up on earlier phases of its development and absorbs into itself essential elements of these former phases. And we were led to attribute special importance in the formation of character to the various vicissitudes which befall the Oedipus complex. So that to set up a fixed norm for human character would be to deny, not only the already acknowledged fact that character is variable, but also all that we know about the way in which such variations arise.

We should be inclined to consider as normal in the social sense a person who is not prevented by any too great eccentricity in his character from adapting himself to the interests of the community. But a description like this is very elastic and allows room for a great number of variations. From the social point of view all that is required is that the character-traits of the individual should not be pushed to an excess; that he should be able, for instance, to find some sort of mean between the extremes of cruelty and over-kindness or between those of avarice and extravagance. We ought above all to avoid the mistake of setting up a norm in regard to the ratio in which the various mental qualities should be combined in any person. It need hardly be said that by this we are not intending to proclaim the ideal of the "golden mean" in all the relations of man to his surroundings.

It follows from what has been said that there is no absolute line of demarcation between the different kinds of character-formation. Nevertheless in practice we do find that they fall fairly naturally into distinct classes.

The best subjects for psycho-analytic investigation are those patients who exchange certain character-traits for others from time to time under the direct observation of the analyst. One young man who came to me for analysis gradually changed his attitude to such an extent under the influence of treatment that he quite got rid of certain markedly unsocial features of his character. Before that he had been unfriendly, ill-disposed, overbearing and grasping in his relation to others, and in fact had exhibited a great number of oral and anal characteristics. This attitude changed more and more as time went on. But at certain irregular intervals violent resistances appeared and were accompanied every time by a temporary relapse into that archaic phase of character-development which he had by now partly given up. On those occasions he would become disagreeable and hostile in his behaviour, and overbearing and contemptuous in his speech. From having conducted himself in a friendly and polite manner he became suspicious and irritable. While his resistance lasted all his friendly feelings towards his fellowmen—including his analyst—ceased, and he took up a completely opposite attitude towards the external world. At the same time as he reacted in this way with aversion and hate for human beings, he centred his desires in an unmeasured degree on inanimate objects. His whole interest was absorbed in buying things. In this way he set up as much as possible a relationship of *possession* between himself and his environment. During this time he was filled with fear that something belonging to him might get lost or stolen. His whole attitude to the external world was thus dominated by ideas of possession, acquisition and possible loss. Directly his resistance began to diminish his oral character-trait of covetousness and his anal one of avarice in regard to objects retreated into the background, and he began once more to entertain personal relationships towards other people and normal feelings about them which continued to develop.

Cases of this kind are particularly instructive, not only because they show the connection between certain features of character and a particular level of libidinal organization, but also because they are evidence of the mutability of character; they show that the character of a person can on occasion rise to a higher level of development or sink to a lower one.

The final stage of character-formation shows traces everywhere of its association with the preceding stages. It borrows from them whatever conduces to a favourable relation between the individual and his objects. From the early oral stage it takes over a forward-pushing energy; from the anal stage, endurance, perseverance and various other characteristics; from sadistic sources, the necessary power to carry on the struggle for existence. If the development of his character has been successful the individual is able to avoid falling into pathological exaggerations of those characteristics, whether in a positive or a negative direction. He is able to keep his impulses under control without being driven to a complete disavowal of his instincts, as is the obsessional neurotic. The sense of justice may serve as an illustration; in a case of favourable development this character-trait is not carried to an excessive pitch of punctiliousness, so that it is not liable to break out in a violent way on some trivial occasion. We have only to think of the many actions done by obsessional neurotics in the way of "fairness": suppose the right hand has made a movement or touched an object, the left hand must do the same. We have already said that ordinary friendly feelings remain entirely distinct from exaggerated forms of neurotic over-kindness. And similarly it is possible to steer a middle course between the two pathological extremes of either delaying everything or always being in too great a hurry; or of either being over-obstinate or too easily influenced. As regards material goods, the compromise arrived at is that the individual respects the interests of others up to a certain point, but at the same time secures his own existence. He preserves to some extent the aggressive impulses necessary for the maintenance of his life. And a considerable portion of his sadistic instincts is employed no longer for destructive but for constructive purposes.

In the course of this general alteration of character, as presented here in rough outline, we also observe that the individual achieves a steady conquest of his narcissism. In its earlier stages his character was still in a large measure governed by his narcissistic impulses. And we cannot deny that in its definitive stage it still contains a certain proportion of such impulses. Observation has taught us that no developmental stage, each of which has its organic basis, is ever entirely surmounted or completely obliterated. On the contrary, each new product of development possesses characteristics derived from its earlier history. Nevertheless, even though the primitive signs of self-love are to some extent preserved in it, we may say that the definitive stage of character-formation is *relatively* unnarcissistic.

Another change of great importance in the formation of character is that in which the individual overcomes his attitude of ambivalence (I speak again in a relative sense). Instances have already been given to show in what way a person's character avoids extremes on either side after it has attained its final stage of development. I should also like to draw attention here to the fact that as long as a severe conflict of ambivalent feelings continues to exist in the character there is always a danger both for the person concerned and for his environment that he may suddenly swing over from one extreme to its opposite.

Thus if a person is to develop his character more or less up to that point which we have taken to be its highest level, he must possess a sufficient quantity of affectionate and friendly feeling. A development of this sort goes hand in hand with a relatively successful conquest of his narcissistic attitude and his ambivalence.

We have seen that the customary view of character-formation did not give us any real clue to the sources of that process as a whole. Psycho-Analysis, on the other hand, based on empirical observation, has demonstrated the close connection that character-formation has with the psychosexual development of the child; in especial with the different libidinal stages and with the successive relations of the libido to its object. And, furthermore, psycho-analysis has taught us that even after childhood the character of the individual is subject to processes of evolution and involution.

In psycho-analysis we view abnormal character in close and constant relation to all the other manifestations of the person's psycho-sexual life. This and the fact that character is not a fixed thing, even in adults, make it possible for us to exert a corrective influence upon pathological character-formations. Psycho-Analysis is by no means simply confronted with the task of curing neurotic symptoms in the narrow sense of the word. It often has to deal with pathological deformities of character at the same time, or even in the first instance. So far our experience goes to show that the analysis of character is one of the most difficult pieces of work which the analyst can undertake, but that it has undoubtedly proved in some cases to be the most repaying. At present, however, we are not in a position to make any general judgement about the therapeutic results of character-analysis; that we must leave to future experience.

Notes

1. Chapter III of *Psychoanalytische Studien zur Charakterbildung*, 1925.
2. Chapter I, "Contributions to the theory of the anal character", *International Journal of Psychoanalysis*, Vol. IV, Pt. 4. Chapter II, "The influence of oral erotism on character-formation", *International Journal of Psychoanalysis*, Vol. VI, Pt. 3.
3. "The castration complex in the formation of character", *International Journal of Psychoanalysis*, Vol. IV, Pt. 1.
4. "The predisposition to obsessional neurosis", *Collected Papers*, Vol. II.
5. *Versuch einer Entwicklungsgeschichte der Libido*, 1924, Chapter I and elsewhere.

CHAPTER SIX

Super-ego

Jones, Ernest (1926). The origin and structure of the super-ego. *International Journal of Psychoanalysis*, 7: 303–311.

From 1913 Freud was interested in the phenomenon of guilt (Freud, 1912–1913, 1916d, 1917e). His interest arose as a problem not fully explained by his early theory of anxiety and libidinal energy. He eventually solved this problem with his structural model (Freud, 1923b) and the notion of the "super-ego" arising as a formation of identity from the introjection of primary objects. For many of his colleagues, the super-ego was a difficult concept to reconcile with his earlier sexual theories and the Oedipus complex. Freud was driven to amplify his idea that the super-ego is heir to the Oedipus complex a year later (Freud, 1924d). He also believed he had settled a range of other problems with his theory of the super-ego.

Jones (1926*), in the paper republished here, subjected the concept to careful and sometimes sceptical scrutiny. He was not the only analyst to do so, but his was the most magisterial statement. He asked a number of questions, including: how can the same institution present itself to the id to be loved instead of the parents and also as an active force criticizing the ego? If the super-ego is the internalization of a primary object, would not the surrendered object be that of the opposite sex? If the super-ego is a moral agent derived from the loved parents, why does it promote its influence with immoral sadistic means?

Others (Abraham, 1924; Alexander, 1929; Ferenczi, 1925; James Glover, 1926; Klein, 1927, 1933; Rado, 1925; Reik, 1924) also had questions or alternative points of view. The evident harshness of the super-ego was widely considered. The serious threat that backs the power of the super-ego is castration but, as Stephen (1999 [1946]) dryly observed, it is unlikely that most children have witnessed an actual parent conducting a castration. Alexander (1929) reflected on the origins of the super-ego in the death instinct rather than from introjected real objects. Ferenczi (1925), Glover (1925) and Abraham (1924) were interested in the pre-genital aspects of morality, and the oral- and anal-sadistic elements in an agency of mind that derives from genital phallicism. The wide critical appraisal of the super-ego concept demonstrates the difficulty for loyal analysts at the time to accept such a radical departure in Freud's views as the structural model of the id, ego, and super-ego. Stephen, in 1946, argued on the basis that maturity is a respect for reality, that the super-ego is a pathological construction since it is based on the unrealistic belief in imminent castration. Such a penetrating criticism, and its credibility, leaves the concept somewhat bruised (Stephen, 1999).

Jones's paper typifies this unease about Freud's concept and in a way is a model of how the questions could be asked of Freud. Despite the uncertainties and questions, the development of the theory of the super-ego has contributed to understanding masochism, guilt, character formation, psychosis, and other psychoanalytic puzzles. However, the question that remains is whether there are particular inconsistencies in the theory, inconsistencies which therefore underlie the wide range of items in psychoanalytic metapsychology that the structural model explained.

It is unusual for the super-ego to be challenged or debated now, and it appears to be a permitted area where various views on a concept may co-exist, as if unnoticed. Many of the problems were discussed over the years, but without Freud's authoritative voice there appears to be no arbiter between competing views and, as in many theoretical developments, progress is shaped like an evolutionary tree rather than a linear progression of knowledge. Jones's paper would be a good start for a review of the steady march towards pluralism in psychoanalytic theory, as well as a current critical reappraisal of the super-ego concept.

References

Abraham, K. (1973) [1924]. A short study of the development of the libido, viewed in the light of mental disorders. In: K. Abraham (Ed.), *Selected Papers on Psychoanalysis* (pp. 418–501). London: Hogarth.

Alexander, F. (1929). The need for punishment and the death-instinct. *International Journal of Psychoanalysis*, 10: 256–269.

Ferenczi, S. (1925). Psycho-analysis of sexual habits. *International Journal of Psychoanalysis*, 6: 372–404.

Freud, S. (1912–1913). *Totem and Taboo. S.E.*, 13: 1–162. London: Hogarth Press.

Freud, S. (1916d). Some character-types met with in psycho-analytic work. *S.E.*, 14: 311–333. London: Hogarth Press.

Freud, S. (1917e). Mourning and melancholia. *S.E.*, 14: 237–260. London: Hogarth Press.

Freud, S. (1923b). *The Ego and the Id. S.E.*, 19: 1–60. London: Hogarth Press.

Freud, S. (1924d). The dissolution of the Oedipus complex. *S.E.*, 19: 173–179. London: Hogarth Press

Glover, E. (1925). Notes on oral character formation. *International Journal of Psychoanalysis*, 6: 131–154.

Glover, J. (1926). The conception of the ego. *International Journal of Psychoanalysis*, 7: 414–419.

Jones, E. (1926). The origin and structure of the super-ego. *International Journal of Psychoanalysis*, 7: 303–311.

Klein, M. (1927). Criminal tendencies in normal children. *British Journal of Medical Psychology*, 7: 177–192.

Klein, M. (1933). The early development of conscience in the child. In: S. Lorand (Ed.), *Psychoanalysis Today* (pp. 64–74). New York: Covici-Friede.

Rado, S. (1925). The economic principle in psycho-analytic technique. *International Journal of Psychoanalysis*, 6: 35–44.

Reik, T. (1924). Psycho-analysis of the unconscious sense of guilt. *International Journal of Psychoanalysis*, 5: 439–450.

Stephen, K. (1999) [1946]. Relations between the superego and the ego. *Psychoanalysis and History*, 2: 11–28.

The origin and structure of the super-ego*

Ernest Jones

It is desirable to state clearly at the outset that this paper is of a
peculiarly tentative character. The special occasion for which it was
written, and the exigency of a time limit, induced me to attack an
intricate theme when my own opinions about it are the very reverse
of mature. Indeed, the essential object of the present contribution is
merely to define a little more closely some of the complex problems
involved and to invite further discussion of them; I would attach
only a very restricted validity to any positive suggestions that may
emerge in the course of the present remarks. The subject itself is
concerned with one of the most important contributions that Freud
has made to the science of psycho-analysis he created, and the spec-
tacle of the following attempt to apprehend his latest teachings will
serve as well as any other to illustrate the ever-pioneering nature of
Freud's work and the fact that his mind remains the youngest and
freshest of any among us.

---

* Article citation:
Jones, E. (1926). The origin and structure of the super-ego. *International
Journal of Psychoanalysis*, 7: 303–311.

The particular problem to be considered here is that of the origin and actual structure of the super-ego, that is, the nature and genesis of the various trends composing it. As Freud himself says, "In other matters—for instance, concerning the origin and function of the super-ego—a good deal remains insufficiently elucidated".[1]

As to the validity and value of the conception itself there will be universal agreement, for the reasons Freud gave when he postulated it can be definitely confirmed in any character analysis, and perhaps in any properly completed analysis. Further, a number of formulations in regard to it would appear to be equally well established. Thus, the genesis of the super-ego is certainly connected with the passing of the Oedipus complex, and the nuclear and essential part of its composition may be regarded as the direct imprint made on the personality by the conflicts relating to this complex;[2] Freud neatly designates it as the heir of the Oedipus complex.[3] Much is known also about the relation of the super-ego to the outer world and to the other institutions of the mind. The function it exercises is perhaps its clearest feature. It is to criticise the ego and to cause pain to the latter whenever it tends to accept impulses proceeding from the repressed part of the *id*. In this connection we may note the improvement Freud has effected in the terminology relating to the idea of guilt. He would confine the expression "consciousness of guilt", or "sense of guilt", to the perception of guilt on the part of consciousness[4] and substitute that of "need for punishment" (*Strafbedürfnis*) when it concerns the unconscious ego, reserving "criticism" for the operation performed by the super-ego. The relation of both these active and passive aspects of the phenomenon to consciousness, however, is a very variable one; either or both may be unconscious, the latter more often than the former.[5]

When, however, we leave these valuable broad generalizations and come to a closer study of the problems involved, a considerable number of awkward questions present themselves. To mention only a few at this point: How can we conceive of the same institution as being both an object that presents itself to the *id* to be loved instead of the parents[6] and as an active force criticising the ego? If the super-ego arises from incorporating the abandoned love-object,[7] how comes it that in fact it is more often derived from the parent of the same sex? If it is composed of elements taken from the "moral" non-sexual ego-instincts, as we should expect from the part it plays in the repression of the sexual incestuous ones, whence does it derive its sadistic, i.e. sexual, nature? These and many other apparent contradictions need to be resolved. Finally, there is every reason to think that the concept of the super-ego is a nodal point where we may expect all the obscure problems of Oedipus complex and narcissism on the one hand, and hate and sadism on the other, to meet.

Before taking up the problems concerning the origin and structure of the super-ego, it is necessary to say something about its general relations, particularly the topographical ones. *Relation to the outer world, the ego and the id.* The ego is the part of the *id* that is altered by the influence of the outer world, and the super-ego is a differentiated part of the ego,[8] again one brought about under the influence of the outer world. On the one hand we read[9] that the super-ego stands nearer to the *id* than does the ego, is independent of the latter and represents to it the demands of the *id*, though the *id* can also influence the ego directly as well as through the super-ego.[10] On the other hand it is just through its connection with the outer world, the reality demands of which it represents, that the super-ego gains its power of affecting the ego.[11] The full explanation seems to be that the super-ego in some obscure way combines influences from both the inner and the outer world, from the *id* and from external reality, and that these are then directed towards the ego.[12]

Relation to Consciousness.—Two statements of Freud's bear on this point. The super-ego may be for the greater part unconscious and inaccessible to the ego.[13] It dips deeply into the *id* and is therefore farther removed from consciousness than is the ego.[14] It is probable that the super-ego may be partly conscious, partly preconscious and partly unconscious; further that its relation to consciousness varies at different times. That it should be as a rule less conscious than is the ego may be explained by its relation to outer reality, for this relation was far closer in the past (in infancy) than it is in the present.

Relation to Repression.—It is the ego, not the super-ego, that performs the act of repression, though it commonly does so in obedience to the demands of the latter.[15] It is important, however, to note that, especially in hysteria, the ego can keep from consciousness, i.e. repress, the feeling of guilt provoked by the super-ego's attack on it.[16] It should be possible in the future to describe this in economic terms as a balance between different amounts of pleasure and pain.

Relation to External Love-object.—Freud writes:[17] "If a sexual object has to be given up, there is not infrequently brought about in its place the change in the ego which one must describe, for instance in melancholia, as an erecting of the object within the ego", and he adds "the nearer closer conditions of this replacement are not yet known to us." Throughout he appears to assume that the super-ego, which we know to be the heir of the Oedipus complex, results in this way from the incorporating of the parental figure that had to be given up in its sexual connection. But the evidence is fairly extensive that, though the super-ego may be derived from either parent and is commonly enough derived from both, it is normally and predominantly derived, not from the love-object that has been abandoned, but from the parent of the same sex. With the boy, for instance, it is derived in the main from the father, and when it is derived from the mother the chances are great that he will be homosexual. Freud himself points out this paradox,[18] but offers no explanation of it. The discussion of bisexuality that follows in the context doubtless explains the facts of there being two types and of their often being mixed, but it in no way accounts for the phenomenon of the more normal type in which the heterosexual person derives his super-ego from the parent of the same sex as himself. It would therefore seem that a necessary condition for the process of incorporation is that the object incorporated must have thwarted the love impulses of the subject.

If this reasoning is sound, then it can only be that the mechanism of super-ego formation normally follows the order which Freud has described in connection with the attitude of a homosexual towards his brothers,[19] namely, that original rivalry of a hostile kind was replaced by a friendly object-choice, which in its turn was replaced by identification. Applying this to the Oedipus situation, and taking again the case of the boy, we must assume that the super-ego usually arises from identification with the father where the initial hostile rivalry had been replaced by homosexual love. In the less usual and less normal case, that of the homosexual man, there are two possibilities open. Either the same mechanism as that just suggested holds good, which means that, the feminine component of his bisexuality being predominant, he deals with his jealous rivalry of his mother by a passing object love followed by identification with her, or else the identification is a means of dealing with hatred proceeding from the fact, characteristic of this type, that his castration fears are more closely connected with the mother than with the father. Both explanations accord with the law that the super-ego is derived from a thwarting object. The two explanations differ in that with the first congenital sexuality would be the ultimate cause of the undue reaction to the mother, with the second this might or might not be so.

It will be seen that here stress is laid on *hostility*[20] being the essential condition of super-ego formation. This one may relate to the predominantly sadistic nature of the later super-ego, a matter which will be discussed presently. To recapitulate for the sake of clearness: it is suggested that the super-ego is derived from the thwarting parent, irrespective of whether this happens to be the primary love-object or not; normally it is a secondary love-object, the parent of the same sex.

The replacement of object-cathexis by identification brings about a profound change in the libidinal situation. The image thus incorporated into the (super-) ego serves itself as an object to the libidinal impulses proceeding from the *id*, so that more of them are directed towards the ego as a whole than previously; this constitutes what Freud terms "secondary narcissism".[21] Along with this goes a desexualization of the impulses, a kind of sublimation, and this important process gives rise to interesting problems. Freud hints that it is due to the giving up of sexual aims implied in the change from allo-erotic into narcissistic libido. To quote his exact words: "The transformation of object-libido into narcissistic libido that takes place here evidently brings with it a giving up of sexual aims, a desexualization, i.e. a kind of sublimation."[22] But narcissistic libido is still sexual, as is even an impulse inhibited in its aim (affection), and both in moral masochism and in the obsessional neurosis we see that the impulses concerned with the super-ego need not be desexualized; it is plain, further, that there are all degrees of desexualization. So that there must be some further factors at work to account for this interesting change when it occurs.

Two further clues are provided elsewhere by Freud. In the first place he points out that the super-ego is not simply a residuum of the object-choices, but also signifies an energetic reaction-formation against them. "Its relation to the ego is not all comprehended in the exhortation 'You ought to be like the father'; it also includes the prohibition 'You may not be like the father' i.e., you may not do everything he does; many things are his prerogative".[23] In other words, the super-ego consists in the incorporation only of the "moral", thwarting, and asexual elements of the object. The allo-erotic libido of the subject's *id* somehow accomplishes the extra-ordinary feat of substituting this loveless image for the previous love-object; by some magic he manages to love with all the strength of his being just that which he had most reason to hate and fear. It is very possible, however, that from the wreckage of his own desires he is able by means of the identification with the father to save at least in a vicarious way the object-relation which the latter bears to the mother; if so, this vicarious gratification would have to be much deeper in the unconscious than the super-ego.

A second and more valuable clue is afforded by the following considerations. If we enquire into the actual composition of the super-ego, the most obvious constituent to be perceived is sadism,[24] usually desexualized. It is presumably to be accounted for as a pregenital regression of the libido that is no longer allowed to be directed towards the love-object; we know that regression is a common sequel to frustration. But this is only the result of a reaction on the part of the endangered ego, which yields to the (castration) threat to its integrity and defends itself by repression of the incestu-ous impulses. This threat to the primary narcissism must also mobilize the non-sexual ego-instincts, notably hate and fear, and probably all those which I have grouped under the name of "repul-sion instincts".[25] The problem that here arises is the relation of the two groups of instincts to each other—roughly speaking, of the hate group[26] to the love group. In *Das Ich und das Es*[27] Freud supposes that any previous connection between the two undergoes a process of "de-fusion". He takes for granted the desexualization of the libidinal impulses as a necessary consequence of the secondary narcissism and suggests that as the result of this desexualization the libido loses its power to bind the aggressive tendencies, which are therefore set free; hence the cruelty of the super-ego. To me at least an alternative hypothesis which he had previously put forward in the *Triebe und Triebschicksale* essay[28] appeals as more likely. In speaking of ambivalence he shows illuminatingly how the ego instincts and sexual instincts mutually influence each other, and how they can form a unity during the pregenital phases of libidinal organization. "When the sexual function is governed by the ego-instincts, as at the stage of the sadistic-anal organization, they impart the qualities of hate to the instinct's aim as well. . . . This admixture of hate in love is to be traced in part to those preliminary stages of love which have not been wholly outgrown, and in part is based upon reactions of aversion and repudiation on the part of the ego-instincts. . . . In both cases, therefore, the admixture of hate may be traced to the source of the self-preservation instincts. When a love-relationship with a given object is broken off, it is not infrequently succeeded by hate, so that we receive the impression of a transformation of love into hate. This descriptive characterization is amplified by the view that, when this happens, the hate which is motivated by considerations of reality is reinforced by a regression of the love to the sadistic preliminary stage, so that the hate acquires an erotic character and the continuity of a love-relation is ensured". One may ask whether this does not describe the changes that occur when the super-ego is formed. That would mean a fusion, rather than a de-fusion, of the two groups. And it may be that the secret of the desexualization of the libidinal impulses, perhaps also the preceding regression of them to the anal-sadistic level, will be found in the influence on them of the hate impulses (ego instincts in general). Whether this holds good for the desexualization and sublimation which Freud[29] suggests occurs at every identification is, of course, another matter. On the other side the libido would give an erotic colouring to the ego impulses, so that the hate would come to partake of the quality of sadism and fuse with the sadism resulting from libidinal regression.

We may now attempt to describe schematically the changes that ensue on the passing of the Oedipus complex and the replacement of it by the super-ego.

A. *Ego Instincts*. These "reactive" instincts are all stimulated by the unfriendly situation in the outer world (parents) that leads to the repression of the incestuous wishes. The hatred for the rival, the half of the Oedipus complex which is presently to be resolved by homosexual identification, arises later in time than these wishes.

Fear. The fear of castration constitutes the kernel of the dread which the ego displays in regard to the super-ego,[30] and this is evidently a displacement from the father. It is continued later as a sensitiveness to conscience, that is, as a sense of guilt.[31]

Hate. This is activated against whichever parent is felt to be the obstacle to the love impulses, whether that be the main love-object or not.

1. Part is repressed, but continues to be directed against the external object or subsequent substitutes for this.
2. Part fuses with the libidinal impulses and helps to give them their sadistic character. This part operates from the *id* via the super-ego and is directed against the actual ego whenever this tends to admit repressed libidinal or hate impulses of such a kind as to bring the risk of re-arousing the external disapproval and danger. This "turning round upon the subject" of impulses previously directed against the parent is a defensive procedure designed to avert the wrath of the parent; it is akin to the mechanism of the self-imposed penance among religious people.

B. *Sexual Instincts.* As was indicated above, the ego defends itself against external danger by repressing the genital impulses directed towards the love-object. Regression to the anal-sadistic level ensues, but the relation of this process to the frustration and to the influence of the ego instincts is not clear. The libido is then re-distributed as follows:[32]

1. A part continues to be directed to the parents, both heterosexually and homosexually, but as a form of libido "inhibited in its aim". This is the ordinary affection felt by the child for its parents. It is apt to be weakened whenever the parent's conduct falls below the standard set by the super-ego, i.e. whenever the identification of parent and super-ego is impaired. Where the affection consciously felt for the parent of the opposite sex is excessive one may suspect excessive identification with that parent, with subsequent homosexual subject-inversion (in Ferenczi's sense).
2. A part becomes secondary narcissism. This is another way in which the allo-erotic impulses can achieve indirect gratification,

for the super-ego towards which they are here directed is in great part a substitute for the parent. In the case where this parent is of the same sex, which is the most frequent one, a previous deflection has taken place from heterosexuality towards homosexuality.

3.   A part regresses and fuses with the hate instincts to constitute sadism. To begin with this is probably also directed from the *id* towards the super-ego, as a substitute for the hated parent, but it passes through the super-ego and is applied (apparently by it) to the ego itself. It operates in the way mentioned above in connection with hate. This part of the libido is normally desexualized, but the change varies greatly in completeness.

4.   It is probable that other active components of the libido follow the same course as the last group. Thus in the attitude of the super-ego towards the ego, particularly in regard to such matters as duty, order, and the like, it is hard not to see traces of the anal component of the anal-sadistic phase. Similarly scoptophilic elements may perhaps be concerned in the careful "watching" exercised over the ego.

We thus see that the super-ego arises as a compromise between the desire to love and the desire to be loved. On the one hand it provides an object for the libidinal impulses of the *id* when the external object is no longer available, whereas on the other hand it represents the renouncing of incest which is the only condition under which the parents' approval (i.e. affection) can be retained.

Notes

1.   *Collected Papers*, Vol. II, p. 250.
2.   *Das Ich und das Es*, 1923, S. 40, 60, etc.
3.   *Das Ich und das Es*, 1923, S. 43.
4   *Das Ich und das Es*, 1923, S. 68.
5.   *Collected Papers*, Vol. II, p. 266.
6.   *Das Ich und das Es*, S. 34.
7.   *Das Ich und das Es*, S. 33, etc.
8.   *Das Ich und das Es*, S. 27, 31.
9.   *Das Ich und das Es*, S. 43, 61, 67.

10. *Das Ich und das Es*, S. 72.
11. *Collected Papers*, Vol. II, pp. 251, 253.
12. *Collected Papers*, Vol. II, pp. 253, 264.
13. *Das Ich und das Es*, S. 47.
14. *Das Ich und das Es*, S. 61.
15. *Das Ich und das Es*, S. 66.
16. *Das Ich und das Es*, S. 66.
17. *Das Ich und das Es*, S. 33.
18. *Das Ich und das Es*, S. 38.
19. *Das Ich und das Es*, S. 45.
20. Cf. Freud's remarks on ambivalence in connection with melancholic identification (*Collected Papers*, Vol. IV, p. 161).
21. *Das Ich und das Es*, S. 34.
22. *Das Ich und das Es*, S. 34.
23. *Das Ich und das Es*, S. 40.
24. The finding is not surprising when one reflects how sadistic and persecutory even ordinary (outwardly directed) morality often is; in the formation of the super-ego we have an example of the "turning round upon the subject", which Freud described in connection with sadism as one of the vicissitudes of instincts (*Collected Papers*, Vol. IV, p. 70). Cf. *Das Ich und das Es*, S. 70, 71.
25. Trans. of the VII. International Congress of Psychology, 1924, p. 231.
26. Freud's "death instinct". I find myself unable to operate with this philosophical concept in a purely clinical discussion.
27. S. 71.
28. *Collected Papers*, Vol. IV, p. 82.
29. *Collected Papers*, Vol. II, p. 273.
30. *Das Ich und das Es*, S. 75.
31. *Das Ich und das Es*, S. 75.
32. It is doubtful if one can apply the term desexualization to the first two of these four groups.

The sense of reality

Ferenczi, Sandor (1926). The problem of acceptance of unpleasant ideas: advances in knowledge of the sense of reality. *International Journal of Psychoanalysis*, 7: 312–323.

Freud gave up his seduction theory to invent psychoanalysis as the investigation of the internal, or psychic, world. External reality was then viewed in a different way—not in terms of its impact on the patient, but in terms of the perceptions the patient had of external figures. The notion of an imago, or internal object (Abraham, 1924) came to the fore, and Freud became interested in the capacity for realistic recognition of external others, or the interruption or disabling of accurate recognition. He dealt with this in his "Formulations on the two principles of mental functioning" (Freud, 1911b). In 1913 Ferenczi argued that Freud had concentrated on the distinction between the pleasure principle and the reality principle, but had done less to describe how a child develops from one to the other.

In that paper, Ferenczi's first on the sense of reality, he proceeded to elaborate several developmental phases prior to a proper objective appreciation of reality; he called these "unconditional omnipotence", "magical–hallucinatory omnipotence", "omnipotence by magical gestures", and "magical thoughts and magical words", before the subsequent renunciation of omnipotence. These phases are in relation to the ego-instincts as autoerotism and narcissism are to the libido.

Ferenczi returned dissatisfied to the theme in 1926, in the paper republished in this volume. He wished to add to the final step—relinquishing omnipotence to allow the objective recognition of an object, even if it is a source of unpleasure as well as pleasure. What impels the infant from denial to acceptance? He relied on Freud's paper "Negation", which had recently been published (Freud, 1925h), and argued that negation is a transition stage between denial and acceptance. Denial repudiated the existence of something unpleasant. A step on from that is negation, the existence of something bad is admitted but is not a part of the self. It is a judgement about the location of the object; it is outside the ego, separate and independent.

He makes the point that the recognition of reality depends on an ambivalence, a love for a satisfying object which can later be hated because it is no longer present and available for satisfaction, but is attributed as outside and separate. Ferenczi further argued that this process of recognizing a separate object is bought, as it were, with the price of a compensation. The compensation for acknowledging and tolerating that the external source of unpleasure does exist, is that the loved pleasure-giving object is found again. The satisfying object has not disappeared for good; and so the gain is this reassurance, and that makes the relinquishing of omnipotence worthwhile. In the process, the loved object which is introjected and judged as the self, in Freud's description, is recognized as also the hated object that is externalized as poisonous.

In some respects Ferenczi's descriptions of the clinging to omnipotence and the wrenching clear from the narcissistic stage is a forerunner of Mahler's separation–individuation model (Mahler et al., 1975), and it also covers ground which Winnicott differently explored with the notion of the transitional object as a means to prolong the sense of omnipotence (1953). Freud also returned to the pathological clinging to omnipotence when, around this time (Freud, 1927e), he described the fetishist. The link that Ferenczi makes between ambivalence and the achievement of the reality principle recurs in Ferenczi's analysand Melanie Klein and the depressive position (1935).

Ferenczi's two papers turn a light upon a theme of fundamental theoretical and clinical importance to psychoanalysts, which many have returned to in their own ways again and again. It is impressive how Ferenczi's ideas here hint at many theories that come later.

References

Abraham, K. (1973) [1924]. A short study of the development of the libido, viewed in the light of mental disorders. *Selected Papers on Psychoanalysis* (pp. 418–501). London: Hogarth.

Ferenczi, S. (1926). The problem of acceptance of unpleasant ideas: advances in knowledge of the sense of reality. *International Journal of Psychoanalysis*, 7: 312–323.

Ferenczi, S. (1952) [1913]. Stages in the development of the sense of reality. *First Contributions to Psychoanalysis* (pp. 213–239). London: Hogarth.

Freud S. (1911b). Formulations on the two principles of mental functioning. *S.E.*, *12*: 218–226. London: Hogarth Press.

Freud, S. (1925h). Negation. *S.E.*, *19*: 235–240. London: Hogarth Press.

Freud, S. (1927e). Fetishism. *S.E.*, *21*: 152–157. London: Hogarth Press.

Klein, M. (1935). A contribution to the psychogenesis of mainc depressive states. *International Journal of Psychoanalysis*, *16*: 145–174.

Mahler, M., Pine, F., & Bergman, A. (1975). *The Psychological Birth of the Human Infant*. London: Hutchison.

Winnicott, D. W. (1953). Transitional objects and transitional phenomena. *International Journal of Psychoanalysis*, *34*: 89–97.

The problem of acceptance of unpleasant ideas: advances in knowledge of the sense of reality*

S. Ferenczi

Not long after I first made acquaintance with psycho-analysis I encountered the problem of the sense of reality, a mode of mental functioning which seemed to be in sharp contrast to the tendency towards flight from "pain" and towards repression otherwise so universally demonstrable in mental life. By means of a kind of empathy into the infantile mind, I arrived at the following hypothesis. To a child kept immune from any pain the whole of existence must appear to be a unity—"monistic", so to speak. Discrimination between "good" and "bad" things, ego and environment, inner and outer world, would only come later; at this stage alien and hostile would therefore be identical.[1] In a subsequent work I attempted to reconstruct theoretically the principal stages in the development from the pleasure-principle to the reality-principle.[2] I assumed that before it has experienced its first disappointments a child believes itself to be unconditionally omnipotent, and further that it clings to

---

* Article citation:
Ferenczi, S. (1926). The problem of acceptance of unpleasant ideas: Advances in knowledge of the sense of reality. *International Journal of Psychoanalysis, 7*: 312–323.

this feeling of omnipotence, even when the effectiveness of its power in the fulfilment of its wishes is bound up with the observance of certain conditions. It is only the growing number and complexity of these conditions that compel it to surrender the feeling of omnipotence and to recognize reality generally. In describing this development, however, nothing could at that time be said of the inner processes that must accompany this remarkable and important transformation; our knowledge of the deeper foundations of the mind—especially of instinctual life—was still too undeveloped to allow of this. Since then Freud's penetrating researches into instinctual life and his discoveries in the analysis of the ego have brought us nearer to this goal;[3] but we were still unable satisfactorily to bridge the gap between instinctual life and intellectual life. It was plain that we still needed that supreme simplification into which Freud has been at last able to reduce the multiplicity of instinctual phenomena; I refer to his view concerning the instinctual polarity that lies at the basis of all life—his doctrine of the life-instinct (Eros) and the death-instinct or destruction-instinct.[4] Yet not until one of Freud's latest works appeared—'Die Verneinung",[5] under which modest title lies concealed the beginnings of a psychology of the thought-processes, founded on biology—have the hitherto scattered fragments of our knowledge been gathered together. As always, here once more Freud takes his stand on the sure ground of psycho-analytical experience, and is extremely cautious in generalization. Following in his footsteps, I shall attempt once more to deal with the problem of the sense of reality in the light of his discovery.

Freud has discovered the psychological act of a *negation of reality* to be a transition-phase between ignoring and accepting reality; the alien and therefore hostile outer world becomes capable of entering consciousness, in spite of "pain", when it is supplied with the minus prefix of negation, i.e. when it is *denied*. In negativism, the tendency to abolish things, we see still at work the repressing forces which in the primary processes lead to a complete ignoring of whatever is "painful"; negative hallucinatory ignoring is no longer successful; the "pain" is no longer ignored, but becomes the subject-matter of perception as a negation. The question naturally arises at once: what must take place in order that the final obstacle to acceptance may be also removed from the path, and the affirmation of an unpleasant idea (i.e. the complete disappearance of the tendency to repression) made possible?

The suspicion also arises immediately that this is a question that is not to be easily answered; but since Freud's discovery this, at least, is clear from the outset: the affirmation of an unpleasant idea is never a simple thing, but is always a two-fold mental act. First an attempt is made to deny it as a fact, then a fresh effort has to be made to negate this negation, so that the positive, the recognition of evil, may really be assumed always to result from two negatives. To find anything comparable to this in the familiar realm of psycho-analysis we should have to draw an analogy between complete denial and the mental state of a child who still ignores everything unpleasant. In the same way I endeavoured some time ago to show that the fixation-point of the psychoses is to be found at this stage,[6] and I explained the uninhibited capacity for constant euphoria that is found in cases of megalomanic paralysis as a regression to this phase.[7] The stage of negation has an analogy, as Freud has shown, in the behaviour of a patient during treatment, and especially in a neurosis, which is similarly the result of a half-successful or unsuc-cessful repression and is actually always a negative—the negative of a perversion. The process by which recognition or affirmation of something unpleasant is finally reached goes on before our eyes, as the result of our therapeutic efforts when we cure a neurosis, and, if we pay attention to the details of the curative process, we shall be able to form some idea of the process of acceptance as well.

We note, then, that at the height of the transference the patient unresistingly accepts even what is most painful; clearly he finds in the feeling of pleasure accompanying the transference-love a conso-lation for the pain that this acceptance would otherwise have cost him. But if, at the close of the treatment, when the transference also has to be renounced, the patient were not successful in gradually finding for this renunciation too a substitute and consolation in reality, no matter how sublimated that substitute might be, there would undoubtedly follow a relapse into negation, i.e. into neuro-sis. In this connection we are involuntarily reminded of a very fruitful work by Victor Tausk, an analyst whose too early death we all deplore. In his "Compensation as a means of discounting the motive of repression"[8] he adduced the weakening of the motives of repression by compensation as a condition of the cure. In a similar fashion we must suspect the presence of a compensation even in the very first appearance of an acceptance of something unpleasant; indeed in no other way can we conceive of its originating in the mind, for this moves always in the direction of least resistance, i.e. according to the pleasure-principle. As a matter of fact we find as early as in Freud's *Traumdeutung* a passage which explains in a similar manner the transformation of a primary into a secondary process. He tells us there that a hungry baby tries at first to procure satisfaction by a kind of hallucination; and only when this fails does it make those manifestations of "pain" that lead to a real satisfaction as their result. We see that here for the first time the mental mode of reaction seems to be conditioned by a quantitative factor. The recognition of the hostile environment is unpleasant, but at the moment non-recognition of it is still more painful; consequently the less painful becomes relatively pleasurable, and, as such, can be accepted. It is only when we take into consideration the fact of compensation and avoidance of a still greater "pain", that we are able in any way to understand the possibility of an affirmation of "pain" without being compelled to renounce the universal validity of the search for pleasure as the fundamental psychical trend. But by doing so we are clearly postulating the intervention of a new instrument into the mental mechanism—a sort of reckoning-machine, the installation of which confronts us again with fresh and possibly still more puzzling enigmas.

We shall return later to the problem of psychical mathematics; meanwhile let us consider the mental content of the materials in relation to which a baby accomplishes the acceptance of reality. When Freud tells us that a human being ceaselessly or at rhythmic intervals observes his environment by "feeling after", "handling" and "tasting" little samples of it, he clearly takes a baby's procedure when it misses and feels after its mother's breast as the prototype of all subsequent thought-processes. A similar train of thought led me in my bio-analytical paper[9] to assume that smelling or sniffing the surrounding world shows a still greater likeness to the act of thinking, since it allows of finer and more minute samples being tested. Oral incorporation is carried out only when the result of the test is favourable. The intellectual difference between a child that puts everything indiscriminately into its mouth and one that only turns to things that smell pleasantly is therefore quite an important one.

Let us keep, however, to the example of the baby that wants to suck. Let us assume that up till now it has always been appeased in good time, and that this is its first experience of the "pain" of hunger and thirst; what probably takes place in its mind? In its primal, narcissistic self-assurance it has hitherto only known itself; it has known nothing of the existence of objects outside itself, which, of course, include even the mother, and could therefore have no feelings towards them, either friendly or hostile. There apparently occurs—possibly in connection with the physiological destruction produced in the organic tissues by the absence of nutrition—an "instinctual defusion" in the mental life as well, which finds expression first of all in unco-ordinated motor discharge and in crying—manifestations which we may quite well compare with expressions of rage in adults. When after long waiting and screaming the mother's breast is regained, this no longer has the effect of an indifferent thing which is always there when it is wanted, so that its existence does not need to be recognized; it has become *an object of love and hate*, of hate because of its being temporarily unobtainable, and of love because after this loss it offers a still more intense satisfaction. In any case it certainly becomes at the same time, although no doubt very obscurely, the subject of a "concrete idea". This example illustrates, it seems to me, the following very important sentences in Freud's paper, "Die Verneinung": "The first and most immediate aim of testing the reality of things is not to find in reality an object corresponding to the thing represented, but to find it again, to be convinced that it is still there", and "We recognize as a condition for the testing of reality that objects which formerly had brought satisfaction must have been lost."[10] We are only tempted to add further that the ambivalence indicated above, i.e. instinctual defusion, is an absolutely necessary condition for the coming into existence of a concrete idea. Things that always love us, i.e. that constantly satisfy all our needs, we do not notice as such, we simply reckon them as part of our subjective ego; things which are and always have been hostile to us, we simply deny; but to those things which do not yield unconditionally to our desires, which we love because they bring us satisfaction, and hate because they do not submit to us in everything, we attach special mental marks, memory-traces with the quality of objectivity, and we are glad when we find them again in reality, i.e. when we are able to love them once more. And when we hate an object but cannot suppress it so completely as to be able to deny it permanently, our taking notice of its existence shows that we want really to love it, but are only prevented from doing so by the "maliciousness of the object". The savage is therefore only logical when after killing his enemy he shows him the greatest love and honour. He is simply demonstrating that what he likes best of all is to be left in peace; he wants to live in undisturbed harmony with his environment, but is prevented from doing so by the existence of a "disturbing object". When this obstacle appears it leads to a defusion of his instincts, so that the aggressive, destructive component comes to the fore. After his revenge is satisfied the other—the love-component—seeks satisfaction. It seems as if the two classes of instincts neutralize each other when the ego is in a state of rest, like the positive and negative currents in an electrically inactive body, and as if, in just the same way, special external influences were needed to separate the two currents and thus render them once more capable of action. The emergence of ambivalence would thus be a kind of protective device, instituting the capacity for active resistance in general, which, like the mental phenomenon accompanying it, recognition of the objective world, signifies one of the means of obtaining mastery over it.

We perceive, however, that while ambivalence no doubt leads to acceptance of the existence of things, it does not carry us as far as objective contemplation; on the contrary, things become alternately the objects of passionate hate and equally passionate love. In order that "objectivity" may be obtained it is necessary for the instincts that have been released to be inhibited, i.e. again mixed with one another, a fresh instinctual fusion thus taking place after recognition has been achieved. This is probably the mental process which guarantees the inhibition and postponement of action until the external reality has been identified with the "thought-reality" (Freud); the capacity for objective judgement and action is thus essentially a capacity of the tendencies of loving and hating for neutralizing one another—a statement that certainly sounds very like a platitude. I think, however, that we can in all seriousness assume that the mutual binding of attracting and repelling forces is a process of mental energy at work in every compromise-formation, and in every objective observation, and that the maxim *sine ira et sine studio* must be replaced by another, namely, that for the objective contemplation of things, full scope must be given to an *equal amount* both of *ira* and of *studium*.

Clearly, then, there are stages in the development of the capacity for objectivity too. In my article on the development of the sense of reality I described the gradual surrender of personal omnipotence, and its transference to other higher powers (nurses, parents, gods). I called this the period of omnipotence by means of magic gestures and words; as the last stage, that of insight derived from painful experience, I regarded the final and complete surrender of omnipotence—the scientific stage, so to speak, of our recognition of the world. In psycho-analytical phraseology, I called the first phase of all, in which the ego alone exists and includes in itself the whole world of experience, the period of introjection; the second phase, in which omnipotence is ascribed to external powers, the period of projection; the last stage of development might be thought of as the stage in which both mechanisms are employed in equal measure or in mutual compensation. This sequence corresponded roughly to the representation of human development broadly outlined in Freud's *Totem und Tabu* as a succession of magical, religious and scientific stages. When, however, I attempted much later to bring some light to bear critically on the manner in which our present-day science is working, I was compelled to assume that, if science is really to remain objective, it must work alternately as pure psychology and pure natural science,[11] and must verify both our inner and outer experience by analogies taken from both points of view; this implies an oscillation between projection and introjection. I called this the "utraquism" of all true scientific work. In philosophy ultra-idealistic solipsism means a relapse into egocentric infantilism; the purely materialistic psychophobe standpoint signifies a regression to the exaggerations of the projection-phase; while Freud's maintenance of a dualism completely fulfils the utraquistic demand.

We are justified in hoping that Freud's discovery of negation as a transition-stage between denial and acceptance of what is unpleasant, will help us to a better understanding of these developmental stages and their sequence, besides simplifying our view of them. The first painful step towards recognition of the external world is certainly the knowledge that some of the "good things" do not belong to the ego, and must be distinguished from it as the "outer

242   INFLUENTIAL PAPERS FROM THE 1920s

world" (the mother's breast). Almost at the same time a human being has to learn that something unpleasant, that is, "bad", can take place within him (in the ego itself, so to speak) which cannot be shaken off either by hallucination or in any other way (hunger, thirst). A further advance is made when he learns to endure absolute deprivation from without, i.e. when he recognizes that there are also things that must be relinquished for good and all; the process parallel to this is the recognition of repressed wishes while realization of them is at the same time renounced. Since, as we know now, a quota of Eros, i.e. of love, is necessary for this recognition, and since this addition is inconceivable without introjection, i.e. identification, we are forced to say that recognition of the surrounding world is actually a partial realization of the Christian imperative "Love your enemies". It is true that the opposition which the psycho-analytical doctrine of instinct meets with certainly proves that reconciliation with our inner foe is the most difficult task that humanity is called upon to accomplish.

When we attempt to bring our fresh knowledge into connection with the topographical system of Freudian metapsychology, we surmise that at the stage of absolute solipsism only Pcpt-Cs, i.e. the perceptual superficies of the mind, is functioning; the period of negation coincides with the formation of Ucs repressed strata; the conscious acceptance of the outer world requires further that hypercathexis of which we are made capable only by the institution of another psychical system—the preconscious (Pcs)—interposed between the Ucs and the Cs. In accordance with the fundamental law of biogenesis the racial history of the evolution of the mind is thus repeated in the psychical development of the individual; for the serial sequence here described is the same as that by which we must imagine the progressive evolution of psychical systems in organisms.

In organic development too we find prototypes of the progressive adaptation of living creatures to the reality of the external world. There are primitive organisms that seem to have remained at the narcissistic stage; they wait passively for the satisfaction of their needs, and if this is denied them permanently they simply perish. They are still much nearer to the point of emergence from the unorganic, and on that account their instinct of destruction has a shorter path to travel back, i.e. it is much stronger. At the next stage the organism is able to thrust off parts of itself that cause pain and in this way save its life (autotomy); I once called this sort of sequestration a physiological prototype of the process of repression. Not until after further development is the faculty for adaptation to reality created—an organic recognition of the environment, so to speak; very fine examples of this can be seen in the mode of life of organisms that are symbiotically united; but the fact is patent in every other act of adaptation. In connection with my "bio-analytical" point of view, we can accordingly distinguish even in the organic between primary and secondary processes—processes, that is, which in the realm of the mind we regard as stages in intellectual development. That would mean, however, that in a certain degree and sense the organic also possesses a kind of reckoning-machine, which is concerned not simply with qualities of pleasure and "pain", but also with quantities. To be sure, organic adaptation is characterized by a certain inflexibility, seen in the reflex processes which are undoubtedly purposive but immutable, while the capacity for adaptation shows a continual readiness to recognize new realities and the capacity to inhibit action until the act of thinking is completed. Groddeck is therefore right in regarding the organic id as intelligent; but he shows bias when he overlooks the difference in degree between the intelligence of the ego and that of the id.

In this connection we may instance the fact that in organic pathology too we have an opportunity of seeing the work of negation (autotomy) and adaptation in operation. I have already attempted to trace certain processes of organic healing (of wounds, etc.) to the flow of a current of libido (Eros) to the injured place.[12]

We must not disguise from ourselves that all these considerations still furnish no satisfactory explanation of the fact that, both in organic and in psychical adaptation to the real environment, portions of the hostile outer world are, with the assistance of Eros, reckoned as part of the ego, and on the other hand, loved portions of the ego itself are given up. Possibly here we may have recourse to the more or less psychological explanation that even the actual renunciation of a pleasure and the recognition of something unpleasant are always only "provisional", as it were; it is obedience under protest, so to speak, with the mental reservation of a *restitutio in integrum*. This may hold good in very many cases; there is evidence for it in the capacity for regression to modes of reaction that have long since been surmounted and are even archaic—a capacity that is preserved potentially and in special circumstances brought into operation. What looks like adaptation would thus be only an attitude of interminable waiting and hoping for the return of the "good old times", differing fundamentally therefore only in degree from the behaviour of the rotiferæ which remain dried-up for years waiting for moisture. We must not forget, however, that there is also such a thing as a real and irreparable loss of organs and portions of organs, and that in the psychical realm also complete renunciation without any compensation exists. Such optimistic explanations therefore really do not help us; we must have recourse to the Freudian doctrine of instinct, which shows that there are cases in which the destruction-instinct turns against the subject's own person, indeed, that the tendency to self-destruction, to death, is the more primary, and has been directed outwards only in the course of development. We may suppose that whenever adaptation is achieved, a similar, as it were masochistic, alteration in the direction of aggression plays a part. Further, I have already pointed out above that the surrender of loved parts of the ego and the introjection of the non-ego are parallel processes; and that we are able to love (recognize) objects only by a sacrifice of our narcissism, which is after all but a fresh illustration of the well-known psychoanalytical fact that all object-love takes place at the expense of narcissism.

The remarkable thing about this self-destruction is that here (in adaptation, in the recognition of the surrounding world, in the forming of objective judgements) destruction does in actual fact become the "cause of being".[13] A partial destruction of the ego is tolerated, but only for the purpose of constructing out of what remains an ego capable of still greater resistance. This is similar to the phenomena noted in the ingenious attempts of Jacques Loeb to stimulate unfertilized eggs to development by the action of chemicals, i.e. without fertilization: the chemicals disorganize the outer layers of the egg, but out of the detritus a protective bladder (sheath) is formed, which puts a stop to further injury. In the same way the Eros liberated by instinctual defusion converts destruction into growth, into a further development of the parts that have been protected. I admit that it is very hazardous to apply organic analogies immediately to the psychical: let it serve for my excuse that I am doing it deliberately, and only with regard to so-called "ultimate problems", where, as I have explained elsewhere, analytical judgements take us no further, and where we have to search for analogies in other fields in order to form a synthetic judgement. Psycho-analysis, like every psychology, in its attempts to dig to the depths must strike somewhere on the rock of the organic. I have no hesitation in regarding even memory-traces as scars, so to speak, of traumatic impressions, i.e., as products of the destructive instinct, which, however, the unresting Eros nevertheless understands how to employ for its own ends, i.e. for the preservation of life. Out of these it shapes a new psychical system, which enables the ego to orientate itself more correctly in its environment, and to form sounder judgements. In fact it is only the destructive instinct that "wills evil", while it is Eros that "creates good" out of it.

I have spoken once or twice about a reckoning-machine, the existence of which I assumed as an auxiliary organ of the sense of reality. This idea really belongs to another connection, which to my mind explains the scientific mathematical and logical sense, but I should like to make a reference, although briefly, to it here. I can make a very useful beginning with the double meaning of the word "reckon". When the tendency to set aside the surrounding world by means of repression or denial is given up, we begin to *reckon* with it, i.e. to recognize it as a fact. A further advance in the art of reckoning is, in my opinion, the development of the power to choose between two objects that occasion either more or less unpleasantness, or to choose between two modes of action that can result in either more or less unpleasantness. The whole process of thinking would then be such a work of reckoning—to a large extent unconscious, and interposed between the sensory apparatus and motility. In this process, as in modern reckoning-machines, it is practically the result alone that comes into conscious view, while the memory-traces with which the actual work has been performed remain concealed, i.e. unconscious. We can dimly surmise that even the simplest act of thinking rests on an indefinite number of unconscious reckoning-operations, in which presumably every kind of arithmetical simplification (algebra, differential calculus) is employed; and that thinking in speech-symbols represents the ultimate integration of this complicated reckoning-faculty.

I believe, too, in all seriousness that the sense for mathematics and logic depends upon the presence or absence of the capacity for perceiving this reckoning and thinking activity, though it is also performed unconsciously by those who do not seem to possess the mathematical or logical faculty in the slightest degree. The musical faculty might be ascribed to a similar introversion (self-perception of emotional stirrings, lyricism) as well as the scientific interest in psychology.

Whether and how far a given person forms "correct" judgements (i.e. the ability to reckon the future beforehand) probably depends on the degree of development this reckoning-machine has reached. The primary elements with which these reckonings are performed are our memories, but these themselves represent a sum of sensory impressions and therefore ultimately are reac-tions to various stim-uli of different strength. Thus psychical mathematics would only be a continuation of "organic mathematics".

However this may be, the essential thing in the development of a sense of reality is, as Freud has shown, the interpolation of an inhibitory mechanism into the psychical apparatus; negation is only the last desperate effort of the pleasure-principle to check the advance to a knowledge of reality. The ultimate forming of a judge-ment, however, resulting from the work of reckoning here postu-lated, represents an inner discharge, a re-orientation of our emotional attitude to things and to our ideas of them, the direction of this new orientation determining the path taken by action either immediately or some time afterwards. Recognition of the surround-ing world, i.e. affirmation of the existence of something unpleasant, is, however, only possible after defence against objects which cause "pain" and denial of them are given up, and their stimuli, incorpo-rated into the ego, transformed into inner impulses. The power that effects this transformation is the Eros that is liberated through instinctual defusion.

Notes

1. The child will learn "to distinguish from his ego the malicious things, forming an outer world, that do not obey his will", i.e. he will distinguish subjective contents of his mind (feelings) from

those which reach him objectively (sensations). "Introjection und Transference" (1909), *Contributions to Psycho-analysis.*

2. "Stages in the development of the sense of reality" (1913), *Contributions to Psycho-analysis.*
3. *Group-Psychology and the Analysis of the Ego* (1921). *Das Ich und das Es* (1923).
4. *Beyond the Pleasure-Principle* (1920).
5. *Imago,* 1925.
6. "Stages in the Development of the Sense of Reality".
7. *Zur Psychoanalyse der paralytischen Geistesstörung.*
8. *International Journal of Psychoanalysis,* 1924.
9. *Versuch einer Genitaltheorie* (Internationale Psycho-Analytische Bibliothek, Vol. XV).
10. In my *Genitaltheorie* I trace back the feeling of gratification—the feeling of attaining *erotic reality*—to a similar recurrence of finding *again* and recognizing *again.*
11. Introduction to my *Genitaltheorie.*
12. *Hysterie und Pathoneurosen.*
13. Cf. S. Spielrein, "Die Destruction als Ursache des Werdens", *Jahrbuch für Psycho-Analyse,* IV, 1912.

CHAPTER EIGHT

Lay analysis

Jones, Ernest (1927). Lay analysis. *International Journal of Psycho-analysis, 8*: 174–198.

In early 1926 Theodor Reik was prosecuted for conducting an analysis without being medically qualified. It quickly blew into a controversy that opened a split between psychoanalysts, including opening a divide between American and European psychoanalysis. Freud (1926e) wrote a pamphlet about it, not being an impartial bystander since his daughter had scant formal qualifications for therapeutic work. His trenchant arguments were not supported in America, where the fear of, and quantity of, medical quacks was rightly a powerful public issue of concern. In America, prompted by Brill (Gay, 1988), laws were passed from 1926 onwards to prohibit lay analysis. The issue threatened to split the psycho-analytic movement once again. So, Jones (together with Eitingon) organized a symposium at the next IPA conference (1927 in Inns-bruck) on the topic. The journal pre-published a number of papers by various analysts and psychoanalytical societies. Jones's paper* was a long and elegant essay devoted to the relations between psychoanalysis and medicine. The entrenched special interests ensured that the Congress did not settle the issue (Bos, 2001), and there were many subsequent political campaigns in a battle that has rumbled on, and occasionally disastrously erupts today (Wallerstein, 2000).

As always Jones's writing is transparently clear, optimistic, and rather concealing of the deep clefts within the psychoanalytic movement. It aspires to a height of magisterial statesmanship, unlike Freud on this topic, who was more blunt and tetchy, and might even have willingly jettisoned the New York Society altogether. Jones's paper held the view that a medical qualification is to be preferred, but not necessary. He carefully investigated the advantages and disadvantages of medical qualification versus lay analysts in three sections; first, the benefits for psychoanalysis, then for the patient, and third, for the analyst. He was less radical in his views than Freud, and campaigned for a medical authority to "prescribe" psychoanalysis when conducted by a lay practitioner. In this way Jones attempted a diplomatic strategy, ultimately partially successful, for keeping open a bridge between Europe and America.

At the time Jones was himself becoming embroiled in a serious political battle. Because of adverse public and professional criticism, the British Medical Association established an inquiry into psychoanalytic treatment. The enquiry, which lasted three years from 1926, considered whether psychoanalysis was an ethical and effective treatment and who should conduct it. Jones campaigned tirelessly, first to be a member of the committee of enquiry and not just a witness before it, then to wear down the medical opposition, and finally to contribute significant passages to the report. Jones disentangled the major issues. These were: (a) the validity of psychoanalytic discoveries and method, (b) training of practitioners, and (c) the medical control over the practice and over non-medical practitioners. The result of the enquiry was as Jones recommended: all treatments should be prescribed by doctors; all practitioners should be properly trained; and only those trained by the British Psychoanalytical Society should call themselves "psychoanalyst". Thus he established the centrality of the British Psychoanalytical Society and its training, authorized by the British Medical Association.

Therefore, Jones considered himself well placed to introduce the IPA symposium by rehearsing the effectiveness of psychoanalysis, its rigour in training, and the protection of the name. The issues still speak to the current, fraught issues of the relations of psychoanalysis to medical science, to managed care, and to the evidence-base of "clinical excellence".

References

Bos, J. (2001). Notes on a controversy: The question of lay analysis. *Psychoanalysis and History*, 3: 153–169.

Freud, S. (1926e). The question of lay analysis. *S.E.*, 20: 179–258. London: Hogarth Press.

Gay, P. (1988). *Freud: A Life for our Time*. London: Dent.

Wallerstein, R. (2000). *Lay Analysis: Life inside the Controversy*. New York: The Analytic Press.

Lay analysis

Ernest Jones

The Central Executive of the International Psycho-Analytical Association informs us that it is their intention to bring forward the question of "Lay Analysis" at the next Congress, so that opinions may be heard and, so far as possible, decisions arrived at in the matter. The Executive desires that the question shall be ventilated as fully as possible before the Congress meets, and has consequently requested the various Branch Societies to further this end by arranging for local discussions on the subject. In order to serve the same purpose we are opening our pages to an international discussion of the question of Lay Analysis.

Ernest Jones

I propose to discuss this topic at considerable length because it would appear to be one of the most important problems concerning the future of psycho-analysis. To justify the length of the present contribution I may advance the consideration that I have had perhaps unique opportunities of studying various aspects of the question. Of the British Society, which has always been the most friendly towards lay analysis, more than forty per cent. of the members are lay, i.e. non-medical: several of these are analysts of the first rank, both in theory and practice. I have therefore had opportunities for continual and direct observation of the valuable assistance that lay analysts can contribute to psycho-analysis, and this apart from the opportunities afforded by long-standing personal contact with the most distinguished lay analysts on the Continent. On the other hand I doubt if any other centre, even New York, provides more occasions than London for observing the activities of wild analysts,[1] both medical and lay.

It is sometimes said that any discussion of the subject among analysts is useless because it is out of our power to influence the matter one way or the other, inasmuch as it will be finally decided by legal judgements or by the attitude of the public or the medical profession. Although Professor Freud evidently does not share this opinion himself, otherwise he would not have troubled to write a book[2] on the subject, a passage in his book might be used in support of those who do. He remarks that no authority can prevent someone who has himself been analysed from analysing others. None of us, however, would seriously maintain that every patient who has been successfully treated is *thereby* fitted to become a psychoanalyst, and that we should not think so is a fact of increasing import. It is easy to under-estimate the influence and authority that the body of psycho-analysts will be able to exercise when the functioning of their Institutes and Clinics becomes more widely recognized. Nor is it thinkable that any official institution will ever issue diplomas or degrees in psycho-analysis, a consummation which is certainly not within sight, without the licensing body being composed of qualified analysts. The prospect would thus appear to be that what our psycho-analytical organization decides to be the fitting qualification for psycho-analytic practice will be a matter of increasing, and ultimately decisive, importance. At the present juncture, therefore, when the conditions and nature of training are being worked out by the International Training Commission, it becomes all the more necessary to probe in a radical manner such questions as the present one.

It is probable that much of the muddled and emotional thinking that one often finds expressed during conversations on the subject, together with the unnecessary heat that is engendered, could with great advantage be avoided if it were more fully realized that many of the divergencies of opinion arise from an imperfect appreciation of the nature of the transitional stage through which the psycho-analytical movement is now passing. Psycho-analysis is at present faced with the formidable task of organizing the knowledge it has so painfully won. This needs to be accomplished both internally (training) and externally (linking with other branches of science).

It will not be denied that both these tasks have had to be considerably neglected in the past in favour of more pressing duties. To begin with, when psycho-analysis had to fight for its very existence one could not afford to be very nice in the choice of supporters; "beggars can't be choosers". Anyone was welcome who was prepared to strike a blow on our side: his only qualification need be that he was sympathetically interested in psycho-analysis. The interest might be thoroughly neurotic in origin, it might be purely temporary and later replaced by opposition, it might be throughout ambivalent, but there was no time to take stock of these fine discriminations; support was support, however short-lived, imperfect or ultimately troublesome. It was only after years of experience, often bitter in the testing, that we were impelled to look more carefully at the support offered us: and this coincided with a diminished pressure for our need of support: psycho-analysis was evidently going to survive, and was even becoming established. We now need a radical revision of the previous attitude, one comprehensible enough in the early desperate days.

For a number of sufficiently obvious reasons, which need not be detailed here, we are agreed to insist that future analysts should receive an adequate training in psycho-analysis before they begin practice. What constitutes "adequate training" is a technical matter for the International Commission and its branches to decide, and fortunately there would appear to be very little disaccord over the main principles concerned. It is important to note that this decision brings with it the necessity, not previously present, for selecting the material to be trained. No serious curriculum of study in any branch of knowledge is open to all and sundry. Everywhere some standard is exacted, of character, of previous education, of attainments in examinations, etc. This will be specially desirable with psycho-analysis, where cranks, failures elsewhere and various abnormal types press forward for admission to the ranks. To eradicate all the character anomalies that are so troublesome in practice often needs several years of intensive analytic work, which could be more profitably employed in the training of several more promising individuals selected beforehand. What so often happens now is that the less satisfactory types we have in mind do not persevere beyond a few months and depart to practise psycho-analysis without let or hindrance, indeed with the prestige of having been "trained by so-and-so". It is in connection with this essential process of preliminary selection that the question urgently arises of the attitude to be adopted towards the would-be lay analyst.

The other half of the task defined above has also a bearing on the same issue. I refer to the *external* organization of psycho-analysis, to the relation between psycho-analysis and science in general. It will hardly be denied that this matter is in a very unsatisfactory state at present and has indeed received little attention at our hands. The reasons for this are familiar. The founder of psycho-analysis wisely chose the course of pursuing his scientific research independently and of addressing himself mainly to those with experience in the same field rather than devoting his time to presenting the detailed evidence for his conclusions to the scientific world at large in the customary manner. His early essays in the opposite direction convinced him that he would only squander his energies by pursuing such a course, and so, to the inestimable gain of the world, he has for the last twenty years mainly directed his writings to those who were prepared to admit without further ado his fundamental principles and methods. The case was similar for the first generation of followers, who eagerly pushed forward in their learning and exploring without pausing to heed the outer world more than was necessary. Experience showed, further, that the difficulties in the way of presenting their work to those without personal first-hand knowledge of its method and its details were of a very special kind and transcended those of which the history of science has any record elsewhere. These difficulties are indeed so formidable that the possibility of their being ever surmounted is a very arguable proposition. If this were answered in the negative, it would mean that psycho-analysis would differ from any other branches of science in being strictly confined to a particular group of people, and that the wide bearings it has on so many other branches of science, and on life and civilization in general, would forever remain unavailable. If this pessimistic and regrettable conclusion had to be adopted, it is hard to predict what would be the practical consequences. We know enough of human nature, however, to surmise that the hothouse atmosphere which would in time be engendered could hardly be the best one for free development and would be more likely to result in narrow sectarian jealousies and unedifying squabbles of the kind that most interfere with the pursuit of truth. The dangers of developing an esoteric cult instead of a branch of science are such that not all workers would find it easy to resist them.

On the other side we are equally alive to the opposite danger, that of our conclusions being weakened, discounted and diluted in the process of absorption by the outer world. This we are determined to resist to the full, and our determination is evinced by a certain hardness and aloofness towards workers in allied fields which has already been commented on by various critics. The problem that faces us, therefore, is how best to steer between the Scylla of esoterism and the Charybdis of absorption. Opinions will vary in answering this question. To those who dread the second danger most the paragraphs that here follow will be irrelevant. For my own part I would declare myself equally alive to both sets of danger, but I am optimistic—or adventurous—enough to hope that a secure course may yet be found that will avoid both.

Any attempt to establish contact with other branches of science, particularly the cognate ones and gradually to permeate them with the discoveries and conclusions of psycho-analysis will necessitate much patient work at presenting our data and clarifying our concepts in a more systematic fashion than hitherto. For this purpose what is quite indispensable is a highly trained body of workers, accustomed to the idea of scientific research and, if possible, with some experience of scientific discipline in other fields. The thorough training just mentioned is equally essential for the aim we have here in view and for the even more important purpose of guarding against any tendency to "absorption", which we have proclaimed to be the second danger.

These considerations put the question of systematic and thorough training in the forefront of our endeavours. No body of work is likely to achieve the status of an exact branch of science and to be regarded as serious by other scientific workers until a precise curriculum of studies pertaining to it has been effectively organized. One of the best definitions of science is "verifiable organized knowledge". This is one of the reasons why psychology in general is still looked at askance by many workers in other fields, and, as for psycho-analysis, the idea is popular enough that the practice of it is dependent mainly on some personal gift, that it is an arbitrary art which can perhaps be supplemented by reading a few books. There have, of course, always been various means of acquiring a knowledge of psycho-analysis, but the organizing of these means into a systematic training constitutes a step of revolutionary significance. It marks the passage of psycho-analysis into the ranks of other sciences and its practice into the ranks of other professions.

These considerations have a twofold bearing on the topic here under discussion; on the question of the selection and general education, as well as special training, of our workers: and on the connection between psycho-analysis and other branches of science. As regards the latter point there can be very little doubt that the nearest and most promising point of contact, the one forced on us by every relevant consideration, is medicine. We cannot escape from some relation to medicine, and the only question is what is this to be. The reasons for this are so obvious as barely to need recounting. Not only did psycho-analysis take its origin in the field of clinical neurology and psychopathology (it has well been said that psycho-analysis stands to psychiatry as histology does to anatomy), but it has always found this its surest basis, though it has of course *extended* widely from this centre into other fields. Psycho-analytical conceptions are for the greater part pathological in origin, a fact which is often brought as a reproach against them. Our material consists essentially of suffering patients in need of help, though here, too, we have extended beyond the usual frontiers of medicine (e.g. character analyses). The vast bulk of this material necessarily comes before medical practitioners, and presumably will always do so, for one can hardly foresee a day when the public will itself make accurate diagnoses between mental and physical afflictions: this fact alone necessitates a close contact with the medical profession. The diagnostic relationship between our problems and, on the one hand, those of the psychoses, conditions which for legal reasons will certainly always be under the care of medical practitioners, and, on the other hand, innumerable organic states, will be dealt with below, but we must here also insist on the extent to which this holds good not merely as a preliminary, but throughout the whole analysis. Even in the theory of psycho-analysis itself—and what is practice without theory?—the doctrine of erotogenic zones, so fundamental for any problem in development, impinges directly on to the somatic, as do so many questions like the chemical basis of the libido, somatic factors influencing changes in the libido, glandular functioning, etc., etc. The innumerable problems connecting psycho-analysis and medicine can be shirked, but they cannot be avoided.

These points seem to me to be easily demonstrable. I now wish to introduce one that is more a matter of personal judgement. In my opinion, and this is formed on purely psycho-analytic lines, the greatest hindrance to the advance of psychology as a science has always been the motive of flight from what may be described as the personal, the human, the natural, the animal in man. We know the ultimate source of this to be the flight from the unconscious, particularly from infantile sexuality. This flight has taken two main forms. The flight into materialism I count as the less serious of the two. It is a recent one, not much more than fifty years old, and it is already showing signs of passing, even in the physical sciences themselves. It is the less dangerous of the two, because after all it is in the direction of the natural rather than the supernatural. Nor has the materialistic bias of medical education, undeniable as this is, proved a very serious obstacle to the study of the psyche. It cannot be chance that the psychologists who have done most to replace the old intellectualistic conceptions by more fruitful human ones have so often been medical men. I refer to such pioneers as William James and Morton Prince in America, Rivers and McDougall in England, Janet in France, and—the sun among the stars—Freud himself. Inside psycho-analysis itself the workers who have been most daring in applying psychological principles in the somatic field have all been medical; Ferenczi, Groddeck, Jelliffe, and Stoddart: lay analysts have shown a justifiable inhibition in this respect.

The other, more serious, form of this flight is, in my opinion, that more directly away from the natural. It may be either expressly towards the supernatural, by one of the many open or disguised forms of religion, or towards what may broadly—and perhaps not altogether fairly—be termed philosophy, by rarefaction of the mind into intellectualization. Now I cannot think of any education that gives a better opportunity for defence against this tendency than the medical one: I say opportunity, for of course it can provide no guarantee. Not only is the training and work throughout naturalistic and biological in its outlook, but, with his daily observation of the continual failure of the human mechanism, it is harder for the doctor than for any other worker to retain any illusion about the isolated superiority of mankind over the rest of the animal world or the belief in an independent and self-determining "soul" that rests on this. To someone like myself, steeped throughout in evolutionary doctrine, of which psycho-analysis itself seems to be nothing but an extension and completion (though, incidentally, the most valuable part of that doctrine), the consideration just adduced must count as being especially weighty.

After this lengthy introduction, the main theses of which are the urgency of raising *and organizing* the standard of psycho-analytic training and the necessity of defining our relations to the neighbouring science of clinical medicine, I will now approach the main topic of this discussion. In doing so we shall gain greatly in clearness and simplicity of outlook if we first narrow down the issue to its essentials by ascertaining what precisely is meant by the question, "Are you in favour of lay analysts?" The following discussion is intended to elucidate this question.

We have first to distinguish between analyses performed as part of a professional livelihood and those performed for any other purpose. The first we may term therapeutic analytic work, though it will at times include training analyses and character analyses. It is what we generally mean when we refer to the work of lay analysts.

A case of the second kind would be where a non-medical anthropologist wished, with the intention of applying in his own field the insight and knowledge he had gained through his personal analysis, to fortify and extend this knowledge in the best way possible by spending a couple of years conducting analyses in a psycho-analytical clinic under trained medical supervision. I cannot imagine that any analyst would have any other attitude than approbation for such a laudable procedure as this. One might reasonably expect that such cases should not be very rare, now that the value of the extensive applications of psycho-analysis is being more and more established; students of religion, of sociology, mythology, literature, etc., etc., should be applying to us for opportunities to further their researches. The facts, however, are stark in the other direction. One distinguished anthropologist, Dr Róheim, has indeed pursued this course, following his own self-analysis and wide reading by performing a few analyses for the express purpose of still further deepening his knowledge. With this single exception, every other student who has come to psycho-analysis from other fields, whether mythology, religion, biology, education, etc., has taken up, usually for whole-time, though occasionally for part-time, professional occupation with therapeutic analyses. We are therefore forced to realize that when lay analysts working in other fields are mentioned, it nearly always means in practice that such workers adopt psycho-analysis professionally and come into the category of the first group. There are, of course, those who deprecate the activities of the first group, but I have never heard any objections raised to those of the second, and most of us would very cordially welcome the appearance of the type in large numbers. To say, therefore, as Dr Róheim does, that applied psycho-analysis stands and falls with lay analysis is very wide of the mark; he is here confounding two groups of lay analysts, and it is not thinkable that any objection would ever be raised to the one group on whom progress in applied psycho-analysis essentially depends.

There are, again, two classes of the first, professional type of lay analyst, and the attitude of medical analysts differs considerably in regard to them. Theoretically the difference is not supposed to exist, but it certainly does in practice. For some adhere to the rule that *no lay analyst should engage in independent practice*, whereas others do not. This rule is so important that it is desirable to be quite clear about the significance and bearings of it. In most countries the chief distinction drawn between the medical profession and the laity in respect of disease is not so much in the actual carrying out of treatment—except in the obvious cases, such as surgical operations, that demand special skill—as in the matter of prescribing treatment. Many forms of treatment can be, and indeed have to be, *carried out* by assistants acting under medical instruction and supervision, but society has become increasingly aware of the disadvantages to the community of allowing anyone to *prescribe* treatment who has not undergone the requisite training in physiology, pathology, etc., that will enable him to make an exact diagnosis of the pathological condition present before deciding on the suitability of the case for this or that form of treatment. The thesis here put forward would apply this universal rule to the practice of psycho-analysis. It means that, whether a lay person carries out an analysis or not, he should in no case prescribe it, i.e. he should not engage in practice independently of the medical profession.

I have never heard a lay analyst actually deny this thesis, though it is unfortunately often neglected in practice. All medical analysts to whom I have spoken are unanimous in supporting it, and even Professor Freud, perhaps the most extreme defender of lay analysts, maintains it absolutely and without any qualification. It goes without saying that the non-analytical part of the medical profession, familiar as they are with the dangers of allowing the functions of diagnosis and prescription to be exercised by non-medical persons, would be wholeheartedly in favour of the thesis, as presumably would be the greater part of the laity.

It would seem necessary to insist on some implications of this rule. In the first place, it should be an absolute one. In spite of the fact familiar to all of us, that the preliminary consultation with a physician is often an entire formality, with no sort of medical question at all arising, the decision of whether it is a case suitable for consultation with a physician should never be left to the lay analyst: to do so would, by begging the question, plunge the whole principle into confusion and impose a responsibility on the lay analyst that cannot and should not be his. Nor would I suggest any exception with children, even with "infant analyses", for the transition between the mental and physical is even readier with them than with adults and, of course, the question of psychosis arises equally with both.

Nor can we overlook the difficulty that in many cases, as Professor Freud has often pointed out on previous occasions, the diagnosis can be determined only during and by means of the analysis itself. It is hard to state what is the proportion of cases in which a physician would be prepared at the outset, and especially from one interview alone, to guarantee that no physical factor is concerned in the clinical situation and that all psychoses can be ruled out; it would doubtless vary with the physician and with his confidence in his powers of diagnosis.

As is well known, many forms of insanity present themselves clinically under the guise of a neurosis. It may be a true neurosis, with absolutely typical symptoms, and the relationship of the two conditions furnishes an interesting theoretical problem. It is not rare for general paralysis to show itself first in the form of a neurasthenic syndrome, for cases of dementia præcox and paranoia to wear a mask of hysterical phobia, of catatonia to wear one of conversion hysteria, and manic-depressive insanity one of obsessional manifestations. The diagnosis of such conditions calls for a knowledge not only of clinical psychiatry, but also of clinical neurology, and could very rarely be entrusted to someone destitute of training in these subjects. It is further known that it may occasionally need months of analytic work before one can come to a decision on these difficult problems; an occasional consultation with a physician cannot wholly replace the advantage of constant observation conducted by the physician.

I have here discussed, and by no means completely, the single matter of diagnosis. It will be pointed out later that this is only one of the many respects in which medical knowledge is valuable in psycho-analytic work. But enough has perhaps been said to establish two propositions: first, that it is undesirable for lay analysts to engage in independent practice, and secondly, that there needs to be a definite selection of the cases judged suitable for treatment at their hands.

We have now, I hope, settled the case of the student lay analyst (definitely in his favour) and of the independent lay analyst (definitely in his disfavour). I need hardly say that I do not propose to say anything about the irregular or wild analyst, for his problem is much the same whether he is medically qualified or not and we are here concerned only with true, i.e. trained, analysts. There remains for our consideration the most delicate question of all, that of the lay analyst working in conjunction with the medical profession.

So far as I know, only three general opinions have been expressed on this topic, though several others are conceivable. They are, shortly put: (1) only medically qualified analysts should conduct psycho-analyses, (2) it is irrelevant whether the analyst is medically qualified or not, and (3) it is desirable that most analysts be medically qualified, but there is no good reason why selected lay persons should not conduct analyses under certain definite conditions. The first two of these may fairly be termed the extreme views, and I have no hesitation in rejecting them both, for reasons that are here expounded.

The first view has certainly the merit of simplicity to commend it, but little else. It is thinkable that some grounds could be brought forward to support it as a temporary expedient in particular regions of the world, but the arguments against its being sustained as a general proposition appear to me to be overwhelming. Whatever may be said about the advantages of all analysts being medically qualified, no one with a knowledge of psycho-analytic work can seriously maintain that it is *essential* for them to be so. The fact cannot be denied that with a large group of cases the analysis can be as well performed by a layman as by a physician. I speak here from unequivocal first-hand experience. That being so, it would seem to me an act of sheer tyranny to forbid, if it were in our power, anyone to conduct psycho-analyses unless he is medically qualified. I see no warrant whatever for such an arbitrary monopolizing of psycho-analytic work.

Those who, like myself, have enjoyed the opportunity of working in constant collaboration with lay colleagues can have little doubt of the inestimable advantages of such co-operation, and would be extremely loth to have to forego them. Contact with other fields of work is always an invigorating stimulus and brings a stream of fresh ideas with it. An open breeze of benevolent and instructive criticism pervades the atmosphere, information from different regions lights up our work at novel angles, and our perspective is throughout enriched and widened. The effects are those of sunlight and fresh air. What may be called applied psycho-analysis has already brought us not only constant confirmation and corroboration but a large amount of knowledge that would otherwise not be at our disposal. Perhaps the most striking example of this has been in the field of symbolism. In a number of instances the investigation of folk-lore, comparative religion, etc., has furnished us with both the interpretation and understanding of recurring symbols that had baffled us in our purely clinical work.

It seems to me, in short, that advance in the science of psycho-analysis would be seriously impeded if all lay workers were excluded. I am speaking here not only of the matter of practice, of the number of skilful practitioners in analysis we should lose by excluding the laity, but of the more important question of losing the contributions they can and do make to our knowledge. With only medical analysts available we might have had to wait long for the contributions that Melanie Klein has made to our knowledge of the psycho-analysis of young children, for those made from the side of religion, mythology and literature by Rank, Reik and Róheim, for those made by Sachs to many technical problems—to mention only a few examples. And it seems reasonable to expect that lay analysts will render equal service in the future, for they have the definite advantage of being able to import into our studies points of view that are foreign to most physicians, to bring ideas and experience gained in other fields to bear on psycho-analytic problems. There is, of course, no guarantee that the same contributions might not be made in time by purely medical analysts, but to confine psycho-analysis to the medical profession would surely mean sacrificing a potential source of strength.

The second of the views enumerated above is championed by no less an authority than Professor Freud and must therefore be examined with special care. To me it appears a distinctly tenable proposition, for it is unquestionably true within a certain sphere. And if, nevertheless, I feel impelled to reject it as being too narrow a formula, this is only because it ignores a series of considerations which to me at least appear to have some importance. The discussion of it may well be combined with that of the third view, and, as it concerns the crucial issue of the whole problem, it will demand a section to itself. We may formulate the issue as follows: Is it a matter of indifference whether analysts on the whole are medically qualified or not, or is it more desirable that they should be? What are the advantages and disadvantages that might be expected to accrue from the adoption by the International Training Commission of one or the other of these alternative views?

In the one case the members of the Commission would say to the lay candidate: "We see no reason why you should put yourself to the trouble, time and expense of becoming medically qualified, for in our opinion it will make no difference to your future psycho-analytic work whether you become so or not". In the other case they would say: "We regard it as highly desirable for you to become medically qualified, and shall refuse to accept your candidature unless you can produce satisfactory reasons why an exception should be made in your case". For the sake of convenience, let us refer to these as Plan A and Plan B respectively.

We have now narrowed the problems down to the last, and most crucial, issue. Before dealing, however, with the individual criteria on which this issue will have to be decided, it will be well to envisage, so far as is possible, what would be the most probable practical consequences of either plan being adopted.

If Plan A were adopted we should have to be prepared for what in my judgement would be a very considerable probability, namely, that n a measurable period of time—perhaps after the present generation of medical analysts had passed away—the profession of psycho-analyst would become predominantly lay. At present most medical analysts first obtained a medical qualification and only subsequently decided to take up the study of psycho-analysis. In the future, when they would usually hear of the psycho-analytic career at an earlier age, they would be definitely discouraged from the arduous and unnecessary study of medicine. Similarly there would be manifested an increasing disinclination for physicians to exchange their profession for one in which they would be informed that their previous medical studies would have no special value and would give them no special advantage; physicians do occasionally become writers, engineers or lawyers, but in inappreciable numbers. The profession of apothecary, linked to the medical one by a thousand ties and once historically united, may be taken as an analogy; the fact that a medical qualification is a "matter of indifference" to the work of an apothecary has the very natural result that no apothecary troubles to obtain such a qualification, and no physician specialises in the work of an apothecary. The two lines of work, though related, remain distinct, and so, it seems to me, it would happen if psycho-analysis were to be regularly regarded as an independent profession rather than as a special branch of medicine.

Added to this would be the increasing opprobrium of a physician's joining a profession which would, rightly or wrongly, be held to contravene the fundamental principles of medical practice; for an independent discipline of psycho-analysis would be avowedly displacing the medical one from what it unanimously regards as one of its legitimate provinces—the care of the mentally afflicted. Indeed, even at the present day in London, one is constantly told that a great reason why so few of the better class of university or medical school physicians contemplate the study of psycho-analysis is because analysts admit to their ranks those who have had neither a medical nor any other scientific preliminary education, so that the study can in the nature of things possess no recognized scientific status. Even in regard to medical analysts one of the commonest criticisms, not entirely unjustified, to be heard from our medical colleagues is their regret that so many are very imperfectly trained in psychiatry, neurology, and even general medicine; what they say about analysts who are destitute of any medical training whatever we know well enough. One may think what one will of these reasons: I am concerned here only to point out one of the probable consequences of Plan A.

But the matter cannot be left at this. If I am correct in these assumptions, there would be still further consequences of the divorce between psycho-analysis and clinical medicine. As psycho-analysis possesses almost a monopoly of the most important part of psychopathology, the tendency of Plan A would be to wrench the knowledge of psychopathology more and more from the medical profession, for the better it succeeded the more would psychical affections be regarded as "non-medical", much in the way that speech affections are at present. This would stifle the hope of those who look forward to steady improvement in the psychological education of the medical profession as a whole. We know not only that most neurotics first consult a general physician, and presumably always will do so, but—what is perhaps even more important—that the part played by psychical factors in organic disease is immensely greater than is now at all widely recognized; if one makes a general survey it becomes quite doubtful whether the general practitioner has more to do with psychical or with physical factors in his daily work.

While the medical profession would thus be starved in its study of psychology, psycho-analysts also would suffer greatly from the lack of adequate medical contact. This important matter will presently be discussed more fully in connection with the inner development of psycho-analysis.

I do not see how anyone can contemplate these real possibilities with equanimity, whether he is more concerned with the well-being of suffering humanity or with the march of scientific knowledge. To my mind, at least, it would signify setting back the clock of progress in no uncertain degree.

Let us now consider the probabilities if Plan B were adopted. Where any good reason could be shown why it was inexpedient for the lay candidate to go through a medical education he would be accepted for training in psycho-analysis, provided, of course, that he proved otherwise suitable (character, previous scientific education, etc.). This should ensure that the contributions and services of valuable lay analysts would not be lost. The majority of analysts, however, would be, as now, medically qualified, so that direct continuity would exist between the psychological and physiological points of view. Psycho-analysis would be regarded as essentially a branch of clinical medicine, gradually replacing—as, in fact, it is already doing—the older branches of "psychotherapy", "medical psychology", or "psychopathology". It would only be a question of time when psychiatrists also would make a regular practice of being trained in psycho-analysis, for I do not regard this expectation as in the least chimerical; the process is indeed already beginning. Once psycho-analysis had obtained a secure foothold in the more psychological departments of medicine, the rest would automatically follow: that is to say, the gradual penetration of psycho-analytical doctrine among the ranks of the profession, and the incorporation of truly psychological, i.e. psycho-analytical, points of view into general medical education. The naturalistic and biological outlook characteristic of both disciplines could only result in their reinforcing and supplementing each other to their mutual benefit. The study of mankind, and especially of suffering mankind, would attain this logical unity instead of being artificially divided into the two separate categories of physical and mental—a division which, try as we may, cannot be effected without doing gross violence to the facts of reality.

After contemplating these imaginary pictures we have finally to close on the issue occupying us, and I would suggest in doing so that it would be advantageous to consider separately the various criteria on which our answers will be based. The criteria in question are the interests respectively of (1) the science of psycho-analysis itself, (2) the large class of persons capable of being helped by means of it, and (3) the analyst. I have named them in what is to me their order of importance; others would perhaps change the order. It is plain that the individual arguments must overlap somewhat in their application; for instance, what is good for the development of our knowledge will be good for the patient, and so on.

A. *The Development of Psycho-Analysis*. This criterion must in turn be subdivided as follows:

1. *Internally*. By this is meant the inner development of the science and art of psycho-analysis irrespective of its expansion outwards.

It is admitted that the inner development of psycho-analysis would be deleteriously affected if all lay workers were excluded, and it is probable that this would be even more so if all medical workers were excluded, for nothing could stultify progress in psycho-analysis more than to divorce it from the medical sciences. If the prediction stated above is correct, however, we are faced with the alternative of the workers being either predominantly lay or predominantly medical.

The innumerable connections between psycho-analysis and the sciences of biology, physiology and clinical medicine (particularly clinical neurology and psychiatry) would appear to be so important that the chief advances in future knowledge may reasonably be expected to come from those having the double training; the greater must surely include the less, so that a person doubly qualified would in most cases make more valuable contributions than one singly qualified.

In the nature of things the layman must confine his attention rigidly to the psychological aspects of his problems, although in reality nature is not so obliging as to make a correspondingly sharp distinction. The theory of neurosis-formation, the basal problems of bio-chemistry, heredity, somatic erotogenesis, etc., would remain a sealed book to him, and he would be more and more reduced to the position of a mere practitioner of an art. Now all experience shows that any divorce of therapeutics from pathology is sooner or later attended by sterilization. We have an excellent example in our own

270 INFLUENTIAL PAPERS FROM THE 1920s

field. Medical psychology made no perceptible progress for nearly a hundred years, mainly because its exponents confined themselves to endless therapeutic hypnotising. It is as a symbol of this criticism that I have always protested against the idea that "psychotherapy" could be regarded as a branch of medicine, instead of "medical psychology", "clinical psychology", "psychopathology", or any such word indicating that the workers in question were students of a science, not simply practitioners of an art.

In choosing, therefore, between the relative advantages of Plan A and Plan B, care for the progress in the inner development of psycho-analytical science would, in my judgement, lead us to attach greater value to the second one.

2. *In relation to general science.* I refer here to the external problem of the gradual acceptance of psycho-analysis by the rest of science, a process of which only the earliest signs are visible to-day. Although there might here and there be a few scientists whose interest and curiosity would be aroused by the sight of a new body of knowledge claiming to possess an independent discipline and status of its own, there can be little doubt that this would only enhance the prejudices of the majority. On the other hand, the idea of psycho-analysis being, like psychiatry, a recognized special department of medical knowledge, and therefore subject to all the educational and professional conditions that go with this, would compel a degree of acknowledgment that would be extremely hard to encompass otherwise. That this would be the unanimous attitude of the medical profession itself goes without saying.

3. *In relation to the general public.* Though this is perhaps a matter of much less moment, it has, nevertheless, a certain practical importance. Without the countenance, and even support, of society at large, any branch of science is sure to languish in time, and this is particularly so in an executive art like psycho-analysis which must depend for its necessary material on the goodwill of at least a section of the public. Now, while there appears to be always a proportion of people whose choice of helper is dictated inversely by the qualification of the helper, who are instinctively drawn towards quacks, there is no doubt that the majority of reasonable beings prefer some guarantee, in the form of training and qualification, that they will obtain what they seek from the helper—namely, the ability based on the necessary knowledge. The progress in this

rational sentiment is incorporated, however incompletely in the laws of every country. It is to be presumed that such people would find a more secure guarantee in the double qualification of psycho-analysis and medicine than in either alone, and a large proportion are justly suspicious of the "healers" who constantly emerge in connection with every aspect of health and disease. In the case of psycho-analysis they fortify this attitude, together with their natural prejudices, by pointing out that they have more assurance of the ethical and professional standards so desirable in such work being supplied by members of the medical profession than by what is to them necessarily the unknown quantity of the lay analyst and his qualifications. Although we know the latter consideration has no real foundations, the prejudice itself is one more of the factors that have to be taken for what they are worth.

These considerations speak unequivocally in favour of as many analysts as possible being medically qualified. In the predictions presented above as consequences of adopting Plan A or Plan B respectively, the view was expressed that the latter would lead to psycho-analysis becoming in time a generally recognized department of clinical medicine, from which position its influence would radiate throughout the medical profession and beyond. One strict condition is necessary, as was remarked earlier in this essay, to ensure that the infiltration of the medical profession should always remain a subordinate aim, and never become the chief one. It should, that is to say, always be subordinate to the furthering of psycho-analysis itself, as is true of every other special medical study: bacteriology and neurology, for instance, do not exist primarily for the purpose of infusing the medical profession with bacteriological or neurological principles, but for the advance of these particular branches of science. The condition in question is, of course, that trained psycho-analysts retain a corporate unity together with a high standard of analytic education.

There is a serious argument on the other side in this connection, on which Professor Freud rightly lays stress; it is, I surmise, the one that inclines him more than any other to favour Plan A. This is the fear that psycho-analysis may become "absorbed" into medicine, particularly into psychiatry, the process being accompanied by such a degree of dilution as to render precarious our hold on the vital truths that are the distinctive feature of psycho-analysis. The possibility is a real one and we have even seen something of the sort at work already, notably in America. The matter cannot be decided by any argument, it being one of individual judgement. Personally my faith both in the essential nature of psycho-analysis, with its inherent power to resist any such encroachments, and in the inflexible steadfastness of thoroughly trained and experienced psycho-analysts is robust enough to enable me to face the prospect with considerable equanimity. In any case we are agreed that there is only one way of effectively meeting this danger and other similar ones; that is, to see, through the functioning of our International Training Commission, that our future analysts are provided with an efficient training.

It will be seen that the importance of this matter of training is again emphasized by the considerations brought forward in the present section. This is so, not only in the connection last mentioned, but in the earlier ones also. No scientist will take seriously the claims of a body of knowledge to be regarded as a branch of science until the discipline and education accompanying it are adequately organized.

I should like also in the present connection to state my opinion, based on years of experience in that continent, that the considerations adduced in the last two sections have a quite special weight in the case of America. Without wishing in any way to give offence to my American friends, I may call attention here to the familiar fact that, because of a series of historical, racial, economic and cultural factors whose influence is quite inevitable, respect for the tradition of knowledge is by no means so widespread in America as in Europe. It is hard for Europeans to realize the almost incredible variety and number of pseudo-scientific charlatans in America, and the even more astonishing high social esteem they enjoy. The scientific professions are fighting gallantly against the clouds of ignorance that this state of affairs betokens, and one sign of their gradual success is the extent to which the charlatans find themselves constrained to pay lip service to technical training by establishing "colleges" and similar institutions; there are already even several such "colleges of Psycho-Analysis", which increase the general confusion. A real Institute of Psycho-Analysis, open to the laity and independent of the medical profession, would unquestionably impose a formidable difficulty in the way of psycho-analysis becoming recognized by responsible people in America. Our American colleagues feel that their only hope is to unite psycho-analysis, as a special branch, with an already established profession, i.e. medicine, and when they take the view that the conditions in America are so different from those in Europe that psycho-analysis there should be *confined* to the medical profession, with some resentment against those European analysts who actively force the opposite solution on them against their judgement, I must say that I find it harder to disagree with them than do some Europeans with less experience of that interesting Continent.

B. *The Interests of the Neurotic.*

1. *The interests of the individual patient.* There are to the individual patient several definite advantages in being treated by a medical analyst, assuming of course an equal level of analytic capability. The pre-analytic education in scientific discipline, including the knowledge of physiological mechanisms, affords a better opportunity for comprehension of a great many neurotic problems, which must be reflected in the practical work. The patient is ensured that the work will be kept to its proper field, and that it will not be allowed to invade the realm of the psychotic or somatic through diagnostic ignorance on the part of the analyst. With some cases, e.g. young or mentally undeveloped persons, patients during pregnancy, puberty or climacteric, etc., etc., a certain amount of general medical advice and supervision, including occasionally sexual hygiene, may be indispensable, and in such cases the advantages of the medical analyst are evident. Any temptation on his part to waste time by dwelling unduly on any such medical aspects cannot be reckoned as a counter-argument, because it would represent an error in technique and we are not here considering erroneous analytic technique.

There is more to be said on the subject of *diagnosis* than has been hitherto. We have considered above the matter of initial diagnosis with the somatic and psychotic possibilities, and also the problem of those cases where the diagnosis has to be established during the analysis itself. There remains the still greater difficulty presented by the frequent interaction between the mental and physical spheres in the course of the analysis. It is certainly not to be disposed of in the cavalier fashion of Professor Freud in his remark that in this respect lay and medical analysts are in the same position because the rules of psycho-analysis forbid physical examination and therefore render consultation with an outside physician necessary. Physical examination is only one of the numerous ways in which medical knowledge can be of use. Let me illustrate this at once by a clear case, one out of many in my experience; most medical analysts could doubtless supply similar ones. A patient, a man in the thirties, mentioned that he had pain in the neighbourhood of the anus when going to sleep. He himself wanted to explain the pain as a paræsthesia, of the kind so common in this region, probably aroused by our current discussion of his anal-erotic complex. Various features, however, in the distribution, quality and occurrence of the pain stirred elements of my medical knowledge, and I urged him to consult a surgeon at once. An early carcinoma of the rectum in an unusually favourable state was found, and a formidable operation performed without delay. That was more than ten years ago and the patient, well and happy, is now engaged in an active professional life. Rectal cancer has in general such a bad prognosis that a very little hesitation and delay would probably have meant a horrible death. It is plain that the lay analyst cannot be expected to run to a physician over every ache and pain his patient manifests, so that he has to share with the patient the responsibility of deciding when such a step is necessary. He can, of course, shirk the responsibility under the plea that he is concerned only with the patient's mind, not with his body, just as a teacher of languages would be; but this would be a small consolation to such patients as the one described above. Nor can he fairly avoid the responsibility; for bodily manifestations, both conversion and "transitory" symptoms, are a considerable part of the material he is dealing with. How is he, with only one-sided knowledge, to surmise whether a temporary attack of vomiting is of psychical origin or is due to food poisoning, whether a colic is due to intestinal complexe or needs to be examined from the point of view of mild appendicitis, or any other of the endless similar problems that occur from day to day? The alertness to danger signals is only one part of the general perspective in regard to physical manifestations which is so advantageous in psycho-analytic work, and the judgement that provides such a perspective is one that can be obtained in no other way than through medical training.

I do not find it easy to think of any advantage that would accrue to the individual patient from his analyst being a layman. Perhaps one might reckon in this connection that a lay analyst, being put to so much less expense, can afford to charge lower fees, which would, of course, be an advantage to the patient; but the whole field of analytical economics, with the question of public clinics, is so complicated and fluid that it cannot properly be dealt with here.

2. *The interests of neurotics in general.* Here may be adduced an argument which is, in my opinion, the most weighty of those supporting Plan A. It concerns the supply of analysts. There can be little doubt that Plan A would have the effect, in a few years' time, of creating a considerably larger number of psycho-analysts than Plan B would; for the decrease it would surely lead to in the number of medical analysts would be more than counterbalanced by the ready access of lay candidates. This increased supply of analysts would, of course, be in many ways to the advantage of the large mass of neurotics. This holds good for the number itself, and perhaps still more for the probable consequence that analysts would then be more widely distributed instead of concentrating, as at present, in a few centres.

There is, on the other hand, one argument in this connection which has to be taken into account in support of Plan B. Reckoning, as we must, with the very imperfect discriminating powers of the general public, a feature familiar enough to everyone engaged in practice, we should have to anticipate many unfortunate results of psycho-analysis being regarded as an independent, and predominantly lay, profession. The medical analyst can cope with the wild analyst in his own profession, for he knows that in the light of open scientific discussion it is only a question of time before the pretensions of the latter will be exposed. As regards the wild lay analyst, he is doubly equipped. But under Plan A the real lay analyst would be in a far less favourable position in regard to the wild lay analyst, for the judgement concerning the two would be pronounced, not in a sphere of scientific discussion, but solely in that of general publicity, with all its unedifying accompaniments of advertisement, newspaper campaigns, etc. The net result, apart from its deleterious effect on the status of psycho-analysis, could only be harmful to the general interests of neurotics that we are here considering.

C. *The Interests of the Analyst*. There are several definite disadvantages to the analyst in not being medically qualified, and only one serious advantage. Among the former I would rank highly the circumstance that the lay analyst must encounter hard and fast limitations to his thought and judgement in many of the problems he has to consider. By this I do not refer solely, or indeed mainly, to the diagnostic doubts that must occur during the course of so many analyses. Even more important is the limitation to his understanding of the ultimate mechanism of the bodily neurotic symptoms and of any fundamental problem concerning the genesis of neuroses altogether. The relation of erotogenicity to the non-sexual functions of the organs concerned (on which so much of somatic symptom-formation depends), the relations of internal secretions to changes in libidinal and other instinctual activity, the chemistry and physiology of the body and the relation of this to the emotional life, are only a few of the problems where it is desirable for the psychopathologist to be able at least to form some general judgement, to be correctly oriented in his perspective.

I hold definitely that a worker who excludes important aspects and connections of his field of activity is at a serious disadvantage as compared with one not thus restricted. Not having the right to think freely on the "medical" aspects of his work, both diagnostic and theoretical, must often bring the risk of inhibiting his powers of original thought. And, as was pointed out above, a pure "practitioner" is rarely such a good practitioner as one who is equally interested in the general pathology and theory of the material on which he is practising.

Even in minor ways, all of which cannot be enumerated here, the lay analyst is placed at a constant disadvantage. To mention only one little example. When a patient has to consult a medical specialist, the lay analyst has little means for checking the latter's recommendations and distinguishing between those that are serious and the numerous *placebos* to which he has so often to have recourse. If a minor operation is advised, or a fortnight's change of air, or a course of medicine that may concern the analytic work (e.g. hypnotics, purgatives, etc.), the analyst has no authority to make his opinion heard on the important matter of having the analysis thus interfered with, possibly at a critical stage. A consultation with the specialist on equal terms is rarely possible, and the analytic situation has to suffer from this lack of harmony.

These limitations under which the lay analyst has unavoidably to suffer cannot make it easier for him to maintain the equable confidence so essential to his work. His disadvantages and inferior position must often bring the temptation to have resort to artificial devices for maintaining self-respect (assertiveness, etc.), thus necessitating an exceptionally high standard of self-confidence and serenity to which everyone, even among the analysed, cannot lay claim.

Against all this the lay analyst can counter with one solitary, though substantial, consideration. He has been spared labour, time and cost in dispensing with a medical qualification. The advantage of this is at its maximum at the time of making a decision, but it constantly recedes as time goes on, while the disadvantages accumulate. One wonders how many lay analysts sometimes doubt in later years if the sacrifice they made to their dislike of labour was not too heavy.

I wish to leave the reader in no doubt about my *conclusions*, and so will present a summary of them here.

To begin with, what is perhaps the most important: no amount of proclaiming that it is a matter of indifference whether analysts are medically qualified or not can, in my judgement, alter the fact that this is in reality not a matter of indifference to the future of psycho-analysis, to its progress either internally or externally. Both the internal and external bonds between psycho-analysis and clinical medicine, which have been discussed above at length, are fundamental in character, and they can be ignored only at considerable cost to psycho-analysis. These bonds impose a relationship between psycho-analysis and medicine, and we have to decide what this relationship shall be. In my opinion, there is no half-way measure in this matter; we have no option but to choose whether we wish the profession of psycho-analysis to be in the future either predominantly medical or predominantly lay. For the authorities, i.e. the International Training Commission, consistently to assert that a medical qualification is irrelevant for the practice of psycho-analysis could only end in making it irrelevant; this would mean reducing in time the medical analysts to a minimum, with fateful results to both the inner and outer development of the subject.

I have given the reasons above why I definitely advocate that psycho-analysis remain an essentially medical organization and discipline. Our endeavours should be directed to influencing first medical psychologists and psychopathologists, then psychiatrists, and through them the rest of the medical profession; from this authoritative position its influence would then radiate to the ancillary sciences, as has often happened before in similar situations. This appears to be quite a hopeful proceeding, the success of which, however, will depend on our maintaining a united corporation of highly-trained analysts.

On the other hand, I can see no valid reason for excluding lay analysts from co-operation in our work. Such reasons as exist appear to me to be far outweighed by the loss psycho-analysis would sustain by the absence of lay colleagues. We know that a lay analyst can in many cases, though assuredly not in all, conduct an analysis quite as well as a medical analyst, and therefore a place should be found for him within the psycho-analytical organization provided certain external precautions be taken. Among these I regard it as essential that a lay analyst should not engage in independent practice; it is necessary that he consult with a physician at the outset of an analysis, and often desirable that he remain in contact with one during its course.

For the reasons previously considered at length I advocate that the International Training Commission urge lay candidates to obtain a medical qualification, and that they exercise a strict selection among those to whom such a course appears inexpedient. The criteria according to which such a selection should be made is a matter on which further discussion will be needed after we have agreed on the preliminary principles; prominent among them I should place type of personality and character and nature of previous scientific education.

The questions which the Congress, and through them the International Training Commission, will have to answer would appear to be essentially three: (1) Are lay analysts to be altogether excluded in the future? (2) If not, are they to be admitted unquestioningly (Plan A) or only after they have shown adequate reasons why they cannot undertake a course of medical study (Plan B)? (3) In the event of a divergence of opinion in different countries what is to be the attitude of the corresponding Training Committees?

This last question, which has hitherto not been discussed and which urgently needs regulating, must be faced in spite of its delicacy, for much of the feeling displayed in connection with the whole matter of lay analysis is bound up with it. The day is fortunately passing when any individual analyst could arrogate to himself the responsibility for training candidates in psycho-analysis, since this is being taken over by the various Training Committees. Assuming that these function in all countries as we hope, they will have to decide on what attitude to adopt with candidates who present themselves from foreign countries. Human nature being what it is, there is no doubt that the feeling of responsibility tends to be much greater if the candidate is a fellow-countryman, and therefore potentially a future colleague, than if he is a foreigner whose possible deficiencies will vanish from sight with his departure and will only afflict distant colleagues. Those analysts who take the view that a little psycho-analysis is better than none may have no compunction in working for a few weeks with a notorious charlatan, who then returns to his native country with the imprimatur of having studied with so-and-so (it not being necessary to specify the satisfactoriness or otherwise of the study), but it cannot be expected that the analysts who have to deal with him on his return to his native land will show unqualified enthusiasm over the proceeding.

I hold definitely that in regard to the present question the various national groups should be accorded a high degree of autonomy. If such a group, which should be in the best position to judge the particular requirements and conditions of their country, come to a definite decision in one direction, then any attempt on the part of any others of the International Association to override this and force a contrary decision on them (e.g. by training analysts from the first country which the Training Committee of that country regard as undesirable) can only lead to friction between the groups and act in the long run deleteriously on the interests of psycho-analysis as a whole.

This consideration among many others shows how very desirable it is for the International Association as a whole to come to some united, and as far as possible unanimous, conclusion about the questions discussed in this essay. For this to happen it is evident that concessions must be made on both sides. By rejecting the various extreme solutions, I have indicated a *via media* which seems to me to be at the same time just, advantageous and practicable.

Notes

1. The expression "wild analyst", an early one of Professor Freud's, is used to denote someone who, without being adequately qualified to do so, asserts that he is practising psycho-analysis.
2. *Zur Frage der Laienanalyse*, 1926. See Review in *International Journal of Psychoanalysis*, Vol. VIII, p. 86.